GREECE
AND
YUGOSLAVIA
AN
ECONOMIC
COMPARISON

Nicholas V. Gianaris

PRAEGER SPECIAL STUDIES • PRAEGER SCIENTIFIC

New York • Philadelphia • Eastbourne, UK
Toronto • Hong Kong • Tokyo • Sydney

Library of Congress Cataloging in Publication Data

C.1

Gianaris, Nicholas V.
   Greece and Yugoslavia.

   Includes indexes.
   1. Greece—Economic conditions—1974–
2. Yugoslavia—Economic conditions—1945–
I. Title.
HC295.G52   1984   330.9495′076   83-27010
ISBN 0-03-071466-4 [alk. paper]

Published and Distributed by the
Praeger Publishers Division
(ISBN Prefix 0-275)
of Greenwood Press, Inc.,
Westport, Connecticut

Published in 1984 by Praeger Publishers
CBS Educational Professional Publishing,
a Division of CBS Inc.
521 Fifth Avenue, New York, NY 10175 USA

Printed in the United States of America
on acid-free paper

To the memory of my mother

PREFACE

Greece and Yugoslavia, as parts of the Balkan Peninsula, are located at the crossroads of Europe, Africa, and Asia and constitute a natural bridge between Europe and the Middle East. Although their economic systems are different, they both tend to accept similar institutions and models of development. This causes a need for closer economic and cultural cooperation between them. However, it should be recognized that there are so many other social, political, and ethnic elements involved, especially in Yugoslavia, that it would be improper to concentrate only on economic issues and disregard noneconomic factors.

At present the main problems facing these two countries are those of reducing inflation and unemployment, raising productivity and satisfying growing demand, cutting down on raw materials and energy consumption, and redressing adverse foreign trade balances. To increase productivity, avoid excessive use of raw materials, and increase exports, the governments of these countries introduce fiscal and monetary incentives to stimulate investment and managerial know-how, particularly in less developed sectors and regions.

Recent economic reforms in Yugoslavia emphasize the novel concept of worker self-management as an evolutionary process that will transform capitalism to socialism and "wither away the state," as the supporters of the system argue, not in the distant future but in our own day. However, bureaucracy, inefficiency, and inflationary trends in price and wage determination continue to plague the Yugoslav economy, and the main dilemma is how to stimulate production through a decentralization and, at the same time, avoid antisocialist tendencies.

Greece, on the other hand, like Odysseus in Homer's epic, returned to her European home after a long period of uncertainty and historical disturbances. The accession of

vii

Greece to the European Economic Community (EEC) is expected to be a prelude to its acceptance of Spain and Portugal, and, it is to be hoped, Yugoslavia. Greece and Yugoslavia, as less economically developed and more agri-culturally-based countries of southeastern Europe, will present problems for the EEC, but, from the point of view of transportation and trade, they will prove vital to the future growth of the community.

The new trends toward closer cooperation between these two countries present new areas for research and exploration. However, it should be recognized that the weakness of comparative analysis of countries with different economic systems remains a major problem and a challenge to economic theory and measurement.

The purpose of this book is to examine the main characteristics of the basically market economy of Greece and the mainly planned economy of Yugoslavia and to review developmental trends toward closer economic cooperation between them and with other groups of countries, par-ticularly the EEC and the Council for Mutual Economic Aid (COMECON) or CMEA. This study will be equally valuable to researchers and to students of comparative economic systems and international economic development.

After a survey of the history of each country's develop-ment, an analysis of recent economic and social aspects, with extensive statistical data in comparative tables, is presented. Chapters contrast the economies of Greece and Yugoslavia and examine special problems of resources and productivity, sectoral and regional investment allocation, differences in tax structures and government policies, and foreign trade directions.

Part I focuses on the socioeconomic background of Greece and Yugoslavia from a historical and organizational point of view. Part II examines domestic aspects of develop-ment from a sectoral and regional point of view and analyzes current economic conditions. Issues of resource allocation, productivity, and taxation are also discussed in this section. Part III deals with international aspects of development of these countries. It includes trends in foreign trade and investment, economic relations with other coun-tries, and the possibilities of closer cooperation and inte-gration.

I would like to express my gratitude to Professors Janis Barry, Suati Desai, George Giannaris, George Karatzas, Laura Nowak, Stergios Mourgos, Constantine Popoulias, John Roche, Adamandia Polis, Harry Psomiades, Dominick Salvatore, George Tavlas, Paul Vouras, and Amin Zeiwel for their valuable comments. My thanks to Bill and Mike Gianaris, David Handcock, and Deborah Johnson for their technical and typing services.

CONTENTS

x

PART II: DOMESTIC ASPECTS OF DEVELOPMENT

PART III: INTERNATIONAL TRADE AND ECONOMIC COOPERATION

LIST OF TABLES
AND FIGURES

PART I

SOCIOECONOMIC BACKGROUND

Part I presents a brief historical review of the socioeconomic problems of Greece and Yugoslavia and examines the postwar trends of the public versus the private sectors of these two economies. Because of their strategic position, both countries have attracted continuous involvement of the great powers in their affairs. Being at the crossroads of three continents, the area beckoned to invaders and superpowers, which, in order to promote their own economic and political interests, directly or indirectly divided the peoples of the region and led them to regional conflicts and even civil wars.

In ancient times, the Hellenes (Greeks) in the southern Balkan Peninsula were the first to leave a record of the people in the area. The Cretan (Minoan) culture, the Achaean or Mycenaean, and later the Athenian civilizations flourished in the basin of the eastern Mediterranean, while Illyrians, it is assumed, and Thracians lived in the western and eastern regions of Yugoslavia, respectively.

During the Roman and Byzantine periods, the economy of the region remained mostly agricultural and pastoral, while under the Ottoman occupation a socioeconomic and cultural decline took place. During the turbulent postliberation and interwar years, Greece and Yugoslavia proceeded slowly and painfully to deal with their rehabilitation and development problems. After World War II, in both countries, particularly Yugoslavia, there were peculiar changes in economic organization and the relationship of the private and public sectors.

1

OVERVIEW

This study attempts a fresh and illuminating survey of the most critical economic problems of contemporary Greece and Yugoslavia and tries to provide an innovative analysis of the economic and social trends in these two countries.

Reforms in Yugoslavia, which incorporate the novel concepts of social ownership and self-management, have been begging for careful treatment for some time. The Yugoslav experience of industrial democracy may be considered a unique example with worldwide significance. A similar system of reforms is being gradually implemented in the economy of Greece, as well as in other countries, in the form of decentralization and socialization. The success of such reforms depends, to a large extent, on managerial efficiency, release of worker energies, and production-sales coordination.

Both economies try to promote the welfare of their citizens through structural changes, growth performances, and income distribution policies. Structural changes and economic growth, in turn, require capital investment, innovations, productivity incentives and modernization in the form of high levels of research and technology; while improvements in income distribution require income policies and institutional transformations emphasizing remuneration according to work performance and direct participation in socioeconomic decision making.

A review of the Yugoslav economy is timely, as many students of comparative systems wonder what course post-Tito Yugoslavia will follow. Will the labor-managed system continue along the same conceptual lines? Will decentralization measures lead to better economic performance and to a higher degree of democratization and socialization of the country? Likewise, a survey of the Greek economy is important, as many observers wonder what path Greece will take now that the socialist government of Andreas Papandreou has come to power.

This study explores such socioeconomic trends in both countries and evaluates policy measures taken by the respective governments. It considers the relationship of both the public and the private sectors as they are affected by growing expenditures of the central and local governments and by the growth of public and semipublic enterprises or the "communities of interest."

THE DILEMMA OF UNEMPLOYMENT AND INFLATION

Expansionary fiscal and monetary policies and a decelerating economic growth generated strong inflationary pressures in both countries. Public sector deficits, particularly in public corporations, and credit expansion to real estate and trade activities, especially in Greece, encouraged speculation and escalated inflation. Such trends distorted investment allocation and slowed down productivity growth.

Because neither country managed to achieve substantial reduction in inflation in recent years, their governments have been forced to take painful corrective action, such as raising interest rates and tightening budgets. These policies, coupled with weakening world markets, have led to a further decline in economic growth and to more unemployment. This contraction in turn contributes to, and is made worse by, demands for new subsidies to sensitive industries and leads to large budget deficits, more money in circulation, and the continuation of the vicious cycle of inflation. As a result, both countries have to deal with such thorny issues as encouraging investment for higher rates of economic growth and reducing subsidies to public or private enterprises and cooperatives.

Reversing economic deterioration in these countries requires a sound medium-term strategy to achieve increased growth and productive employment while avoiding structural rigidities and rekindling inflation. Expenditures on productive economic infrastructure, on government-sponsored educational and training programs, and on research facilities for new technology and high productivity may be considered the kind of investment that creates jobs, increases production, lowers inflation, and restores a strong balance of payments position. However, the governments of Greece and Yugoslavia find it difficult to resist grass-roots pressure for wage increases to counteract the effect of higher prices, even though such increases swell currency in circulation and fuel inflation. In their effort to stimulate growth, they try to encourage state-owned enterprises to increase production by giving management and workers more freedom to decide on matters of production, pricing, and distribution. On many occasions, though, this economic freedom, together with wage raises for civil servants and the armed forces, backfires by stimulating inflation, as drachmas and dinars in circulation run ahead of available goods. Moreover, the policy of continuing to shield unprofitable enterprises from the disciplines of the marketplace to prevent unemployment may make things worse. On the other hand, companies protected through subsidies may hoard labor, thus creating a shortage of manpower in certain sectors and lowering labor productivity. This is the main dilemma both countries face as they oscilate between the Scylla of unemployment and the Charibdis of inflation.

For the sake of higher efficiency and growth, more initiative and technical innovations are needed. Investment incentives, provided at present by both countries, are expected to stimulate production and employment. Ceteris paribus, more income would be created, which would be mostly spent to generate more employment and further income through the multiplier effect. Moreover, that part of income that might not be spent but saved would be channeled back into the economy, through the financial intermediaries of Greece and Yugoslavia, introducing new investment (acceleration) and generating a new stream of spending and additional demand, which would, in turn, increase employment and income. Such an interaction of a positive multiplier and accelerator would propel the economy forward, stimulate utilization of idle resources and eventually reduce inflation through higher production.

INTERNATIONAL ECONOMIC RELATIONS

The geographical location of Greece and Yugoslavia in relation to markets of Europe and the Middle East and makes them important for business opportunities. As we shall see later, this is particularly so for Greece, whose trade and investment position has been substantially enhanced by its improved economic relations with Middle East Countries.

In previous years both countries borrowed large sums from other countries, which enabled them to finance new investment and imports. This, in turn, led to heavy foreign debt, particularly in Yugoslavia, and weaker currencies. At present, high priority is given to righting the trade imbalances and earning enough hard currency to repay debts and preserve creditworthiness.

A modest economic expansion, pursued with "stop and go" fiscal and monetary policies, may be designed to spur growth, control inflation, improve the balance of payments, and stabilize exchange rates of the currently devaluated drachma and dinar. However, in the efforts to improve the trade balance, care should be taken to avoid reduction of such imports that may create shortages of parts and needed raw materials. On the other hand, structural changes and regional investment policies should not play a major role in retarding industrial growth and technological innovations to the extent of severely impairing the countries' international trade position.

Both countries are in the midst of a transition that may eventually culminate in the emergence of a new form of economic and social organization, which may prove to be a paradigm for other countries to follow. Moreover closer cooperation between them and the other Balkan countries might be used as an example for a possible convergence of the EEC and COMECON. It is also expected that Greece's membership to the EEC will pave the way for the inclusion of Portugal and Spain, and possibly Yugoslavia.

Recently, the Balkan region, and particularly Greece and Yugoslavia, along with Albania, again became an arena of competition between the Soviet Union and the United States, particularly after the death of the Soviet leader Leonid Brezhnev in October 1982. Yugoslavia, facing severe foreign exchange problems, turned to the United States and other Western countries for loan and credit support and at the same time turned more strongly to the Soviet Union as a trading partner. Greece faces similar problems of international relations: with excessive balance of trade deficits and currency devaluations, it strives for more trade with both Western bloc and Eastern bloc countries.

2

A HISTORICAL PERSPECTIVE

A SHORT HISTORY OF THE ECONOMY OF GREECE

Because of the geographical location and composition of Greece, the main economic activities of the inhabitants were and still are shipping and trade. From the times of the Minoan (Cretan) and the Homeric civilizations (about 3400-750 B.C.) to the Athenian Golden Age (5th century B.C.), the Greeks were distinguished by their maritime and commercial activities along the shores of the Black Sea and the eastern Mediterranean(1).

The Achaeans and the Dorians, descendants of the same Hellenic race, migrated from the Alps and central Europe about the beginning of the second millenium B.C. Under the pressure of the Thracians and Illyrian barbarians, they infiltrated and finally colonized central Greece and many coastlands of the eastern Mediterranean. A branch of the Achaeans became the architects of the Mycenean civilization, which was influenced by the Minoans.

Other people, such as the Ionians and the Aeolians, who probably originated in the northern Greek mainland, were driven south. After the successful siege of Troy in about 1200 B.C. by the Myceneans, an amalgam of Achaeans,

Ionians, Aeolians, and even the pursuing Dorians settled in the coastlands of Asia Minor, now part of Anatolia Turkey. Smyrna and Miletus became great cultural and commercial cities after the eleventh and tenth centuries B.C. respectively. Later, these cities together with others on mainland Greece and the islands, established many colonies along the coasts of Spain and Italy (Syracuse, Taranto, Crotone) and Libya (Apollonia and Cyrene), as well as on the coast of Adriatic and Black Seas and along the Danube River (Histria and Gallatis in Romania, Vachia in Yugoslavia). In these colonies, which remained in close touch with the mother country, commerce, craftsmanship, art, and philosophy were developed. However, the people of mainland Greece remained primarily agricultural and pastoral.

From the sixth to the third century B.C., Athens had become an important economic and cultural center. As other city-states, such as Sparta, Corinth, Cleitor, Thebes, and later Salonika, developed, trade and handicrafts greatly expanded. The appearance of silver and iron coins facilitated transactions and improved trade not only among the city-states but also between Greece and other Mediterranean lands. Moreover, economic and political unions or confederacies, such as the Achaean League during the sixth and the third centuries B.C., were established to formulate common economic and foreign policy on coinage, tariffs, and the removal of trade barriers.

However, Greek philosophers, including Plato and Aristotle, opposed profit making and interest taking in trade transactions and loans. Interest, named tokos or "child" of the "parent" principal in a metaphorical sense, was considered unnatural and immoral. Money cannot (literally) have a child; two drachmas cannot bear a baby drachma, in a natural sense, as human beings or other creatures can. Despite such philosophical arguments, profit and interest were the prime motives in trade and banking activities, which were enhanced after the invention of coins.(2)

Problems of Public Finance

With the establishment of political democracy in Athens came the development of public finance. The constitution of Solon (4th century B.C.) abolished bondage and gave people a share in the government in a democratic fashion. However, together with the people's right to share in government affairs came their obligation to pay taxes in proportion to their incomes, derived primarily from landed property. (The first tax was levied in 428 B.C.)

Thus the richest class (pentacosiomedimni) with evaluated property (timema) of 6,000 drachmas or more and income higher than 500 drachmas per year would pay 24 percent income taxes; the second income class (knights) with estimated property of from 3,000 to 5,000 drachmas and an annual income of from 300 to 500 drachmas would pay 20 percent income taxes; while the third income class (zeugites) with property estimated at from 1,800 to 3,000 and an annual income of from 150 to 300 drachmas, would pay 13.3 percent income taxes. Finally, poor people (thetes) with less than 150 drachmas in annual income were exempted. In wartime, when higher government expenditures were needed, heavier taxes were imposed.(3)

This tax system, which Plato seemed to support in his Laws, can be characterized as a form of progressive taxation based on income differentiation. Taxed incomes were estimated primarily on the basis of landed property. Although there were tolls at the gates of the city-states and sales taxes at times, income taxes, levied according to property, prevailed mainly because of fewer difficulties in assessing the tax base. Regarding tariffs, it was suggested, primarily by Plato, that duties should not be levied on imports or on exports and that imports of unnecessary luxuries and exports of necessary commodities be prohibited.

As Xenophon pointed out, government revenues were also collected from the silver mines of Lavrion, near Athens. In addition to aliens' duties (Metoikion) and the rents from public warehouses and other buildings, the inexhaustible mines of silver provided large amounts of revenues.(4) The proprietor of the mines was the state, and those who worked in them were obliged to pay the public a tribute of one twenty-fourth part of the silver found. The state either operated the mines itself or leased them out to private entrepreneurs, who could also form joint-stock companies. With an efficient administration, national revenue could be improved and, in periods of peace, used to construct public buildings and trading vessels, increase foreign trade, and train youth.

Originally, the citizens of Athens voluntarily contributed to the support of many public works. However, a number of officials became fully occupied in governmental services and many citizens participated, on a rotating part-time basis, in the activities of the city-state assembly (Ecclesia) for pay. Then public expenditures grew rapidly and reserves suffered, especially during the Peloponnesian War. Under the pressure of raids from Sparta and other hostile city-states, people from the countryside fled into Athens, which provided for their sustenance from public funds (Theoricon or Theoric Fund). This welfare system increased the proportion of idle persons, reduced production, destroyed the treasury, demoralized the citizens, and accelerated the decline of Athens. Furthermore, deficiencies in the public finance system of Sparta led to the decline of that city-state.(5) The narrow tax base of property, the income of merchants and artisans, and excises on a few commodities could not support the state's needs for defense and other expenditures for long periods. Similar phenomena can be observed today not only in market economies with a growing public sector, such as that of Greece and the other EEC countries, but also in socialist economies with many functions and services performed by the public sector, as in Yugoslavia and the COMECON countries.

Trade Expansion

In addition to the general national wealth of the mines of Lavrion, there was the valuable, splendid marble of Mount Pentelicus used for the construction of the Parthenon and other monuments as well as for export. Also, honey was produced in Attica, Thebes, and Corinth, and olives, wine, and other agricultural products in the plains and hills of these areas. Some of this produce was sold abroad. Export and import trade thrived primarily through the warmwater ports of Piraeus and Salonika and those of the Aegean islands, which have always facilitated trade between West and East and with Mediterranean lands to the north.

To expand trade, the seafaring Greeks established a number of colonies among the coast of the Balkan Peninsula and the eastern Mediterranean. Further improvement of commercial activities and crafts took place when Philip II, emperor of Macedonia, and his son Alexander the Great unified the Greek city-states (338 B.C.). Alexander, a student of Aristotle, marched through the Middle East to Persia and still farther eastward to the banks of the Indus River, where a number of colonies were established, and the culture of Greece was extended. This Greco-Macedonian state survived until the Romans conquered Greece along with the other Balkan areas during the second century B.C. and formed a foundation that culturally influenced the subsequent Roman and Byzantine empires.

The conquests of Alexander the Great opened new horizons to Greek trade or emporium from the eastern Mediterranean coasts to the rich markets of the far-off East. The main commodities exported by the Greek cities at that time were metals, pottery products, textiles, and similar industrial goods. By then trade had assumed an international character, following on political evolutions and very often preceding them. The products exported by the Greek cities were mostly industrial because the soil was not rich enough for large quantity production and the export of agricultural products. Trade during the Roman and Byzantine periods was, more or less, a continuation of the ancient Greek trade. Even during the long period of the Turkish occupation, trade was dominated by Greek merchants, both in the vast Ottoman Empire and in a number of cities in Western Europe.

ROMAN CONQUEST AND BYZANTIUM

Under the Roman rule, Greece (named Achaea), except Macedonia, suffered a steady economic decline, while the Illyrian lands, particularly Dalmatia, thrived in trading raw materials and slaves. The main contributions of the Romans to the economies of the conquered lands were the development of a well-organized transportation network, the security of life and property, and the establishment of an efficient apparatus of public administration. Under these conditions, a large number of trade centers with theaters and numerous local industries developed. Although the Latin language was spread throughout the area, Greek culture influenced the Roman rulers and administrators, to the extent that the invaders were themselves conquered culturally by the country they conquered physically. Greek architecture had a marked influence on that of Rome, and educated Romans sent their children to Athens to study. General Sulla and later other Romans shipped home much Greek sculpture and kept Athenian workshops busy making replicas (after the sack of Athens in 86 B.C.).(6)

Salonika became an administrative and trade center of the Romans and the Byzantines. Its advantageous location at the crossroads of the Balkans made it an important commercial city. People and products moved from Adriatica to Byzantium and vice versa mainly through Egnatia Street (still used in Salonika).

The Aegean islands, particularly Delos and Rhodos, were used by the Roman armies and merchants as way stations for the transport of merchandise and slaves from the Middle East.(7) After the separation of the eastern section of the Roman Empire, cultural and commercial activities moved largely to New Rome (Constantinople), which became the capital of East Rome or Byzantium (326 A.D.).(8)

The emperors of Byzantium introduced a common (Hellenic) language and (Christian) religion and stimulated trade by reducing taxes and making administrative reforms. Silk production, pottery, jewelry, and shipping were the main industries that flourished in Constantinople, which became an international trade center. Constantinople remained for some ten centuries the economic and political heart of the Byzantine Empire and the center of the Greek Orthodox religion and intellectual life. However, the spread of Christianity changed the ancient Greek culture, caused the closing of ancient Greek temples, and ended the Olympic games after the fourth century.

From the fourth century onward, Slavic tribes infiltrated Byzantium and gradually created agricultural settlements primarily in present-day Yugoslavia and Bulgaria and occasionally in Thessaly and even in the Peloponnesus. However, the southern part of the Balkan Peninsula, the coastal areas and the islands, kept their traditional Hellenic character.

During the ninth century, two missionary brothers from Salonika, Cyril and Methodius, introduced the Cyrillic alphabet, based on the Greek. They were also responsible for the Byzantine (Eastern Orthodox) religious and cultural influence on large segments of Slavic population. Together with other scholars, they nurtured Byzantine culture throughout the Balkans. To this day some religious and cultural aspects of Byzantium have been preserved (since the tenth century) by many monasteries, mainly that of Mount Athos near Salonika.(9)

With the increase in imperial expenses, the weight of taxation became greater. The main levies were land taxes and hearth taxes. The latter may have been payable by every head of household while the former seem to have included taxes on arable and pasture land, vineyards, and mountain land. For humanitarian reasons, tax relief was accorded lands that had suffered disasters. Local administrators, at times, resorted to the use of labor services in road construction, shipbuilding, and similar public works, instead of levying provincial taxes.(10)

During the millenium of Byzantium, Athens wasted away, but Salonika kept its commercial importance and became a vital port in the Mediterranean. After the eleventh century, the empire and its capital city began a slow process of decline. However, a number of scholars fled or were summoned to western Europe, carrying with them Greek philosophy and culture, "the seeds" of which "grew into some of the finest flowers of the Renaissance."(11) Crete came under the Arabs for over one hundred years around the ninth century and Candia, now Herakleon, became an important commercial port during that period.

In 1204, the same year that Constantinople fell to the Crusaders, Venice occupied Crete, a rich and lovely island, as Homer called it, strategically located amidst the dark blue sea, almost equidistant from Europe, Asia, and Africa. Crete, which remained for over four centuries under Venetian rule, developed a prosperous commerce, as did other islands and Greek coastlands, where old Venetian fortresses can be seen today. Also, Franks, anxious to enjoy the sun, climate, and pleasant way of life of Greece, established their feudal system in various parts of the country, particularly in Achaea and Athens, as did the Genoese along the Anatolian coast and on various Aegean islands in the thirteenth century.

Venetian and Genoese merchants competed fiercely with the Greeks for the capture of the lucrative Mediterranean markets. They established a number of commercial outposts in many islands and coastal areas where they were engaged in trade and banking activities. With the Crusaders they occupied Constantinople (1204-1261) and drained the financial resources of the Byzantine Empire by collecting tariffs and not paying taxes. Most of the land of Hellas (Greece) was distributed among Venetian and Genoese barons, and a feudal system was established.

After 1204, Constantinople and other territories of Byzantium were mercilessly pillaged by the soldiers of the Fourth Crusade. Economic mismanagement, high taxes, currency debasement, and the luxurious living of the Byzantine rulers led the empire to the point of bankruptcy. Moreover, internal strife and external invasions, mainly by Mongols from the east, brought about the final collapse and the occupation of the empire by the Seljuk Turks. Conquests by the Latins from the west and the Turks from the east made the Byzantine Empire look, as Charles Diehl, a French historian, characterized it, like a slender, dislocated, miserable body upon which rested an enormous head.

From a sociopolitical point of view, the roots of Modern Greece, so the story goes, are sunk in Byzantine soil, and the attitudes of the people stem from that time.(12) The importance of the Church (at least of its wealth), the centralized bureaucratic state headed by hereditary rulers, the dominance of personalities in politics, and the primacy of politics over economics in policy discussions are mostly the heritage of the Byzantine and Ottoman mentality. On the other hand, the system of centralized public administration was largely borrowed from France.

OTTOMAN OCCUPATION

In 1345, John Cantacugenus, a Byzantine official, invited the Ottomans to support his bid for the throne. In 1349, the Ottomans were invited again to help save Salonika from the Serbs (under Stephen Dushan). Thus the Ottomans, further strengthened by additional troops, began to settle down on eastern Thrace (Gallipoli). From 1354 onward they began pushing westward to the rich lands of Macedonia and Thessaly. Eventually they captured Andrianople (1360) and Salonika (1430).

Constantinople fell in 1453, Athens in 1456, and the Peloponnesus in 1460. Chios and many other Aegean islands, which were occupied by the Genoese for three centuries, fell also to the Ottoman Turks in 1566.

The Turkish newcomers distributed conquered lands to their warriors and collaborators (spahis). This practice helped to ensure their permanent settlement and occupation of Greece and other Balkan areas for some four centuries. The forceful recruitment of infant Christian males converted to Islam (janissaries) and the toleration of the Christian religion also helped establish and sustain Ottoman rule in the area for such a long period. To promote trade and industry, the Turkish sultans renewed the economic privileges that Venice enjoyed under Byzantium and even tried to repopulate occupied areas with merchants, primarily experienced and seafaring Greeks. From time to time, Venetian fleets gained control of many coastal areas and islands, including the Ionian Islands (1386-1797) and the Peloponnesus (1687-1718).(13)

During the years of Ottoman occupation, trade was conducted mainly by Greek merchants and to a limited extent by Jews, Armenians, and Macedonean and Vlachian traders and artisans. A number of commercial and cultural centers gradually developed such as Athens, Salonika, and Ioannina. Raw materials and other merchandise were transported among the Mediterranean ports primarily by the Aegean mariners, especially after the Greek ships were permitted to fly the Russian flag as a result of the Russo-Turkish Treaty of Jassy (1792). Moreover, a number of handicraft industries and production cooperatives, including that of Ambelakia in Thessaly manufacturing cotton thread, were created.

The Ambelakia enterprise was an outstanding example of a handicraft cooperative. It was founded in 1795 in Mount Ossa in Thessaly. Its initial capital, estimated at 100,000 francs, was gradually increased to 20 million francs by 1810. The Cooperative had two branches, one agricultural, and one manufacturing, which provided raw materials and which produced and sold textile products primarily to Central Europe. The cooperative also provided free meals to its poor members and maintained schools and hospitals. Its dyed yarns became famous in European markets, competing effectively with similar British products. However, after the introduction of steam engines, Britain's cotton thread became cheaper than that of Ambelakia, which was spun by manual labor.

Shipping industries also operated along cooperative lines, at that time, with seamen, captains, lumber merchants, and carpenters pooling their resources and sharing the profits. However, a large portion of the ships was destroyed during the revolution against the Turks.(14)

In all of the other areas occupied by the Ottomans, however, heavy taxation, export tariffs, and the bureaucratic centralism of their empire discouraged rapid expansion and modernization of production enterprises. Large fertile areas of the Balkan region that had become prosperous during the Byzantine period and the Frankish and Venetian occupations were left idle after the Ottomans captured them.

Toward the end of the eighteenth century, a number of teachers were sent to Western Europe by rich merchants, shipowners, and a few Phanariots (high clergy and Greek elite) to revive studies of the Greek past.(15) These teachers became interested in bringing the French Revolution's principles of liberty and equality to Greece, and one of them, Rhigas Pheraios (Valenstinlis), formed a revolutionary organization Philike Hetairia (Society of Friends) and composed revolutionary battle hymns to encourage the Greek rayahs (semi-slave subjects) to participate in the struggle for liberation from the Turks. For this reason he was captured and executed in 1798.

From an economic and social point of view, the feudalistic system of western Europe prevailed, to a large extent, in Greece and Yugoslavia during the Byzantine and the Ottoman periods. Aristocrat landlords and Turkish chiefs (pashas and agas) lived luxuriously while the masses lived in poverty. Between them was the class consisting of a few well-to-do local people who retained and enlarged their privileges and their large properties, sometimes though collaboration with the foreign masters.

In each village area there was a Christian Kodjabashis responsible for the collection of taxes, which were delivered to the Turkish masters. Haratsi was a heavy tax imposed on Christians as a punishment for not converting into Islam. Another form of taxation was the decati, levied every year on produce. The most fertile lands in each area were confiscated by the Turkish chiefs, who transformed them into their own estates (chifliks). When the owners and tillers of the land objected, they were summarily executed or tortured by Turkish troops. Under such conditions, many people gave their property to monasteries, which were exempt from property confiscations (vakoufia). As a result, large and rich farms and properties were accumulated by the monasteries (metohia). Even today a number of monasteries in Greece own such farms, which are cultivated by the monks or leased to individuals or agricultural cooperatives.

During Ottoman rule, a number of Phanariots served as administrators and even dragomans of the Porte (in Constantinople). They became rich and powerful under the Turks and, as a result, they opposed the rebellion of the rayahs. They remained a group apart, hated by many Greeks struggling for their freedom. High priests, with some exceptions, were criticized for their exhortation to resignation and acquiescence in Ottoman rule and the prevailing authority.(16) This attitude retarded intellectual progress and discouraged efforts at political liberation. However, local priests helped preserve the Greek language and heritage in secret night schools and sparked resistance in the villages. As members of the elected councils, together with the village headmen and teachers, they were responsible to the Ottomans for tax collection and other administrative duties. At the same time, though, many of these councils helped unite the Greek people against their oppressor.

Heavy oppression and economic exploitation of the Greek and other Balkan rayahs by the Moslem rulers resulted in the struggle for liberation against their masters, which started in Morea (Aghia Lavra at Kalavryta) on March 21, 1821.(17) Helped by Greek merchants and mariners living abroad, as well as other philhellenic societies and governments in Europe and elsewhere, the Greek klefts (revolutionaries) managed to liberate their land and establish a free Greek state that included the Peloponneus (Morea), Sterea Hellas, and Thessaly (by 1928).

GROWTH OF MODERN GREECE

After liberation from the Ottoman occupation in the 1820s, Greece began the process of rehabilitation and development under difficult economic and sociopolitical conditions. Over 200,000 people had lost their lives. Houses, olive orchards, and vineyards had been largely destroyed. Most of the land belonged to the Turks, who owned eighteen times as much land per capita as did the Greeks. Even after liberation, land distribution was slow and highly unequal. The primates and other powerful persons helped themselves first, acquiring title to large and rich Turkish estates. Only one out of six peasants had land of his own. Land appropriations through legal recognition of squatters' rights and title gains (if land was cultivated continuously for a period varying from 1 to 15 years) helped land distribution somewhat but gave rise to frequent litigation and violence among the peasants.

The struggle for independence and nationhood distracted the infant nation from economic development. The area of the new nation was small (about one-third of its present size), as was its population (some 753,000 people). It included central Greece, below the Arta-Volos line in Thessaly, the Peloponnesus, and the Cyclades Islands in the Aegean Sea. The rest of what is today Greece was then still in Ottoman hands, except the Ionian Islands, which were controlled by the British.

The new Greek nation began its life under the influence of the great powers. Even the political parties were based on Russian, British, or French interests. Ioannis Capodistrias and Theodore Kolokotrones were connected with the first, Alexander Mavrocordatos with the second, and Ioannis Kolettis with the third. The first republic was established in 1827 as a result of the first constitution, drawn up by the revolutionary founding fathers in the Convention of Troizin. Ioannis Capodistrias, an educated cosmopolitan who had served as Russia's secretary of state, became the president of the republic (1827-31). After his assassination by chieftains of the Mani area (from the Mavrocordatos family), the protecting powers, primarily Britain, selected Prince Otto of Bavaria, a Roman Catholic, to be king of Greece without consulting the Greeks.

During the thirty years of his reign, 1833-62, King Otto, introduced in autocratic system of centralized administration, which, ever since, has resulted in a slow-moving bureaucracy. He also imported his own artisans and a brewer, Fuchs (Fix), whose firm remains active even today in Athens. In 1862 Otto was deposed by a revolt ignited by students and middle-class intellectuals. By that time, the population had doubled, as had the shipping industry, while foreign trade had more than quadrupled.(18)

When the new and small Greek nation was established, all the fertile plains of Thessaly and Macedonia remained in Ottoman control. However, in the hills and plains of Attica and Boeotia and the coastlands of Peloponnesus, the farms produced cereals, olives, grapes, and other fruits as in ancient times. Grapes, combined with resin from the pines of Attica, were and still are used to make retsina, a pungent local wine. Athens, Thebes (where Oedipus lived in ancient times), Patras, and Corinth were the main market towns for such products. After 1833, when the capital of Greece was transferred from Nauplion, Athens gradually increased in wealth and became a magnet city, as it had been in ancient times. Most of the Greek islands, however, remained poor, and a number of their inhabitants emigrated to other countries.(19)

The typical Greek peasant was engaged in subsistence farming. Agricultural techniques were poor. Rudimentary tools and wooden plows were still in use. Crop rotation was little known, and wasteful scattering of seed by hand was widespread. Lack of transportation limited the available markets for agricultural products. Grain was mostly imported from Trieste, Alexandria, and the Black Sea ports. Taxes in the form of tithes on threshing floors were heavy and unjust, and collection was time consuming.(20) Grain had to remain piled up for months awaiting the tax collector's inspection. Fowls, pigeons, and other birds, as well as rats and other creatures, assembled at the threshing floor to get their share of the poor harvest of the peasants. Animal husbandry was neglected, agricultural credit was limited, and interest rates ranged from 20 to 24 percent on mortgage loans and from 36 to 50 percent on personal loans.(21)

To pay for grain imports, Corinth grapes, currants and later tobacco were exported primarily to Britain, Austria, and Germany. Currant exports steadily increased from 6,000 tons in 1821 to 42,800 in 1861 and 100,700 tons in 1878. Industrial development remained in the embryonic stage. However, shipping kept its traditional importance. Lumber merchants, carpenters, captains, and seamen pooled their resources along cooperative lines to build and operate new ships. A limited number of small, labor-intensive enterprises were developed in the Piraeus-Athens area, Syra, and Patras, especially after 1882 when the Charilaos Trikoupis' administration expanded the transportation network. By 1877, there were 136 plants in Greece employing 7,342 workers.(22)

Through fighting and negotiations, the Greek state expanded, slowly and tortuously, to incorporate territories and peoples of Greek background. Such territories included: the Ionian Islands from Britain in 1864; the rest of Thessaly in 1881, Crete (liberated in 1898), Macedonia and Epirus in 1913, the Eastern Aegean Islands in 1914, and Thrace in 1919, all from the Ottomans; and the Dodecanese in 1948 from Italy. The Treaty of Soevres provided that Smyrna and its environs, as well as eastern Thrace, be turned over to Greece, but the Treaty of Lausanne (1923) eliminated this. Cyprus, with a population of 600,000 (about 82 percent Greek and 18 percent Turkish) and rich in copper, achieved its independence from Britain in 1959, after enduring centuries of foreign occupations. However, Aphrodite's Isle has always been a pawn on the Mediterranean chessboard. It is still a source of contention between Greece and Turkey, as Turkish troops have occupied 42 percent of the island since 1974.

As a result of new acquisitions, Greece's production capacity increased significantly. Production of grain, cotton, and tobacco in Thessaly, Macedonia, and Thrace improved domestic economic conditions and helped increase exports. The city of Kavalla became an important port for tobacco exports. However, much of Epirus, with rugged mountains, eroded lands, and limited means of transportation, remained an economic liability to Greece. This is why many people left it for other areas and industrial centers in search of a better living.

The following is a brief description of the frequent political changes that were responsible for the economic and social instability in the country at that time.

In 1863, Prince William George of the Danish Glucksberg dynasty was enthroned in Greece at Britain's recommendation. King George I of the Hellenes and his descendants were to rule Greece, primarily through obedient conservative governments installed by rigged elections, until 1967, with some interruptions (mainly 1924-35 and 1941-46). On the economic front, the country was plagued by financial difficulties. Large amounts of money were borrowed mainly for military expenditures to police the long new borders and to promote the idea of "Greater Greece." A number of economic concessions were given to British-owned public utilities and other foreign companies.

Trading and professional groups were dissatisfied with economic conditions under George I, and popular discontent with the monarchy increased. Then in 1909 young army and navy officers revolted and demanded the removal of Prince Constantine from the army, where he exercised dynastic influence.(23) They summoned Eleutherios Venizelos, a Cretan revolutionary and statesman, who became prime minister of Greece in 1910. On October 1912, Greece, along with other Balkan nations, entered the war against Turkey. King George went to Salonika to celebrate its liberation by the Greek army. He was shot and killed there in March 1913, and his son became King Constantine I of the Hellenes.

King Constantine I, who married the sister of Kaiser Wilhelm II of Germany, and prime minister Venizelos, a liberal politician, were in almost constant disagreement over constitutional questions and Greece's alliances, as were the voters (royalists versus Venizelists). The former wanted to join the Central powers, dominated by Germany; the latter pushed for Greece's entrance into the war on the side of the Allies (Britain, France, and Italy).

After Venizelos formed his own agreement in Salonika and declared war on Bulgaria, the king, also under pressure from the Allies, left Greece in 1917. His second son, Alexander, then became king, reigning until 1920, when he was fatally bitten by two pet monkeys. Constantine was then recalled by a plebiscite. But the Allies refused to recognize him and withdrew their support from Greece. This was the main reason for the defeat of the Greek army in Asia Minor, although earlier victories had brought it within striking distance of Ankara, the capital of Turkey. This defeat led Colonel (later General) Chicholas Plastiras and a group of officers in the island of Chios to issue an ultimatum in September 1922 demanding the abdication of the king. When Plastiras came to Athens, six leading advisers of the king who were considered responsible for the catastrophe in Asia Minor, were court-martialed and executed. Then George, the eldest son of King Constantine I, became King George II. He, in turn, left the country in 1924 and remained in exile until 1935.

After the Greek expedition in Asia Minor (April 13, 1919) and the disaster thereafter (autumn 1922), a massive population exchange took place. Some 1,500,000 Greeks left Asia Minor, where their ancestors had lived for possibly thirty centuries, for Greece, and 400,000 Turks left Greece for Turkey, while another 40,000 Greeks and 40,000 Bulgarians were exchanged between Greece and Bulgaria. Although there were serious housing and employment problems at the beginning, in the long run the progressive and industrious refugees proved to be a great asset to the Greek economy. A rug industry was transplanted from Asia Minor, and new textiles, pottery, copper ware, and shipping were developed by the skilled labor of the refugees.

As a result of the policy of conciliation and friendship pursued by Eleutherios Venizelos and Kemal Ataturk, president of Turkey, as well as other leaders of the Balkan countries, trade and development in the area were stimulated. Genuine efforts to achieve closer economic cooperation among the nations of the Balkan Peninsula were made after 1924, primarily by Alexander Papanastassiou, a premier of Greece and Nicolas Titulescu, foreign minister of Romania. In a number of conferences among the Balkan states, emphasis was given to further collaboration in tariffs, tourism, credit, and protection of agricultural products.(24)

During the period of the second republic of modern Greece (1924-1935), economic and political instability led to a brief dictatorship (January-August 1926) by the chief of the army staff, General Theodore Pangalos, who was also the leader of the Republic Officers' League. As in all dictatorships, puritanism was proclaimed. Thus, a law was passed that forbade women's skirts to be more than fourteen inches from the ground.(25) On August 1926 General Kondyles overthrew the dictatorship and held elections, which failed to give the republicans enough votes to govern, and a coalition with royalists was formed. There was no tradition of discipline and obedience in Greece, and disagreements among political leaders persisted. In 1927, the Bank of Greece was established to stabilize the currency and the balance of payment. In 1928, Venizelos returned and became prime minister. At that time unemployment, inflation and other economic problems were growing. They were further aggravated in the early 1930s because of the worldwide depression. After attempted military coups by General Nicholas Plastiras in 1933 and 1935 failed because of lack of popular and army support, a plebiscite restored the monarchy and King George II returned at the end of 1935.

In August 1936 General John Metaxas and King George II imposed a dictatorship and instituted martial law, suspending constitutional liberties. Freedom of the press was abolished, and opponents were jailed or sent to isolated islands (especially Anafe, where some prisoners were forced to take castor oil for "ideological" cleansing). Also, Greek classical dramas and Pericles' orations were censored. Metaxas, who had been educated in Nazi Germany, turned more and more to Germany for trade while the palace was sympathetic to Britain.(26) Despite the introduction of minimum wages and social insurance, Metaxas' dictatorship was unpopular with the liberty-loving Greek people, as were other dictatorships.

Suddenly Benito Mussolini, the Italian dictator, launched an attack against Greece from Albania on October 28, 1940. The poorly equipped Greek troops managed to push the invading Italians back to Albania, probably because, as Napoleon's dictum goes, "in war the proportion of moral to material factors is as three to one." However, Greek troops, fighting on so many fronts, were unable to resist the well-equipped armored units of Adolf Hitler, which on April 6, 1941 penetrated far into the country, while Piraeus, the main port of Greece, was heavily bombed.

Greece, under occupation by Germany, Italy, and Bulgaria (in Macedonia and western Thrace), suffered heavy losses. During the first year of occupation the Germans printed inflationary money and drained the country of needed resources, while imports dropped significantly because of the Allied blockade. Some 450,000 people died of starvation alone, primarily in Athens. Adults and children suffered from malnutrition, malaria, and tuberculosis. Factories were destroyed, transportation and communications throughout the country almost disappeared, and about three-quarters of the country's large commercial fleet was sunk. Civilian massacres were carried out by the Nazis throughout Greece. At Kalavryta alone, a town near Patras, 1,300 unarmed persons were gunned down on December 13, 1943 while all the houses were burned to the ground.(27)

Within five months of the occupation of Greece, EAM (the National Liberation Front), a political resistance organization with people from all walks of life, was created.

Later on (April 1942) ELAS (the National Popular Liberation Army), the military arm of EAM, started offensive activities against the Germans. EPON (the United All-Greece Youth Organization) were also formed to train and provide recreation for young boys and girls. ETA (the Caretaking Committee for the Partisans) was responsible for helping feed and equip the partisans. Another resistance group of some importance was EDES (the Greek National Democratic League), organized by Colonel Napoleon Zervas mainly in Epirus. Zervas was preoccupied with promoting his own interests, and his group did not manage to expand as EAM did. Instead, it grew weaker and gradually turned to secret collaboration with the Axis, while EAM-ELAS took the initiative in fighting the Germans and reforming the countryside.(28)

During World War II, the strategic position of Greece became apparent. As Winston Churchill said, "the spasms of Greece ... stood at the nerve center of power, law and freedom in the Western World."(29) The British had more than 50 missions working with the partisans in Greece and Yugoslavia and provided equipment and munitions to the resistance groups, mainly to ELAS and EDES, during the struggle against the Axis. Because of the Nazi occupation and the hardship suffered by the inhabitants during that time, local conflicts appeared in many parts of the country. Some people, promoted by selfishness, jealousy, political differences, and previous disputes about property and personal interests , made accusations against others to the occupation authorities or to the partisans of EAM-ELAS. At that time the British, seeing the growing communist domination of EAM-ELAS, secretly supported with ammunition and sterling the formation of new organizations composed primarily of former officers and right-wingers (such as EO or the National Organization), which turned against EAM-ELAS. On the other hand, certain heads of the EAM-ELAS resistance groups committed a number of crimes at the suggestion of local political representatives. In many instances, people were killed by both sides not for serious political or ideological reasons and without due process and supportive evidence. Local people did not trust each other and frequently resorted to conflicts, hatred, revenge, and even open group fighting. The dismal situation in which the nation found itself toward the end of the occupation period was the background for the severe civil war that followed (1946-49).

As a result of the Moscow Conference in October 1944, Winston Churchill and Josif Stalin agreed that Britain would "have ninety percent of the say in Greece, and go fifty-fifty about Yugoslavia."(30) The Yalta Conference in February 1945, with Churchill, Franklin Roosevelt, and Stalin, accepted this arrangement.

Churchill decided to crush EAM-ELAS, which had been gradually infiltrated and dominated by the communists, to support the government of George Papandreou (an old-line republican with oratorical and maneuvering skills), and finally to restore King George II. On October 4, 1944 British troops of "Operation Manna" entered Patras and after ten days reached Athens. On December 3, clashes between ELAS and the police (mostly German collaborators) started in Athens, and clashes between ELAS and the British went on until February 1945. After a rigged plebiscite, royal rule was installed in 1946. Before the people could lift their heads above their starvation and tragedy, mutual hatred between left-wing and right-wing groups flared up into a serious civil war which persisted until 1949.(31) In the meantime King George II died, and his brother Paul I became king in 1946.

On March 31, 1947 Britain terminated all aid to Greece, and soon thereafter all of its troops were withdrawn. Thus British political and economic tutelage in Greece, which prevailed for more than a century, came to an end. On May 22, 1947 $300 million aid was initially appropriated by the United States (under the Truman Doctrine), most of which went for the army and the expenditures of largely corrupt public administrations. American experts were assigned to administer the program and to supervise related policies.(32)

During the internal conflict, Yugoslavia provided sanctuary to the Greek communist battalions until 1948, when Tito broke ties with Stalin. As a result of military support from the United States and the closing of Yugoslav borders, the civil war came to an end and Greece and Yugoslavia established friendly relations in 1950.

With the promulgation of the Truman Doctrine, American aid, favoring mainly military needs at the neglect of other economic considerations such as inflation and unemployment, began flowing into Greece and Turkey. As Walter Lippman remarked, these two countries had been selected "not because they are specially in need of relief, not because they are shining examples of democracy . . . but because they are the strategic gateway to the Black Sea and the heart of the Soviet Union."(33)   Venal politics, ineptness, nepotism, and corruption were rampant in Greece, which has so often been plagued by social-political turmoil.   The country's political and economic life was in a state of bankruptcy.   As former Prime Minister George Papandreou observed, there was "a people worthy of their history" but "a leadership unworthy of the people."(34)   Greece was perhaps the only country in which enemy collaborators continued to exercise power after World War II instead of being prosecuted. Mostly, they became right-wing royalists, who used direct and indirect (psychological) terrorism on the part the dossier-keeping security forces, paramilitary right-wing organizations, such as the X-Group, the TEA (National Security Batallions), and the rural gendarmerie, to coerce the electorate to vote for conservative governments favorable to the royal family.   Complaints of fraud and intimidation at the polls were common, while criticism of the high costs of maintaining the royal family was widespread.   The annual salary of the king alone was $566,000 or more than three times that of the president of the United States.

Such political and socioeconomic pressures prevented the Greeks from exercising their passion for talk and argument about domestic politics or politiki (derived from polis, the word for city in ancient times), and turned their discussion instead to international events.

In 1952 Greece and Turkey became members of NATO (the North Atlantic Treaty Organization).   United States advisers exercised control on weaponry and had great influence on important decisions through the palace and the Greek army command, not only on military but also on political and economic matters.   American military and economic aid to Greece amounted to about $100 million per year.(35)

After an official visit by President Tito to Greece in 1955, better relations were developed with Yugoslavia. Trade agreements were also concluded with other Balkan and Eastern European nations.

Frequent elections, with a great deal of gerrymandering and vote-rigging were the main characteristics of the postwar crowned democracy of Greece.   Unstable governments and mounting social and economic problems led to extensive emigration of workers and educated people to Canada, Australia, the United States, and later to West Germany.

In the years following the elections of 1961, which were criticized by the two main opposition parties (the Center Union and the United Democratic Left) as dishonest and fraudulent, the monarchy came under mounting challenges. King Constantine II, who succeeded his father Paul in 1966 at age 24, was greatly influenced by his mother, Queen Frederika, a German by origin, who had dictatorial desires. On the other hand, strong individualism and the cult of personality in Greek politics led politicians to spend time beating dead political horses and digging in old records.(36) All this and the absurd actions of the king, who wanted to rule as well as to reign, together with the blessings of NATO and the United States, led to the military coup in April 1967. The end of the monarchy took place in December of the same year, after the king's unsuccessful attempt at a coup against the dictatorship of Colonel George Papadopoulos.

On the economic front, the reforms of 1953 by Spyros Markezinis (the minister of coordination) which included devaluation of the drachma (from 15 to 30 drachmas per U.S. dollar), improvement in public administration, and incentives to attract foreign investments (Law 2687/1953) somewhat improved domestic and foreign trade conditions. With political and fiscal stability in the late 1950s, money deposits increased, exports improved and the wheels of industry began moving more rapidly. Instead of buying gold sovereigns and land or luxury apartments, people put their money in savings accounts for investment financing.

In addition, increasing numbers of tourists from Europe and America came to enjoy the sun-drenched haven and Homer's "wine-dark" sea of Greece. However, unemployment and underemployment remained high, and the gap in per capita income between the city and the countryside increased. Government subsidies on wheat, tobacco, and other crops did not accomplish much. Instead, together with large military expenditures, they increased budgetary deficits. Moreover, the growth of imports over exports had detrimental effects on the balance of payments and the international position of the country.

During the period 1947-66 total United States aid to Greece amounted to $3,749.4 million, about half of which ($1,854.3 million) was military assistance and half economic aid. The largest part of the aid $3,410.9 million) consisted of grants, and the rest ($338.4 million) of loans. Technical assistance was terminated in 1962 and major economic aid was ended in 1964.(37) Only military assistance under the auspices of NATO, continued thereafter. Together with aid, U.S. influence was so extensive that many people criticized the foreign policy of the conservative governments as slavishly following the United States.(38)

Although a number of investment incentives were offered, entrepreneurs were reluctant to invest in anything other than family enterprises. Under the protection of foreign investment, however, a number of new ventures, such as the Esso-Pappas petrochemical complex in Salonika ($200 million) and the Aluminium de Grece, exploiting the rich mineral deposits of bauxite ($125 million), were completed by 1966. However, large amounts of investment continued to be channeled into housing and urban land speculation, particularly in Athens, while the gap in the balance of trade was widening. (More analysis on problems of economic growth, public finance, and foreign trade is provided in later sections.)

A SHORT HISTORY OF THE ECONOMY OF YUGOSLAVIA

The economic history of Yugoslavia is related to the territorial complexity of the area, the expansionary trends of different neighboring powers, and the related resistance of the native peoples as well as their efforts to absorb and unite with each other. The valleys of the Danube, the Sava, and the Morava have served as the main gateways of migrating people and invading armies for centuries, while the Dinaric Alps and the other Balkan mountains served as a bastion against these movements.

Although little is known of the inhabitants of the present Yugoslavian Republic before the coming of the Slavs, many archeological remains attest that the area was peopled even at the early times of the Iron Age (Hollstat period). However, about the fifth century B.C., the Greeks were the first to mention that the Illyrians had occupied the area west of the Vardar and north of Epirus, driving the Thracians to the central and eastern regions of the Balkan Peninsula. During the seventh, sixth and fifth centuries B.C., a number of Greek trading colonies were established in such locations on the coast of the Adriatic Sea as Vis (Issa), Korcula (Korkyra nigra), Hvar (Pharos), Trogir (Tragurion), and Split (Salona). However, the interior had been affected little, if at all, by the spread of such trading colonies. Moreover the infiltration of "Celtic" peoples from the north at the beginning of the fourth century B.C. had little and only temporary influence on the Illyrians.(39)

Trade interruptions by pirates from the Illyrian coasts and the expansionary policies of the Roman Empire led to repeated Roman expeditions from the year 229 B.C. until A.D. 9, when Tiberius annexed the area named Illyricum, which at times incorporated areas from Vienna to Athens. The transportation network and the effective Roman administration stimulated commerce and mining operations, particularly in gold, silver, and copper, in the area.(40) The eastern part of the Roman Empire from near Lake Scutari to the river Sava was separated administratively by Diocletian (A.D. 285). After A.D. 395, this eastern part became the Byzantine Empire, with its own Greek-speaking Orthodox world, contrasted to the Latin-speaking Catholic world of the western part of the Roman Empire.

With the collapse of the Roman Empire, Visigoths, Huns, Ostrogoths, and some other groups captured the whole coastal area of Dalmatia. This was reconquered by Justinian, the Byzantine emperor, by A.D. 535 but then captured and devastated by the Avars coming from the Danube plain during the second half of the sixth century. At the same time and into the seventh century, the Slavs dispersed by the Avar menace in eastern Europe moved southward as far as the Peloponnnesus. By A.D. 650 they occupied Illyria and settled there permanently. They were mainly the Slovenes and the Croats, who came under Roman Catholic influence, and the Serbs in the south who were influenced by the Orthodox church of Constantinople. Although the Croats used the Latin and the Serbs the Cyrillic alphabet, they both continued to speak the same (Serbo-Croat) language, while the Slovenes and the Slavs of Macedonia continued to use different languages. At the beginning of the 10th century the Magyars, a Finno-Ugrian race, established itself in what is now Hungary and separated the southern Slavs from the others in the north. The remnants of the Roman provincials, primarily

Vlachs, were scattered in different mountainous areas and were gradually slavicized.

During the period of the Byzantine and Ottoman empires, Dalmatia's city-states came repeatedly under Venice or Hungary, but they managed to preserve a high degree of autonomy. As a result, the development of industries, fisheries, and seaborne commerce, primarily with neighboring Italian cities, brought real prosperity to the area. However, the interior economy remained primarily agricultural and pastoral. Gradually, though, and as a result of the economic awakening in Europe especially during the thirteenth and fourteenth centuries, production of cereals, hemps, flax, wine, oil, and other agricultural products greatly increased in the fertile basins of the Ibar, the Vardar, the Drim, and the Morava rivers, supplementing the cattle, pigs, wool, and skins that always kept a prominent position in domestic and foreign markets. Furthermore, with the help of immigrants from Italy and Germans from Hungary (named Saxons), the mining of silver, gold, copper, and tin, particularly in the north, proved to be important for the economic development of the country and the hiring of workers by the rulers of the region.

The Serbs, under Stephen Dushan (1331-55), achieved a high level of prosperity, along with the expansion of their country from the Danube and the Drima rivers to Dalmatia, Albania, and northern Greece (up to the Gulf of Corinth). The transportation network that the Romans had established, particularly the east-west roads, proved to be beneficial for agricultural and mining products and the expansion of domestic and foreign trade during that time.

When the Ottomans first came into the Balkan Peninsula, they established military and administrative officials in strategic regions. Turkish chiefs (beys) received large tracts of land (chifliks); while Turkish peasants were transported from Asia Minor, mainly Konia, and were implanted in different areas.

The Turkish conquerors did not press heavily on the Christian subjects (rayahs) during the early years of occupation, and taxation was not excessive. Large regions (pashaliks) were subdivided into provinces (nahies). Each province had an elected native chief (obor-knez) and each village a knez (headman), who were responsible for tax assessment. The obor-knez represented the natives to the Turkish Kadi, who presided in each nahie, and was responsible to the pasha, the governor of larger regions (pashaliks). Nevertheless, some nobles managed to keep their lands and their independence, as long as they paid the taxes, being responsible directly to the pashas. This administrative system proved to be successful at the beginning.

The Turkish authorities stood above local conflicts and let the knezes do the dirty work of collecting taxes and policing their own native people. However, when the central authority gradually lost control and the kadis and pashas became corrupt, heavy oppression was exercised upon the Yugoslavs and other Balkan rayahs.

During the period 1797-1814, the economic conditions of the eastern provinces from Carniola to Dalmatia and Ragusa, under Napoleon's rule, were greatly improved.(41) The administrative system of these "Illyrian Provinces", with Ljubljana as capital, was reorganized. Roads were built, trade was revitalized, and intellectual life, influenced by the liberal ideas of the French Revolution, was stimulated. From 1815 to 1849 the area came under the Austrian Empire.

Directly or indirectly, neighboring big powers opposed cooperation among the Balkan countries so that they could continue to exercise their influence in the area. Thus in 1906 Austria objected to tariff negotiations between Serbia and Bulgaria and imposed high duties on livestock passing through Austria-Hungary (the pig war). Since nine-tenths of Serbian exports were involved, such restrictions would have led to the economic collapse of the country if new markets had not been opened in western Europe and exports facilitated via Salonika.

Macedonia, which extends roughly from Lake Ohrid in the west to the river Nestos (Mesta) in the east, and between the mountain Kara Dagh and Sar Planina in the north and the Aegean Sea in the south, remained a troubled area for a long time. Because of its strategic location, its great port of Salonika, and its fertile plains, it was always coveted by the neighboring countries, mainly Bulgaria, Greece, and Yugoslavia. Before liberation from Turkish occupation, rival educational activities, nationalistic propaganda, and even revolutionary secret societies, such as the Internal Organization or VMRO (1893), the Greek Ethniki Hetairia (1894), and the Bulgarian Supreme Macedo-Adrianopolitan Committee (1895) quarreled in their efforts to gain the support of the people of Macedonia, which at that time included the three

Turkish vilayets of Salonika, Monastir (Bitolj) and Kosova. The passion for education was so strong that parents were often induced by scholarships to enroll their children in schools belonging to rival races. Thus, sometimes a "Greek" father would have "Bulgarian," "Serbian," and "Roumanian" children.(42) Moreover, armed groups, such as the Bulgarian komitadjis in the east, the Greek bands (mainly Cretans) in the south, the Serbs in the north, and Albanians in the west, renewed their activities against each other and against local people opposing their aims.

As a result of the long Turkish occupation and the frequent raids by the revolutionary and nationalistic bands, the development of land and mineral resources of the country was neglected. The Ottoman landlords (beys) were interested in the short-run returns of the occupied lands and neglected their long-term development. River banks were allowed to erode, irrigation projects were neglected, many people were homeless, and agricultural and mining methods remained backward. However, the fertile plains of the countryside and the unexploited rich mineral wealth provided high potential for the production of cereals, fruits, cotton, tobacco, and wine as well as silver, iron, lead, bauxite, and manganese. Slavonia, Croatia, and Voivodina (Hapsburg provinces) were more advanced in agriculture and industry than Serbia, Montenegro and Macedonia (former Turkish territories).

With the departure of the Turks, both Greece and present-day Yugoslavia remained underdeveloped. About 80 percent of the population was engaged in agriculture and less than 10 percent in industry. While in Greece a great number of latifundia remained, in Serbia and other Yugoslav regions land was split among the peasants. Serbs did not have the same opportunity to emigrate as the Greeks, and this, coupled with the rapid increase in population, led to extensive fragmentation of peasant property.(43) Under such conditions, even the Zadruga (village cooperative) gave way to the individual farm unit. The pressure of population increase forced the peasants to grow mostly corn, barley, and wheat and reduce the land for pasture.

Under tariff protection, a number of industrial units were established at the beginning of the twentieth century. They included milling, sugar refining (established mainly by German concerns), meat packing, brewing, textiles, mining, and other industries for the processing of raw materials.

Also, more roads and shipping facilities were created. Railroads were built from Austria and Hungary to Trieste and Fiume through Slavonia and Croatia (1846), and from Vienna through Yugoslavia to Salonika (the Orient Express) and Constantinople.

The last railroad was built by a French firm in 1888 and was expanded by the Serbian government in 1912. However, the financing of economic development required rapid growth of money and credit, which in turn led to high government spending and indebtedness. Thus government expenditures in Serbia increased from 12.5 million francs in 1869 to 120.1 million in 1911, while public debt rose from 2.3 million francs in 1867 to 903.8 million in 1914.(44) The debt, primarily owed to Austria, Germany, and France, was guaranteed and paid by the revenue from taxes on tobacco, salt, liquor, and petroleum, over which the government, together with foreign bond-holders had control.

The need for money to pay taxes and buy agricultural tools and other industrial products forced the peasants to borrow primarily from village usurers and pay high interest rates reaching, at times, 120 percent.

THE ESTABLISHMENT OF MODERN YUGOSLAVIA

The modern Yugoslav state was born out of the collapse of the Central powers in World War I. Its formation was the result of the Declaration of Corfu on July 20, 1917, signed by Nichola Pashich as Serbian premier and Ante Trumbich as president of the Yugoslav committee in exile. This agreement, which was supported by Russia and the United States, provided for a constitutional and parliamentary monarchy under the Karageorgevich dynasty and the union of all Serbs, Croats, and Slovenes. On November 26, Montenegro joined Serbia and by December 1, 1918 the new kingdom of the Serbs, Croats, and Slovenes was proclaimed in Belgrade. The main defect of the new state, South Slav Kingdom, seemed to lie with the domination of the other ethnic groups by Serbia, a fact that condemned it to domestic disturbances and even the danger of full-scale civil war.

In spite of internal political strife, weak federalism, and foreign pressures, Yugoslavia managed to achieve a satisfactory degree of economic progress in the interwar years 1919-30. Transportation and communications were improved, tourism increased, especially on the Dalmation coasts, and agricultural production rose significantly, allowing exports to exceed imports. As a result, the Yugoslav war debts to the United States and Britain were repaid, the dinar was stabilized, and foreign investments were attracted. The textile industry, using machinery from Germany in payment of reparations, advanced rapidly, and the growth of domestic and foreign investment increased the material wealth of the country. Public administration was reorganized and even the name of the state was changed to Yugoslavia (in 1929).

As a result of the universal depression after 1929 and of domestic sociopolitical unrest, the Yugoslav economy deteriorated in the 1930s. Exports fell dramatically, German reparation payments stopped (in 1931) and the deficits in the balance of trade increased. The dramatic decrease in prices of agricultural products forced the government to buy up imported products in exchange for more of its own products. Limited storage facilities and lack of bank credit worsened economic conditions. Increases in taxes and decreases in administrative salaries and pensions intensified social unrest without improving the economy.

Cattle exports decreased as slaughtering increased and peasants, unable to pay their debts, became embittered at usurers and the urban gentry (gospoda). Bankrupt cities were widespread, currency controls were intensified, and foreign credit was not available. To pacify the poor peasants, the government suspended debt payments for more than a year. The whole economic picture was dismal, especially in 1932-34. Then, the economic influence of Nazi Germany penetrated the country further with the Commercial Treaty of 1934 and the new preferential treatment of Yugoslav exports in pigs, cattle, wheat, and other raw materials. By 1938 Yugoslav exports to Germany accounted for 36 percent of total exports, while imports from Germany were close to 33 percent of total imports.(45)

Despite the efforts of the Balkan Entente (Greece, Romania, Turkey, and Yugoslavia) to preserve peace in the area, economic pressures and aggressive acts by Germany and Italy divided the Balkan nations again. With Italy's attack upon Greece on October 28, 1940 and the Bulgarian alliance with Germany and Italy, the situation was further complicated. Encouraged by the Greek success in the battles in

Albania against Italy, the Yugoslavs refused to allow Italian troops to cross Yugoslavia to outflank the fighting Greeks. Instead, they expressed interest to help Greece defend Salonika, where they had an outlet for their foreign trade (the Free Trade Zone). Furthermore, Turkey warned Bulgaria that she would support Greece in case of a Bulgarian attack.

On April 6 Hitler's troops in Bulgaria entered Yugo-slavia and Greece simultaneously. In a few days and after intensive air attacks on Belgrade, Yugoslavia was in the hands of the Axis, as was Greece. The Italians conquered Dalmatia, the Hungarians reached Osijek and Novi Sad, and the Bulgarians occupied most of Macedonia. The Germans occupied northern Slovenia, while Croatia (except Dalmatia) and Montenegro were nominally designated independent.(46) Albania took western Macedonia and Kosovo. The puppet state of Croatia was left to the control of Ustashi fascists under Ante Pavelic, who turned against the Orthodox popula-tion of Bosnia and Serbia as well as against the Jews.

During the years of German occupation, a nationalistic group operated in Serbia (the Chetniks) under Draza Mihajlovich, a former officer who wanted to restore the exiled government of King Peter II. Both Ustashis and Chetniks turned against the partisans of the National Libera-tion Movement under Tito and gradually collaborated with the occupation forces of Germany and Italy.

Tito, the Croat metalworker Josip Broz who joined the Austrian army and later the Bolsheviks in Russia, managed to mobilize and unite large segments of the Yugoslav population against the occupation forces of Germany and Italy. Al-though he headed the communist party in Yugoslavia since 1938, as chief of the wartime partisans he declared that all the peoples of Yugoslavia, regardless of party or religion, must join hands against the fascist occupation forces. In his efforts he was helped by efficient colleagues such as Alex-ander Rankovich, Edvard Kurdelj (from Slovenia), and Miholo-van Djilas (from Montenegro). On the battlefield as well as in diplomacy, Tito (the Lion of Belgrade, as he was called later) proved to be effective enough to unite the long-embattled ethnic groups of Yugoslavia and to be president of the country for thirty-six years (from 1944 until his death in May 1980 at the age of 88). He was also able to combine the Orthodox Christian Serbs and Montenegrins with Roman

Catholic Croats and Slovenes and make room for Moslem, Hungarian, Albanian, and other minorities.

In his efforts to reform the economy of the country, Tito was supported by the poor peasants, who were exploited by the landlords and neglected by the Yugoslav governments during the interwar years. Among the fundamental reforms introduced immediately after the war were: the replacement of the prewar currencies by a new dinar in a ten-to-one ratio; the confiscation of the property of Nazi collaborators; strict rent controls; limitation of land ownership to those who cultivated it (35 hectares for individuals and 10 hectares or 100,000 square meters for institutions); and nationalization of about 80 percent of the country's industry, including mining.(47) Also, banking and insurance activities, wholesale and foreign trade, and foreign-held property were placed under direct state control.

However, Tito's policy of purchasing food and other agricultural products at fixed low prices and putting heavy taxes on profits turned many peasants against the regime. Strong opposition also came from religious groups, particularly the Catholics, who accounted for 32 percent of the population in 1953, compared to 41 percent Orthodox, and 12 percent Moslems.(48)

The first Five-Year Plan for economic development was introduced in 1947 with the aim of restoring the economy after the war's devastations (1.7 million people dead and close to 50 billion dollars material losses) and increasing production through high rates of investment. It was an ambitious plan emphasizing heavy industry and based upon promised Soviet technical assistance and loans of over $300 million. However, after the dispute with the Soviet Union and the other Cominform countries in June 1948, implementation of the plan was gradually abandoned. Also, collectivization of the land, into which some two million peasants were coerced in 1949-51, was abandoned by 1953 because low incentives for production resulted in food shortages.

After the break with the Cominform, Yugoslavia turned to the West for trade and aid. By 1958 about $2.5 billion in aid was given primarily by the United States, Britain, and France. Despite the reconciliation efforts by Nikita Khrushchev in 1955 and the mutual suspicion of Western and Yugoslav leaders, relations with the Western countries continued to improve. Industrial production and Yugoslav manufacturing exports to the West increased significantly.

Although peasants could withdraw their land and livestock from cooperatives after 1953, some 216,000 hectares of land remained under 507 working cooperatives by 1958. The new policy was to encourage the formation and strength of general cooperatives in which the peasants would cultivate their own land but participate in joint efforts for buying agricultural tools, seeds, fertilizers, and breeding stock, and which promoted the marketing of their products.(49) This policy was reinforced by abolishing the system of forcing the peasants to sell their products at fixed prices and fixing taxes in advance on an agreed estimated yield. Further support was provided by the government through improvements in transportation, irrigation, marketing, and refrigeration facilities. However, migration of peasants to the cities necessitated purchase of their land by the government, which then organized them into state farms.

Extensive economic and political decentralization was introduced with the establishment of the workers' councils on June 26, 1950. This institution was incorporated in the constitution of 1953. With these new measures, the powers of the six federal republics were increased and more authority was delegated to the communes. The workers' councils, elected biannually in enterprises as well as universities, hospitals, and similar economic units, would decide on production, marketing, income distribution, and work conditions. However, their freedom was somewhat reduced in matters of tax payments, except for investments, salaries, and price determination, especially after 1954. Tourism was encouraged, Yugoslavs were permitted to travel abroad, work incentives were offered, and productivity was improved. Although some limitations were reintroduced by the 1957-61 and 1961-5 Five-Year Plans, the overall process of decentralization continued. Nevertheless, in the political field decentralization was less effective than in the economic field.(50) Further decentralization was introduced by the constitution of 1963, which expanded the principle of workers' management and gave more economic and sociopolitical independence to the assemblies of the republics and the communes.

Tito's longevity in power helped him to carry through not only his concepts of Yugoslav federalism and ethnic unity but also his innovative economic program of labor-managed enterprises, explained in more detail later. For the formation and implementation of this economic program, which may be considered the first in the world in its application, Edvard Kardelj, Tito's colleague as partisan and economic advisor until his death (1979), played a significant role.

In the international field, Tito was among the first leaders, together with India's Nehru, Indonesia's Sukarno, and Egypt's Nasser, to create and promote the third world nonalignment group of nations in the late 1950s. In consequence to that policy, he introduced and maintained throughout his presidency Yugoslavia's nonaligned relations. He gave the country a global prominence that could be maintained only with great difficulty by his main successors, Lazar Kolisevski, Stevan Doronjski and Stane Dolanc. Under Tito, Yugoslavia built up good political and trade relations with the two main superpowers. These relations, together with a domestic arms industry that supplies 80 percent of the army's needs, bear strongly on the security and safety of the country. Good relations were also created with Yugoslavia's seven neighbors. With Italy, the perennial Trieste issue was settled, as was that with Austria involving the Slovene minority in Carinthia. Moreover, there are elements of genuine friendship with Hungary and all the other Balkan neighbors, particularly Romania and Greece. However, from time to time, there were disturbances with Bulgaria and Albania regarding minorities in Macedonia and Kosovo respectively. But such disturbances did not seem to be instigated by the official governments of the neighboring countries. They may be the result of ethnic groups inside or outside the country, which may continue to play cats-paw for future provocations by the big powers, as frequently happened in the past.

Despite speculations that the Yugoslav federation might be in trouble after Tito's death, the country remains largely calm. Only in Pristina, the capital of Kosovo, were there disturbances in which Albanian nationalist riots left nine people dead and scores injured in 1981. Some 300 people were sentenced to jail terms of up to 15 years, and 60 students and 5 professors were dismissed from the University of Pristina. Kosovo is the poorest province of Yugoslavia, populated mainly by people of Albanian descent. As a result of the riots, mistrust between majority Albanians and minority Serbs and Montenegrins increased.

There may still be agitating groups of ethnic separatists, nationalists, or Cominformists inside or outside Yugoslavia, but they possess limited influence, if any at all.

More serious problems for the successors of Tito are the debilitating effects of inflation, which runs around 30 percent, and the pressures of the various republics and economic sectors to increase or at least keep their share of an insufficient investment pie. The main dilemma for Tito's successors, who do not enjoy his charismatic authority, will be how to keep and promote the twin legacies–unity and self-management socialism. On matters of income distribution, 10 percent of the population grabs 45 percent of total national income and the motto "jobs for the party boys" prevails while more than 90,000 workers are unemployed.

A difficult problem for the post-Tito system of rotation in government may be the continuation of the status quo and the lack of reforms because of the short-run (one year) authority of the rotating presidency among the seven republics and the two provinces. Thus, Mika Spietza replaced Petar Stambolits as the president of Yugoslavia (May 1983).

Economic and diplomatic relations with other countries were improved and Yugoslavia gained many friends among third world nations as a result of the nonaligned movement, an important conference of which took place in Belgrade in 1961. Trade with both communist and Western economies was expanded, especially with the EEC, cooperation with which did not require political alignment. Although economic growth in the 1960s slowed down and inflation and external debts increased, the country was rapidly industrialized and the standard of living of the poor Yugoslav peasants and workers was greatly improved.

Greece and Yugoslavia were perhaps the only Balkan countries that have not had a war or any military conflict between them. On the contrary, they were allies during World Wars I and II. A number of abortive discussions on a Balkan federation have been held since 1945. Nevertheless, closer cooperation has been advanced not only between Greece and Yugoslavia but between them and other neighboring countries. Thus in 1953 the now moribund Balkan Pact was signed by Greece, Yugoslavia, and Turkey. This has been superseded by bilateral summitry of greater importance, particularly in the 1970s and early 1980s.

From a geopolitical point of view, both countries, as well as the whole Balkan region, again attract big powers' influence and competition. Thus U.S. representatives frequently visit Greece to negotiate the future of U.S. military bases and related matters. Soviet Prime Minister Nikolai Tikhonov visited Greece and Yugoslavia recently to urge more independence from the West and the creation of a nuclear-free zone in the Balkan Peninsula,(51) along with more trade and investment between the Soviet Union and these two countries, primarily Greece. Also, Chinese representatives (among them party leader Hu Yaobang) recently visited Yugoslavia (May 1983) and Romania to urge policies independent from both the western and eastern blocs.

NOTES

1. G. Botsford and E. Sihelr, eds., Hellenic Civilizations (New York: Columbia University Press, 1915), chpts. 1,2; and G. Botsford and C. Robinson, Jr., Hellenic History, 5th ed. rev. by D. Kagan (London: Macmillan, 1971), chaps. 1-3. For the period of Minoan (Cretan) civilization see Adam Hopkins, Crete: Its Past, Present and People (London: Faber, 1977), chap. 2. For the years 800-500 B.C. see C. Strarr, The Economic and Social Growth of Early Greece: 800-500 B.C. (New York: Oxford University Press, 1977).

2. The first coins appeared in Lydia (Asia Minor) and in the Aegina island (near Athens), during the 6th century B.C.. By that time, the Greek merchants managed to prevail over the Phoenicians in seabound trade. For more details, see Norman Angell, The Story of Money (New York: F.A. Stokes, 1929), chap. 4. Further valuable information is provided in T. Glover, The Challenge of the Greeks and Other Essays (New York: Macmillan, 1942), p. 78; and C. Stanley, Roots of the Tree (London: Oxford University Press, 1936), p. 24. For related philosophical discussions see E. Barker, The Political Thought of Plato and Aristotle (New York: Dover, 1959), chap. 9; and S. Lowry, "Recent Literature on Ancient Greek Economic Thought," Journal of Economic Literature, March 1979, pp. 65-86.

3. For more details see Andreas Andreades, A History of Public Finance in Greece (Cambridge, Mass.: Harvard University Press, 1933), pp. 53-9; Augustus Boeckh, The Public Economy of Athens (New York: Arno Press, 1976), chap. 5, pp. 494-510.

4. Xenophon's Works, trans. C. Ashley et al. (Philadelphia: Thomas Wardle, 1843), pp. 681-91. Also M. Austin, Economic and Social History of Ancient Greece: An Introduction (Berkeley: University of California Press, 1977).

5. J. P. Mahaffy, Rambles and Studies in Greece, 2d ed. (London: Macmillan, 1878), chap. 6; and Arnold Toynbee, Some Problems of Greek History (London: Oxford University Press, 1969), part III.

6. J. Carey and A. Carey, The Web of Modern Greek Politics (New York: Columbia University Press, 1968), pp. 31-33.

7. During the Roman period, Greece (Achaea) abounded in learning, but she was not self-sufficient in grain. J. Day, An Economic History of Athens under Roman Domination (New York: Arno Press, 1973), chap. 7; W. Tarn and G. Griffith, Hellenistic Civilization, 3d ed., rev. (London: E. Arnold, 1952), p. 266; and J. Toutain, The Economic Life of the Ancient World, (New York: A. Knopf, 1930), p. 232.

8. Byzantium was the name of the city given by the Dorians of Megara (a city of the Greek mainland west of Athens) who had established colonies at the eastern end of the Propontis (Sea of Marmara) in the Dardanelles during the seventh century B.C.

9. There, monks continue to follow the Byzantine tradition and even to live "isolated from all female life, whether hens, nanny goats, or women." Carey and Carey, The Web of Modern Greek Politics, p. 36. See also D. Nicol, The End of the Byzantine Empire (New York: Holmes and Meier, 1979), chap. 4.

10. Arnold Toynbee, Constantine Porphyrogenitus and His World (London: Oxford University Press, 1973), pp. 176-84; and J. Bury, A History of the Eastern Roman Empire (New York: Russell and Russell, 1966), chap. 7. Also, Moses Finley, The Ancient Economy (Berkeley: University of California Press, 1973), chap. 6.

11. Carey and Carey, The Web of Modern Greek Politics, p. 35.

12. B. Ward, The Interplay of East and West (London: Allen and Unwin, 1957), p. 22.

13. John Lampe and Marvin Jackson, Balkan Economic History, 1550-1950 (Indiana: Indiana University Press, 1982), chap. 1; and D. Zakynthinos, The Making of Modern Greece: From Byzantium to Independence, trans. K. Johnstone (London: Basil Blackwell, 1976), chap. 6.

14. L. S. Stavrianos, The Balkans Since 1453 (New York: Holt, Rinehart and Winston, 1958), pp. 276, 298-99.

15. For the cooperative nature of Ambelakia industries see J. Kordatos, T'Apelakia Ki'o Mythos Gia To Syneterismo Tous (Athens: K. Strate, 1955), chaps. 4, 8. For the support of the Greek mercantile diaspora, see the valuable articles in R. Clogg, ed. The Movement for Greek Independence, 1770-1821 (London: Macmillan, 1976).

16. Nicholas Kaltchas, Introduction to the Constitutional History of Modern Greece (New York: Columbia University Press, 1940), p. 11.

17. More details on Nicholas Giannaris, The Province of Kalavryta: A Historical and Socioeconomic Review (New York: Calavrytan Fraternity, 1983), chap. 3.

18. C. Crawley, "Modern Greece, 1821-1930," in W. Heurtley et al., A Short History of Modern Greece (Cambridge: Cambridge University Press, 1965), p. 101.

19. Peloponnesus and the poverty-striken Cyclades islands, particularly Delos (the great shrine of Apollo), Mykonos, Naxos, and Syros, with their barren soil and over-fished seas, had a better cultural and economic life under Venetian than Ottoman control, primarily in artistic and tourist activities. Carey and Carey, The Web of Modern Greek Politics.

20. Loan sharks, thieves, and the power of the strong prevailed in many regions. Dominant classes and political elites with oligarchic clienteles exercised decisive influence upon the people. At the same time, the growing commercial bourgeosie failed to exercise its political power.

21. Stavrianos, The Balkans since 1453, pp. 296-99.

22. Ibid.

23. For more details of this revolt and the formation of a new constitution in 1911, see Victor Papacosma, The Military in Greek Politics: The 1909 Coup d'Etat (Kent, Ohio: Kent State University Press, 1977).

24. Nicholas V. Gianaris, The Economies of the Balkan Countries: Albania, Bulgaria, Greece, Romania, Turkey, Yugoslavia (New York: Praeger, 1982), chap. 3. Also, Aurel Braun, Small-State Security in the Balkans (Totowa, N.J.: Barnes and Noble Books, 1983), pp. 40-44.

25. Edward Foster, A Short History of Modern Greece, 1821-1926 (London: Methuen, 1958), p. 160.

26. H. Richter, 1933-1946: Dio Epanastasis kai Antepanastasis Stin Ellada (Two Revolutions and Counter-revolutions in Greece), 2 vols. (Athens: Exantas, 1975), trans. from German; and J. Koliopoulos, Greece and the British Connection, 1935-1941 (Oxford: Clarendon Press, 1977), chap. 4, 6.

27. For a detailed review, see Nicholas Giannaris, The Province of Kalavryta, chap. 4.

28. For further comments see C. Woodhouse, Apple of Discord: A Survey of Recent Greek Politics in Their International Setting (London: Hutchinson, 1948), pp. 146-47; and C. Myers, Greek Entanglement (London: Rupert Hart-Davis, 1955), chap. 10, 18.

29. Winston Churchill, Triumph and Tragedy: The Second World War, vol. 6 (Boston: Houghton Mifflin, 1953), p. 325.

30. Ibid., pp. 885-86.

31. For more detailed events see George Giannaris, Mikis Theodorakis: Music and Social Change (New York: Praeger, 1972), chap. 2; S. Xydis, Greece and the Great Powers, 1944-1947 (Thessaloniki: Institute for Balkan Studies, 1963), chap. 2; E. O'Ballance, The Greek Civil War, 1944-1949 (London: Faber and Faber, 1966), chaps. 4, 5.

32. For a detailed review see C. Munkman, American Aid to Greece (New York: Praeger, 1978), chap. 4; H. Psomiades, "The Economic and Social Transformation of Modern Greece," Journal of International Affairs 19 (1965), 194-205; Theodore Coulombis, The United States, Greece and Turkey (New York: Praeger, 1983), chap. 1; and articles in Theodore Couloumbis and John Iatrides, eds.. Greek American Relations: A Critical Review (New York: Pella, 1980).

33. Walter Lippmann in the Herald Tribune, April 1, 1947, reprinted in S. Rousseas, The Death of a Democracy: Greece and the American Conscience (New York: Grove Press, 1967), p. 84.

34. S. Rousseas, The Death of a Democracy, p. 83. See also W. McNeill, The Greek Dilemma (London, Victor Gollancz, 1947), pp. 75-76; and Carey and Carey, The Web of Modern Greek Politics, pp. 164-68.

35. For more details on U.S. involvement in Greek political affairs, see A. Papandreou, Democracy at Gunpoint (New York: Doubleday, 1970), chaps. 1,2; T. Coulombis, Greek Political Reaction to American and NATO Influence (New Haven: Yale University Press, 1966), chap. 14; and W. McNeill, The Metamorphosis of Greece Since World War II (Chicago: University of Chicago Press, 1978).

36. Post-World War II governments came and went one after another in Greece with the following Prime Ministers: P. Tsaldaris 1946-47; J. Sopholis 1947-49; N. Plastiras 1950; S. Venizelos, 1950; A. Papagos 1952-55; C. Caramanlis 1955-63; G. Papandreou 1963-65; (after G. Athanasiades-Novas and E. Tsirimokos failed to form a government) S. Stephanopoulos 1965-66; Ioannis Paraskevopoulos 1966-67; P. Kanellopoulos 1967; military dictatorship, controlled by Col. G. Papadopoulos 1967-73, and Maj. D. Ioannides 1973-74; C. Caramanlis 1974-80; J. Rhallis 1980-81; A. Papandreou 1981-.

37. Carey and Carey, The Web of Modern Greek Politics, pp. 164, 213.

38. A new agreement between Greece and the United States signed in 1983, allows U.S. military bases in Greece for another five years, but they have to be dismantled 17 months after the five-year period expires. "Greek Panel Approves Accord on U.S. Basis," New York Times, October 21, 1983.

39. For a comprehensive review, see Stephen Clissold, ed. A Short History of Yugoslavia: From Early Times to 1966 (New York: Cambridge University Press, 1966), chap. 1.

40. The importance of agriculture was very much recognized throughout the Roman period. Richard Duncan-Jones, The Economy of the Roman Empire: Quantitative Studies (London: Cambridge University Press, 1974), chap. 2.

41. For a brief historical review, see Fred Singleton and Bernard Carter, The Economy of Yugoslavia (New York: St. Martin's Press, 1982), chap. 2.

42. For such first-hand observations see H. Brailsford, Macedonia: Its Races and their Future (London: Methuen and Co., 1906), p. 102.

43. For more details, see J. Tomasevich, Peasants, Politics and Economic Change in Yugoslavia (Stanford, Calif.: Stanford University Press, 1955), p. 206.

44. At that time, and since 1878, Serbia has had its own national government. For detailed historical developments, see L. Stavrianos, The Balkans Since 1453, chap. 24.

45. M. G. Zaninovich, The Development of Socialist Yugoslavia (Baltimore: John Hopkins Press, 1968), p. 33.

46. Occupation authorities were responsible for expulsion and forced migration of many Yugoslavs. Some 220,000-260,000 persons were deported or transferred to various camps to work in German factories. Leszek Kosinski, "International Migration of Yugoslavs During and Immediately After World War II," East European Quarterly, June 1982, pp. 183-98.

47. Phyllis Auty, "The Postwar Period," in Stephen Clissold, ed., A Short History of Yugoslavia (New York: Cambridge University Press, 1966), pp. 236-40.

48. Zaninovich, The Development of Socialist Yugoslavia, p. 171.

49. In the early 1960s, more than 90 percent of the peasants belonged to such cooperatives. Phyllis Auty, "The Postwar Period," pp. 247, 250.

50. Although criticism of governmental policies was permitted, the advocacy of other forms of government was not allowed. This can be inferred from the arguments of Milovan Djilas, for which he was sentenced to seven years in prison. See his recent article, "Yugoslavia's Crisis," New York Times, November 23, 1983.

51. Marvin Howe, "Greece Joins Soviets in Urging Deep Arms Cuts," New York Times, February 25, 1983. For a similar letter to the other Balkan nations by Prime Minister Andreas Papandreou of Greece, see "Greece Asks Balkan Arms Parley," New York Times, May 18, 1983.

3

ECONOMIC ORGANIZATION: PUBLIC VERSUS PRIVATE SECTORS

PUBLIC SECTOR FUNCTIONS

One of the most important questions of economic policy in our day is, What is the optimum size of the public versus the private sector, if any? Despite criticism of the bureaucratic public sector in many countries, including Greece and Yugoslavia, it has been proved that, as income increases, demand for government services increases still more. The demand for public services includes, among other social necessities, social security and medical services, education, defense, administration of justice, domestic security, support for those who are unemployed and unable to work, environmental protection, and subsidization of certain sectors in the economy. All these elements loom significantly in government disbursement and lead to the growth of the public sector proportionally more than total production.

Fiscal operations in general and government spending in particular weigh heavily in the aggregate demand and the economic fluctuations of Greece and Yugoslavia. Moreover, defense expenditures are relatively large in both Greece and Yugoslavia, varying from around 20 percent to more than 30 percent of total budget spending, depending on political and territorial disturbances, which are so frequent in the Balkans. Technological changes in weaponry, rapidity of obsolescence, and the nature of the equipment-intensive military establishment increase government outlays and impose a heavy burden on the budgets of both countries. In addition, subsidies allocated to a number of economic sectors and production units are responsible for large portions of government spending, particularly in Yugoslavia.

Another cause of rising budget expenditures is the increasing cost of public services due to inflation, which runs at rates around 20 percent or higher in both countries. Moreover, population mobility and its concentration in urban centers, especially in Athens and Salonika in Greece and in Belgrade and Zagreb in Yugoslavia, augment the need for public services and municipal facilities.

The ever-increasing use of cars, buses, and planes for transportation and the need for more electric power and other public utilities necessitate growing public investment because the private sector is either limited in certain areas or hesitates to undertake and implement long-term capital investment in these countries.

The growing role of transfers and the problem of adjusting income distribution among different groups of population, mainly among different regions, are additional causes of government intervention and of increased expenditures in both countries. Such expenditures, together with welfare payments, which aim at reducing large income inequalities, are growing rapidly, particularly in Greece. Moreover, improvements in medical services and technology move the population bulge farther up the age scale and intensify the fiscal problem of social security payments.

The economic role of government, which expanded during the last half-century while social objectives were pursued in both countries, as well as in many other Western countries, is under intense criticism. Mandated spending programs, such as interest payments, unemployment benefits, and other welfare costs, are difficult for governments to control because, whether explicitly or implicity, they are indexed and increase with rising prices.(1) Such spending based on indexed entitlements, which are considered in economic theory as automatic stabilizers, may on many occasions stimulate inflation. From that point of view, it becomes difficult for the governments of Greece and Yugoslavia to exercise fiscal discipline, reduce budget deficits, and implement anti-inflationary policies.

Increases in the wages and salaries of civil servants, which absorb sizeable amounts of government expenditures in Greece and Yugoslavia, are largely indexed a priori and follow, more or less, the rates of inflation through discretionary decisions made by the responsible ministry or other public authorities. Also, social security payments are indexed to the cost of living.

A more difficult problem arises in defense spending. Many defense items, such as planes, tanks, guns, and the like, are purchased abroad. As long as the prices of such items are going up, larger amounts of government expenditures are required for their purchase. The domestic economy, then, is drained of valuable financial resources while inflationary pressures persist.

Depending on the amount of resources (land and natural resources, labor, capital, entrepreneurship or management), the productivity or efficiency per unit of resources, and the gain from foreign trade, total production of goods and services is different. As Figure 3.1 shows, total production in Yugoslavia is about twice that of Greece. The allocation of resources to different economic activities can be carried out by the private sector, operating through the market mechanism of supply and demand, or by the public sector, operating through government revenue and expenditure. Figure 3.1 presents the production frontiers and the portions of private and public sector outputs in both countries. The public sector, inclusive of all forms of government, absorbs about 30 percent of the GDP (gross domestic product) in Greece and 37 percent in Yugoslavia.

Economic growth in both countries, through increments of factor resources and technological improvement, brings about an outward shift in the production frontier, indicating higher production in both public and private sectors. As long as demand for and production of public goods is growing proportionally more than that for private goods (as it did during the postwar years, particularly in Greece), the new output mix is changing in favor of the public sector. Under competitive conditions, the market mechanism would determine the preference of the people regarding these two sectors. However, in Greece, and more so in Yugoslavia, policymakers or planners modify product mixes, through

Figure 3.1. Output of Private and Public Sectors in Greece and Yugoslavia, 1980, in billion U.S. dollars. Public Sector for Greece is General Government Expenditures; for Yugoslavia Consolidated Expenditures.

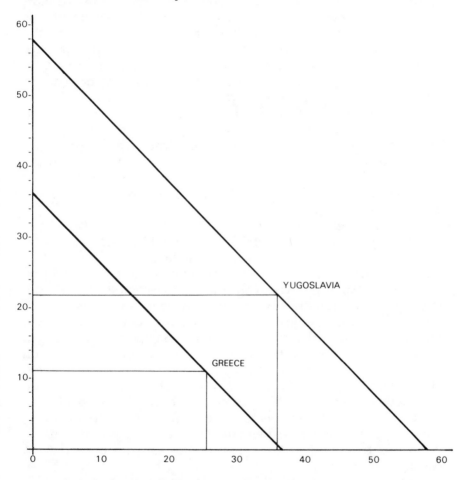

Source: OECD, Country Surveys; and National Accounts, various issues.

controls or fiscal and monetary measures, in order to reduce monopolistic conditions and correct distributional injustices.

In addition to its social function, the public sector plays an important role in the performance of the overall economy. As a matter of practice, the public and private sectors are largely complementary and interdependent. Through the creation of an environment conducive to private investment, and through the establishment of needed infrastructure, as well as provision for regulation or the absence of it, the public sector can have a decisive impact on the private sector and the economic development of the country. In Greece and Yugoslavia, as in many other market or planned economies, the public sector provides a wide range of economic and social services in such areas as education and vocational training, provision of electricity and water, transportation, communications, infrastructural investment, and a host of other activities that affect production, distribution, and growth. If such public services are inadequate or unreliable, the private sector and the economy as a whole will be less efficient.

In both countries a good proportion of economic activity is performed by public and semipublic or parastatal enterprises. Such enterprises are, to a large extent, subsidized by government, and taxpayers have to bear the brunt of additional expense to cover the cost-revenue difference. Despite privileges in taxes and interest subsidies, which public enterprises enjoy in competing for scarce capital and materials, such entities are frequently hampered by political pressures and the weight of government bureaucracy, which restricts work incentives and tends to reduce efficiency. More often than not, bureaucrats and politicians try to serve themselves instead of the public. Nevertheless, public or semipublic enterprises perform an important role in infrastructural and industrial investment where the private sector is unable to provide the necessary finance and organization required.

During the postwar years, in order to accommodate unemployed workers, bureaucrats and politicians have stuffed the offices of these enterprises with unneeded personnel. As a result, operational cost is high relative to revenue, and excessive budgetary deficits appear year after year. Out of 20 large public and semipublic enterprises in Greece, for example, 12-14 had big deficits in recent years.(2) The main reasons for such deficits are high labor cost, low productivity, and bureaucratic inertia. Laying off tenured employees is difficult or impossible in these enterprises. What remains to be explored is the introduction of new technology for higher productivity and the adjustment of labor cost to related price and revenues.

Recent increases in the prices of electricity and telephone communications are expected to transform the deficits of the Public Power Corporation (2.5 billion drachmas in 1981) and the Organization of Telecommunications of Greece (4.7 billion drachmas in 1981) into surpluses. These two semipublic enterprises are important for the economy of Greece because they provide needed infrastructure and investment for further development and employ 60,000 people out of 135,000 employed by the 20 large public and semipublic enterprises mentioned above.

Although there is no way to escape the interaction between the public and private sectors, it is difficult to determine what policies or what blends should be adopted by each country. For the public sector to be more of a benefit than a burden to the economy, good public management, sound industrial and agricultural policies, and an effective financial system are all important. For example, the widespread practice, carried out by the governments of Greece and Yugoslavia, of keeping interest rates artificially low in order to stimulate investment in particular sectors tends to discourage saving and to encourage the inefficient use of investment. Moreover, this practice of capital subsidization is associated with greater centralization in decision making concerning the rationing of capital. However, a well-conceived, albeit limited, structure of government regulations on credit markets may be required to discourage any development of monopolistic practices by major banks with strong ties to industries. This has been a familiar phenomenon in Greece.

Another field where the public sector plays a vital role in the economy is that of exerting a protective or "inward-looking" policy or, conversely, displaying the lack of it. In both countries, there may be a need for protecting certain infant industries from foreign competition from the EEC or other more advanced countries. Industries manufacturing metal products are a case in point. Greece and Yugoslavia are rich in mining resources, such as bauxite, aluminum, iron, tin, and nickel. Instead of exporting these products in the form of raw materials and importing them back as finished metal products, it would be more logical to stimulate their manufacture into final goods by domestic industries. This may require protection for a time until the infant industries are capable of standing on their own feet and can survive competition. However, the period of protection should not be long. Otherwise, such protection, which is, in effect, a tax on consumers of imported goods or a subsidy to domestic producers of substitutes, would perpetuate inefficiencies in these industries at the expense of the rest of the economy.(3) Furthermore, protection may also work against saving foreign exchange because exporters may be forced, through protective tariffs, to pay more for their imported inputs and thereby become less competitive.

TRENDS IN PUBLIC EXPENDITURE

In Greece, the outlay for the public sector (general government) increased from 19 percent of GDP in 1960 to 22 percent in 1970 and 32 percent in 1980. The increase in general government taxes was even higher, creating a small surplus every year during the period 1953-72. This surplus was devoted mostly to investment in the public sector. However, during the period 1950-52 there were annual deficits in the budgets of the general government, mainly because of the rehabilitation process after World War II and the civil war. After that period, there were budget surpluses, despite the fact that payments from social security were higher than contributions. However, since 1973 there have been growing deficits financed by public borrowing and/or by a growing money supply.(4)

In Greece the public sector, in a broad sense, includes not only central government and state and local government, but also public enterprises (which account for about 20 percent of the central government) and social insurance institutions, such as the Institute of Social Insurance and the Organization of Agricultural Insurance. The budgetary expenditures for the Greek central government include the regular or administrative outlays, those for public investments, and payments for consumer goods.(5)

Greece spends the highest proportion of national income on defense of all NATO countries. Military expenditures, according to a NATO decision, should rise by 3 percent per year in constant prices. In current prices they are expected to increase by more than 20 percent in Greece to cover the rate of inflation also. Such sizable expenditures present serious problems in the public sector and the entire economy of Greece because part of the defense material is purchased from abroad in dollars, which have been appreciating drastically during recent years (about 40 percent in 1981, and 25 percent in 1983). Moreover, no part of military expenditures is applied to productive ventures.

Although there are signs throughout Europe and other Western economies that indicate that public spending is approaching its economic and political limits, the public sector in Greece continues to expand rapidly. Governments in many Western countries recognize that they cannot have economic growth without incentives to invest, which can be achieved by shifting resources from the governmental consumption sector back to the investment sector.(6) That is why government consumption spending, which rose rapidly during the postwar years, started tapering off--it was not so much because of the disorganized popular resistance as because governments began taking the lead themselves. However, this task is difficult for Greece and Yugoslavia because of the reaction of many vested interests and the disturbances that persist in the eastern Mediterranean area.

However, in Greece, where people still tend to look to government to solve almost all their problems, public spending continues to increase at a faster rate than total output. As mentioned previously, such spending takes place mainly in the form of subsidies in the areas of health, social security, education, transportation, housing, and agriculture, as well as for defense. The increase is accounted for by government spending primarily in consumption or in transferring wealth from one group to another.(7) It has the advantage of improving income distribution but often reduces incentives to work and slows down economic growth. Thus, while public spending in Greece for social insurance against illness or unemployment may raise the level of social welfare, it may, at the same time, exaggerate budget deficits and drain investment funds. Also, government spending in advanced education may prove to be socially counterproductive as long as it is used for training young people in honorific professions for which there are no demand and no satisfying jobs available.

Total expenditures of the public sector in Yugoslavia increased from 32.2 percent of GDP in 1960 to around 40 percent in 1980. In the self-managed communities of interest, budget expenditures are about half of the total public sector's expenditures. They are determined, together with contributions or taxes, through consultation with the assemblies of the communities in accordance with the specific needs and possibilities of each community and in line with the growth of the economy.(8) From that point of view, there is not much point in carrying out any countercyclical policies through utilization of expenditures within the self-managed communities of interest.

As Figure 3.2 shows, public expenditures in Greece gradually increased from less than 20 percent of GDP in 1950 to 32 percent in 1980. However, public expenditures in other Western European countries absorb far higher proportions (40 to 50 percent) of GDP. This is particularly so for the EEC countries and Sweden.(9)

In Yugoslavia, central government expenditures, including social security payments after 1958, varied from 34 percent of GMP (gross material product) in 1953 to 27 in 1960, 22 in 1970, and 17 percent in 1980. These large variations may be attributed primarily to the trial-and-error approach to decentralization and economic reforms introduced particularly in the 1960s and 1970s. However, disregarding the unusual increase in the expenditures of 1964, the overall trend of central government expenditures from 1953 to 1967 was downsloping, indicating a gradual shift from central government to "communities of interest" and "special funds". In 1967-72 such expenditures remained more or less stable and declined thereafter.

Yet the thrust toward decentralization and self-management in Yugoslavia led to an extensive institutional fragmentation of public expenditures, higher administrative costs, lack of proper coordination, and losses in economies of scale. Moreover, poorly performing enterprises had to pay as much in taxes as the more successful ones. Productive investments were not properly coordinated with economic fluctuations, while the state was no longer contributing as much as before.

Expenditures for defense and subsidies in Yugoslavia are taken care of primarily by the federal government, while spending for public administration, social activities, and investment is the main responsibility of republics, cities, and

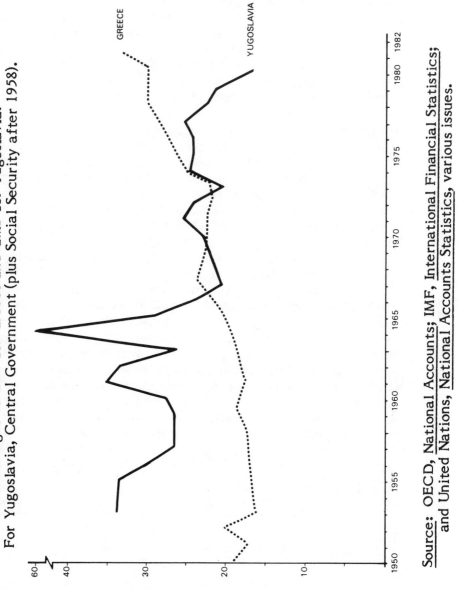

Figure 3.2. Expenditures of General Government as Percentages of GDP for Greece and GMP for Yugoslavia. For Yugoslavia, Central Government (plus Social Security after 1958).

GREECE

YUGOSLAVIA

Source: OECD, National Accounts; IMF, International Financial Statistics; and United Nations, National Accounts Statistics, various issues.

the communes. Also, housing expenses are the exclusive responsibility of the cities and the communes. Out of the total budgetary expenditures of about 20 percent of GMP, the federation accounts for around 12 percent, republics and provinces about 3.5 percent, and cities and communities about 4.5 percent. In addition, there are a few extra-budgetary institutions or accounts, such as the FAD (Fund for Financing the Accelerated Development of the Underde-veloped Regions), the Federal Fund for Financing Exports, the Federal Fund for Financing Investment, Education Com-munities Fund, Social Insurance Funds, Road Funds, and Water Funds. The federal share of extrabudgetary expendi-tures is close to 23 percent of the total and the remaining of the 77 percent belongs to the republics and the communes.

In Yugoslavia, federal budgetary expenditures for na-tional defense and public administration absorb about 50 percent of total expenditures. Subsidies to poor communities absorb 15 percent, and subsidies to enterprises selling at prices lower than the cost of production absorb 20-22 percent of total expenditures. Administrative expenditures for the republics and provinces account for 27 percent and for the communes 55 percent of their total expenditures respec-tively.(10) The largest part of the remaining expenses goes to investment and grants, primarily to less developed areas.

In our previous analysis, the size of the public sector was measured by relating budgetary activities to GDP or to national income. However, for the evaluation of the behavior of public sector expenditures over time in the countries considered, related income elasticities were used.

Table 3.1. Income (Y) Elasticity of Government Expendi-tures (G), $\Delta G/G \div \Delta Y/Y$

	1950-60	1960-70	1970-80
Greece	0.95	1.35	1.48
Yugoslavia	0.86	0.70	1.15

Note: For Greece general government; for Yugoslavia central government expenditures.

Source: OECD; National Accounts, various issues. IMF, International Financial Statistics, Yearbook, various issues.

Table 3.1 presents the percentage change in government expenditures over the percentage change in national income, that is, the income elasticity of government expenditures. For Greece, this elasticity was lower than one during the 1950s and higher than one for the 1960s and 1970s; while for Yugoslavia it was lower than one during the first two decades and higher than one during the last decade. This means that the public sector (all forms of government) in Greece was growing proportionally a little less than the overall economy during the 1950s, but it kept growing far more than proportionally during the 1960s and 1970s. One can observe a similar trend of a growing public sector at a rate proportionally higher than that for national product or income in the four large countries of the EEC (France, West Germany, Italy, and the United Kingdom). Thus the EEC elasticities of government expenditures, with respect to GDP, were more than one and growing from 1.03 during 1950-60 to 1.13 in 1960-70 and 1.35 in 1970-80.(11)

In Yugoslavia, on the other hand, central government expenditures grew proportionally less than national income during the 1960s but relatively more in the 1970s. This indicates that the impact of decentralization of central government was stronger in the 1960s than in the 1970s. Year-to-year variations in the proportion of central government expenditure to national income in Yugoslavia in the 1970s was not as much as during the previous two decades. The trend of this proportion was to grow slowly after 1967. This may be because of the growth in social security payments, which are included in central government expenditures, as the IMF (International Monetary Fund) data indicate.

The growth of expenditures was covered by higher taxation and/or higher public debt. Thus for Greece borrowing to finance government deficits increased from 10.5 percent of national income in 1960 to 22.2 percent in 1970 and about 30 percent in 1980; for Yugoslavia total debt declined gradually from 24 percent of national income in 1960 to 16 percent in 1970 and around 10 percent in 1980.(12)

Government consumption expenditures in Greece rose from 12 percent of national income (average propensity to consume) in 1960 to 13 percent in 1970 and 16 percent in

1980, while the marginal propensity to consume by government increased from 12 percent in 1950-60 to 14 percent in 1960-70 and 18 percent in 1970-80. In Yugoslavia both average and marginal propensity to consume by government were stable and close to 20 percent of national income during the postwar period. Income elasticities of government consumption for Greece grew from 0.93 in the 1950s to 1.13 in the 1960s and 1.38 in the 1970s, while for Yugoslavia they were constant and almost unitary during the three postwar decades. Social security payments and investment by government pushed the overall government expenditures in 1981 to 36 percent of national income for Greece and about 40 percent for Yugoslavia.

The governments of both countries try to mitigate inflation by stabilizing demand mainly through moderation in the growth of the public sector. In addition, other measures, such as restrictive credit ceilings and income guidelines are used. However, the relatively weak outlook for world trade, cost pressures, and inflationary expectations present problems for anti-inflationary and economic growth policies.

To reduce the growth in expenditures, the Yugoslav government imposed a ceiling on the increase in nominal earnings for most public sector employees and discontinued a number of investment projects in many government sectors and in "noneconomic" activities. However, the increase in defense spending, the special fund payments to Montenegro to compensate for damage caused by earthquakes, as well as growth of expenditures on civil and war pensions (which are indexed to the cost of living), have largely offset the contractionary impact of other measures. Although most other public sector bodies are constitutionally obliged to have broadly balanced accounts, the above three items, which are principally the responsibility of the federal government, have led to a high federal deficit (20 billion dinars in 1980). Because wages and investment (both subject to high domestic multiplier rules) were reduced in real terms, the Yugoslav rate of economic growth will most likely be reduced in the foreseeable future.

CENTRAL VS. LOCAL GOVERNMENT

There are certain public or collective activities, such as

defense, which the central government can provide more efficiently than local governments. Also, a number of public or quasi-national goods of social importance can be coordinated or efficiently allocated by higher-level governments. At the same time, stabilization and redistribution policies, as well as economies of scale in tax administration, can be better achieved by central than by state and local government. However, for a large spectrum of public services, subnational authorities can make efficient decisions for their regions that approximate those of the market mechanism. Local representatives in Greece and Yugoslavia, as well as in many other countries, are under greater pressure to relate tax costs and public benefits on a regional level rather than on a central bureaucratic basis.

Decentralization in government authority allows for more direct participation of the local population in cultural, economic, and political decision making. People in cities, towns, and villages are much more interested in solving their own regional problems than in having it done by a remote and impersonal bureaucracy. The greater the decentralization of the public sector, therefore, the greater the participation of citizens in the decision-making process and the greater the efficiency in solving regional and local problems. However, in order for local authorities to be able to perform such functions effectively, they need the required financial resources.

Certain functions now performed by the central government of Greece could easily be delegated to local authorities. This would facilitate the process of decentralization, reduce central government bureaucracy, and provide for a source of revenue for the local authorities. A recent authorization for municipalities and communities throughout the country to issue housing permits, for example, seems to be an appropriate step in the right direction. The permit fees will now go where they belong, that is, to the local authorities and not to the central government. Other examples include traffic accident reports, marriage licenses, licenses for extending water lines and constructing or expanding roads in remote villages, and the like.

By the same token, great centralization in government authority involves, among other things, greater inefficiency and waste of valuable resources. The slow-moving central government bureaucracy is usually unable to conceive and implement efficiently projects of local importance. Most of the time the dead hand of the central government acts as a drawback to the developmental efforts of those immediately involved at the local level. More often than not, the central bureaucrats fail to see and understand the real need of specific regions and communities. This explains, to a great extent, their propensity to embark on a highly wasteful prestigious projects that have little to do with the real needs and aspirations of the people. It seems, therefore, that inefficiency goes hand in hand with government centralization. Moreover, centralization leads to the suffocation of individual and collective initiative at the regional and local levels and encourages corruption at high levels of government.

Despite growing criticism of central government expansion, Greece seems to continue to follow the path of greater centralization.(13) The tendency becomes evident when one looks at the relative magnitude of central versus state and local government expenditures. While central government expenditures, as a proportion of general government expenditures, increased significantly during the postwar period, those of the local government declined at a steady rate. Moreover, the gap in the relative size of these two forms of government tended to widen during the last two decades.

As Figure 3.3 shows, central government expenditures in Greece increased from 62 percent of the total public expenditures in 1960 to 70 percent in 1980. On the other hand, the share of state and local government expenditures in general government declined from 16 percent in 1960 to 9 percent in 1980. Thus, although there has been a slight improvement in the trend from 1975 onward, the relative shares of local and state government on the one hand and the central government on the other explain the widening gap between those two forms of government in Greece.

In sharp contrast to what is happening in Greece, decentralization trends continue and local governments are strengthened in the four largest EEC countries, that is, in France, West Germany, Italy, and the United Kingdom. Thus the share of central government expenditures in these four countries taken together declined from 58 percent of general government expenditures in 1960 to about 55 percent in 1980 while that of local government increased from 10 to 13 percent between 1960 and 1980. Similar declines in central

Figure 3.3. Greece: Relative Expenditure Shares of Local and Central Government in General Government.

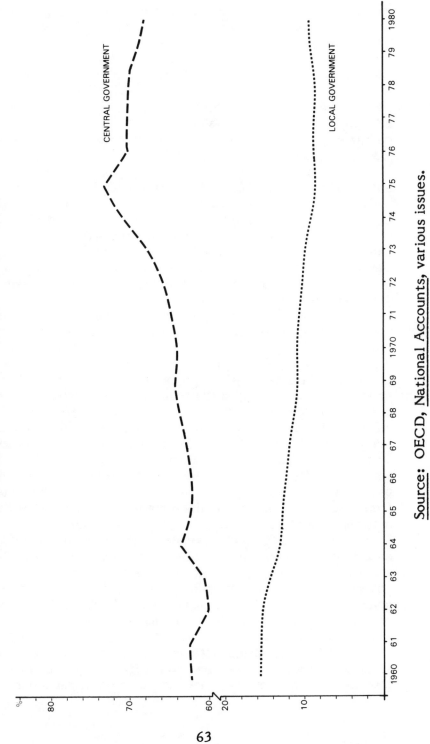

Source: OECD, National Accounts, various issues.

government and increases in state and local government shares can be also observed in Australia, Canada, and the United States.

The same messages are conveyed when one considers the elasticity of state and local government expenditures with respect to general government expenditures. The figure for Greece was considerably less than one during all the time intervals considered, in sharp contrast to the other EEC countries, where it was either very close to one or considerably greater than one.

To summarize: when elasticity is estimated for the entire period from 1960 to 1980, it is seen that it is very low (.55) for Greece, and well above one for the other EEC countries (1.12). The standard interpretation of these values for elasticity is clear. The figures imply that, on the average and for the entire period, when general government expenditures were increasing by 1 percent in the EEC countries, the state and local government expenditures were increasing by 1.12 percent. In Greece, however, with an increase in the size of general government by 1 percent, there was a corresponding increase of only .55 percent in the size of local government.(14)

The main reason for the centralization observed in Greece, contrary to what happens in the EEC and other countries, is that local authorities are deprived of tax revenues from some of their own services. To meet their expenses local governments, that is, municipality and community authorities in the EEC countries, depend primarily on their own revenues, collected primarily from property income taxes and sales taxes. In Greece, on the other hand, the main part of the limited municipal and community revenues comes from the provision of certain services, primarily sanitation, maintenance of cemetaries, and sidewalk leasing.

A good part of such revenues is collected along with the electricity bills by the Public Power Corporation. More specifically, about 57 percent of the total revenue of local government in Greece comes from other "subsectors of general government"; 21 percent from "property income receivable"; 16 percent from "indirect taxes"; and 6 percent from "direct taxes."

It should be noted here that in other countries a wide variety of additional services are offered by the local authorities. Those services include elementary, secondary, and (in the case of New York City) higher education, police and fire protection, hospital care, and mass transportation facilities, as well as court functions. It is expected, therefore, that higher levels of revenue will be needed in order for the local authorities to finance these additional services. From a sociopolitical point of view such extensive delegations of power to local authorities would diffuse the decision-making power to more people and strengthen democratic institutions.

It is paradoxical that even in some socialist or centrally planned countries, including Yugoslavia, the trend is towards more decentralization, while the opposite was true for Greece during the postwar years.

Furthermore, it can reasonably be expected that in Greece there will be pressure to reduce central government transfers to local governments. There are several factors working in that direction. For one thing, a reduction in tariffs on imports, to about half their present levels, is expected in the years ahead. At present tariffs represent about 22 percent of the value of imports. However, they are expected to be reduced to 10-12 percent as a result of Greece's accession to the Common Market and the harmonization of her trade and tax policies. (More on the relationship between tariffs and imports will be covered in a later section.)

Moreover, as a result of Greece's membership in the EEC, the introduction of a value added tax by 1984 will probably generate less tax revenues than the present turnover and other taxes. The reason is that Greece's industrial sector is not as advanced as that of the EEC and, therefore, the production stages for which taxes are collected are fewer. As will be explained later in more detail, Greece will collect value added taxes only for the final retail stages on imported commodities, while exporting countries will reap most of the taxes for the intermediate stages of production.

It becomes evident, therefore, that Greece might be forced to introduce sizeable sales taxes--to the degree permitted by the EEC agreements--and/or massive direct income and property taxes. This will be necessary in order to keep revenues at the same levels or, more realistically, to increase them in equal proportion to the expected increases in central and local government expenditures. The alternative for Greece would be growing budgetary deficits, the financing of which would tend to increase inflation.

Recent decentralization measures in Greece delegate a great part of administrative authority to municipal and community governments. Local governments in the rural regions and block organizations in large cities are the basic units of decision making concerning their own affairs. Prefectual (nonmarchy) councils, in which representatives of local towns, trade unions, banks, and utilities participate, will coordinate regional decisions while a small administrative unit will supervise the implementation of the decentralization mandates.(15) With this type of bottom-up decision making, in which initiatives would be derived from the general populace, manipulation of the state for private benefit (rousfeti) and the paper power of the miniczars and the elite class of the bureaucracy will be reduced or eliminated.

In order to bolster the financial base of the municipalities and give them fiscal muscle, the central government transferred controls of forests, mountain terrains, lakes, and all beaches (covering some 60 percent of Greece's surface area) to local authorities. Moreover, local governments can raise revenue by opening up parks and tourist resorts and collecting local property taxes and natural resource user taxes, in addition to revenue sharing and investment financing from the national budget. The Five Year Plan of 1983-87 provides for the gradual emancipation and financial independence of the provincial localities. However, since there are so few experts and mass organizations to implement decentralization, mass education programs are needed to make local people familiar with a more democratic way of decision making. To avoid the vicious circle of "keeping power to transfer power," incentives for popular participation in community affairs and decisions are needed even at the cost of some initial disorganization.(16)

Overcentralization and bureaucratization in Greece kill initiative and create unhealthy economic dependencies. As a result, the economy lacks the necessary managerial skills to run decentralized collective activities. To use the services of well-trained bureaucrats and other managers to push for local self administrations, that is, to use centralized means for decentralized ends, involves the risk of creating a new elite that may consolidate its power and allocate excessive benefits to its members far above the average working person, as happens to some extent in Yugoslavia. In spite of all difficulties, however, there are some interesting examples of decentralized and cooperative activities. Thus when houses were built in Kalamata, in southern Peloponnesus, 50 percent of each house was owned by the municipality, 25 percent by the workers who built it, and the remaining 25 percent by those moving in. In Zakynthos, an Ionian island, a plant producing and selling cheese domestically and abroad was established by a village cooperative. In Fthiotida, central Greece, a mineral water bottling company, based on self-management, was set up. Similar "socialized" enterprises, including skiing centers, hotels, and other services are planned in Kalavryta in northern Peloponnesus and other places. Moreover, a mine employing 2,500 workers and a refrigerator-television enterprise (one of the most up-to-date in Europe), with 1,100 workers, instituted an embryonic form of worker participation in business decision making. In the latter, in a mass meeting the workers decided to accept a 150-dollars monthly pay cut. The firm, covering more than its costs, began to repay part of its enormous debt.(17) It appears, therefore, that appointing sound and efficient managers is the key to making such enterprises with worker participation competitive with other private or public enterprises. In such endeavors, overorganization and bureaucracy as well as underorganization and managerial inefficiency associated with nepotism and favors, so familiar in Greece, should be avoided.

In Yugoslavia, a comparison of government expenditures indicates that, during the postwar years up to 1971, emphasis was given to the republic and local governments at the expense of the federal government. As Figure 3.4 shows, federal government expenditures declined from 58 percent of total budgetary expenditures in 1958 to 50 percent in 1971, while republic and local government expenditures increased from 42 percent to 53 percent. However, a significant increase in federal government expenditures and a dramatic decline in republic and local government expenditures took place after 1971.

Differentiating between the republics' budgets and those of local governments, we can observe how this decline was caused by lower local government expenditures while the republics kept about the same level of expenditure (around 15 percent) throughout the postwar years.

Budgetary expenditures of the combined public authorities (federal, republic, and local) decreased, from 22 percent of GDP in 1958 to around 15 percent in 1980. However,

Figure 3.4. Expenditures of Federal, Republic, and Local Government in Yugoslavia.
(Percentages of total budgetary expenditures)

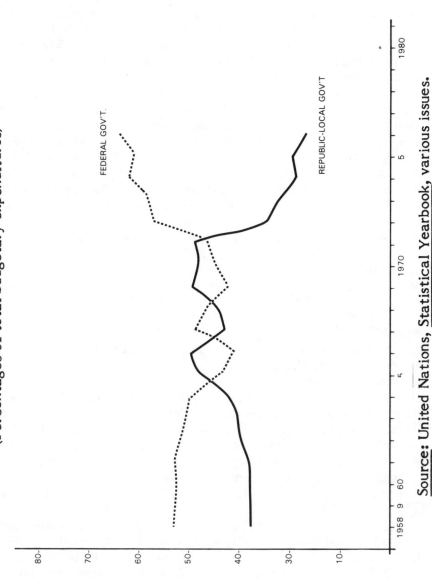

FEDERAL GOV'T.

REPUBLIC-LOCAL GOV'T

Source: United Nations, Statistical Yearbook, various issues.

68

expenditures of communities of interest and special funds kept on growing during the postwar years, causing the overall public sector expenditures to grow from 32 percent of GDP in 1967 to about 40 percent in 1980.

In Yugoslavia, the elasticity of the expenditures of republics and local government with respect to the expenditures of "combined public authorities," where federal government is included in addition to the republics and local governments, was more than one (1.3) during the 1960s. But it declined significantly to 0.5 during the 1970s. This means that decentralization from federal to local governments increased during the decade of the 1960s. In the 1970s, however, the decentralization process was shifted from the local authorities to "communities of interest," which absorbed 39 percent of total revenues in 1966 and 50 percent in 1975. On the other hand, the expenditures of the republics as percentages of the total budgetary expenditures, were more or less the same during the postwar years.

BUDGETARY DEFICITS

There is an important question about deficit financing in countries, like Greece and Yugoslavia, that undergo serious price inflation. This is because there is a basic connection between deficit financing and inflation. It seems that monetary expansion is a consequence of printing money to cover the difference between government expenditures and tax revenue. This is particularly so for Greece and Yugoslavia, where domestic borrowing to finance budget deficits is used to a limited extent. Levying taxes, on the other hand, is an unpopular practice, in addition to the distorting effects upon incentives that taxes always have. Therefore, what remains is to have the central bank make up the difference of expenditures over tax receipts by printing money. This is an easy practice in Greece and Yugoslavia, where the central banks are under the direct control of the government and do not enjoy much independence on matters of managing money and formulating monetary policy.

Two major questions may be asked in connection with the trend in growing public expenditures: (1) Is the relative expansion of the public sector producing adverse macroeconomic effects by crowding out private investment or is it only a question of private consumption being replaced by government consumption? (2) Is this expansion the result of a growing demand for government services on the part of the taxpayers and, therefore, are they willing to bear the burden of additional taxation?

Although there is strong criticism of the bureaucratic public sector, it would seem difficult to argue that the expansion of the public sector has detrimental effects on the performance of the overall economy. When the public sector invests, particularly in public utility projects where the private sector is unable or hesitates to do so, there are expectations of economic stimulation. These expectations arise in the same manner as with private investment since they are based on the positive effects of the multiplier and the accelerator. In the case of a slackening economy, any form of public spending would have beneficial effects on the market sector demand and production by offsetting the deflationary impact of a rising propensity to save.(18)

When the market sector devotes a comparatively higher proportion of spending to investment and exports, there might arise expectations for a better growth performance. Hence, it would be difficult to establish causality of a growing public sector leading to low growth performance, since the opposite tendency of high growth might occur. In many cases it depends on the managerial efficiency and technological innovations affected by the decision makers in charge of public enterprises and the public sector in general.

Regarding the second question, that is, whether the taxpayers are willing to support a growing public sector and pay more taxes, the answer seems to be in the negative, particularly for Greece. The sociopolitical structure of the country permits us to accept the argument that the state imposes taxes, frequently suppressing unions and other groups of taxpayers, instead of monitoring their demand for government services.

However, it should be recognized that the main area of governmental activities and expenditures lies in services of a general sort, such as civil administration and defense, which cannot be sold at a price to individuals and are collectively consumed. Hence there is no automatic mechanism by which one may compare cost with benefits of government services, and it is difficult to determine how far government expenditures may go.

There seems to be a close relationship between budget deficits of the central government and inflation in Greece. Thus the deficits of recent years, as percentages of government revenue, were about the same as the rises in consumer prices and the increases in money supply (around 20 percent) above the real rate of economic growth.(19) In spite of the efforts of the socialist government of Greece to reduce the budget deficit, it still remains about 17 percent of total economic output. Given that the velocity of money remained fairly constant (5.3), it can be concluded that the growth in money supply, which was primarily used to finance budgetary deficits, was responsible for inflation. In other words, additional money issued for financing government expenditures (not backed by taxation or borrowing from the public), led to an almost proportional increase in inflation. To finance the budget deficit, the government issues a promissory note to the Bank of Greece and "borrows" the needed funds. The Bank of Greece, in turn, prints additional money and delivers it to the government. However, it may be possible for the bank to lend money belonging to pension funds and insurance institutions. Such institutions are required by law to deposit a certain proportion of their collected funds with the central bank free of interest. This manner of financing deficits is an indirect way of borrowing funds from the public and is not as inflationary as that of issuing additional money.

The total deficits of the public sector in Greece were 210 billion drachmas in 1980, 304 billion drachmas in 1981, and 337 billion drachmas in 1982 or 13 percent of GDP (compared to 2.5 percent in France and West Germany). This represented 70 percent of the total tax revenue.

Defense spending (6.2 percent of GNP in Greece and 4.3 percent in Yugoslavia in 1979) absorbs large amounts of public sector revenue. Also, a large proportion of these deficits comes from public enterprises and separate public institutions dealing with urban transportation, electricity, railways, airlines, and water distribution. It was 34 billion drachmas in 1979 and 45 billion in 1980 or 37 and 21 percent respectively of the total deficits of the public sector. In 1981 it reached 49.6 billion drachmas and in 1982 76.5 billion drachmas.(20) The main reasons for deficits in public enterprises were: First, prices of their services were kept at low levels for political reasons. Second, they were stuffed with excessive personnel during the postwar years to accommodate unemployed constituencies of the politicians in power. As a result, administrative costs remained high, revenues were low, and the deficits, which were covered by government budgets, were growing.

For effective operation, the management of public enterprises needs to be independent of political pressures and the control of the central government. That is, decentralization is needed. Moreover, periodic price adjustments of their products are needed to match the country's general rate of inflation and increases in costs. This happens in France almost every year.

Public sector deficits are partially covered by domestic and/or foreign debt. According to statistics issued by the Bank of Greece, a large part of the deficits is covered by printing new money and parts by foreign debt. Ceteris paribus, foreign debt that is monetized domestically is also inflationary. Such deficits are primarily used for financing consumption and not new investment, which could increase supply and help eventually to mitigate inflation. Moreover, at times, parts of deficits are covered by promissory notes, mainly from insurance funds. This form of deficit financing absorbs funds that would be largely allocated to capital formation. This in turn would stimulate production and suppress inflation.

MONEY SUPPLY, VELOCITY, AND DEFICIT FINANCING

There was a significant increase in money supply, which was related to the growing public sector and price rises in Greece, and more so in Yugoslavia, during the last decade. As Figure 3.5 shows, the money supply in Greece increased 4.6 times (from 55 billion drachmas in 1970 to 310 billion in 1980). Given that the velocity of money, that is, the ratio of GDP over money supply, remained relatively constant and close to 5, the increase in money supply, over and above the real economic growth, was therefore related to an increase in prices. The extremely stringent Greek credit policy allowed such strong central control as to make the Greek system almost similar to that of Yugoslavia.

A far higher growth in money supply took place in Yugoslavia during the 1970s, as Figure 3.6 indicates. It increased some ten times (from 40 billion dinars in 1970 to 470 billion dinars in 1980). However, money velocity declined from 5.1 in 1970 to 3.3 in 1980. The increase in money supply, though, was so dramatic that it not only overcame the declining velocity and the growth in real production but it also generated further price rises.(21)

As was mentioned earlier, an important reason for an increase in money supply is the financing of budgetary deficits. As long as tax revenues are not sufficient to cover government expenditures, the governments of Greece and Yugoslavia frequently create money mostly to purchase goods and services, to pay their employees, and to pay off previous debts. This is a common practice in these two countries, where government borrowing from the public is not widespread as in other countries, notably in the United States. Fiscal needs, therefore, affect monetary policies and force these governments to cover budget deficits by printing new money, regardless of the prevailing economic and market conditions. In countries with democratic governments, as in Greece, politicians tend to press for the creation of money to finance local projects, particularly when election time approaches. However, extra money creation, which leads to a limited positive inflation rate, may be fiscally desirable to discourage hoarding and to encourage productive investment.

By exercising monetary monopoly and printing additional money, the governments of these countries can obtain real revenue. Depending on the transactions demand for money, individuals will give up real goods and services to obtain additional money in order to facilitate transactions, even if the prime level is somewhat higher than previously.(22) Moreover, by paying off previous debts with monetary units that have somewhat less value per unit than before, these governments gain real revenues, as they do through progressive taxation.

Taxation on capital or wealth in both countries is limited or nonexistent. Therefore, a tax on income from capital can be avoided by keeping capital stock idle. But this practice reduces the use of available resources and retards growth. In the case of keeping liquid capital stock, an inflationary money creation is similar to a tax that acts retroactively, after the decision is made on how much capital to hold in liquid form.

However, future expectations about money creation for deficit financing and the siren wails from inflation affect

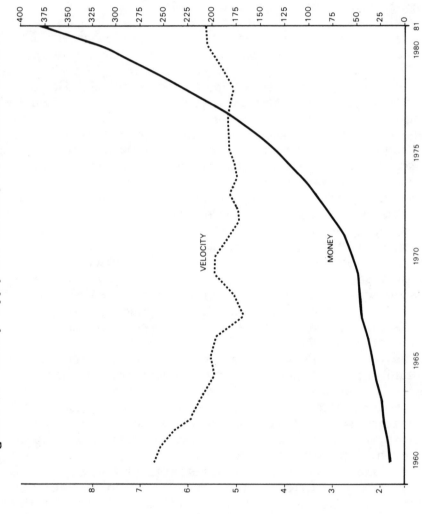

Figure 3.5. Money Supply and Velocity (GDP/M) for Greece.

Source: OECD, National Accounts; and IMF, International Financial Statistics, various issues.

74

Figure 3.6. Money Supply and Velocity (GDP/M) for Yugoslavia.

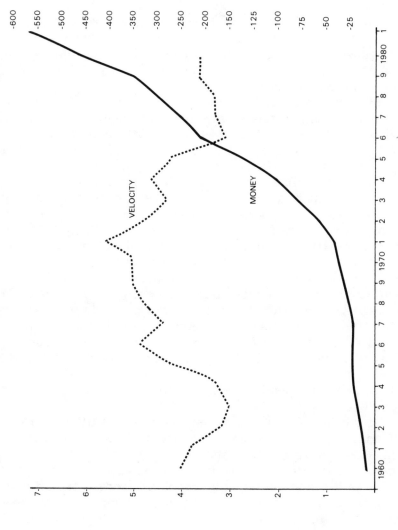

Source: OECD, National Accounts; and IMF, International Financial Statistics, various issues.

75

such behavior and tend to push interest rates to high levels. Such monetization of deficits puts a great burden on monetary policy and has adverse effects on industries that depend on borrowed money.

To facilitate industrial development, postwar Greek governments created or supported commercial and investment banks for the purpose of channeling investment into new industries and expanding old ones. However, these banking institutions were primarily involved in lending operations, providing mostly credit for other forms of spending than investments in industry.

As mentioned earlier, in both Greece and Yugoslavia, increases in money supply are used frequently to finance growing government deficits. A substantial portion of such deficits is the result of subsidization or aid to enterprises that failed the competitive market test and whose revenues are fallen to less than the costs of their operations. Government regulations and controls in Greece and Yugoslavia may be considered another source of deficits because of the high administrative expenditures associated with them and the largely unjustified stifling of productive investment arising from them. In such government bureaucracies there are interest groups certainly concerned with doing the job assigned to them by society, but frequently they do that in ways beneficial only to themselves. Policy recommendations for fine tuning the economy by budgetary deficits, at times, turn out simply to stultify the economy through perpetuating self-serving bureaucracies and unleashing waves of inflation and high interest rates. However, in cases of high unemployment, deficit spending can be a significant stimulant to a sagging economy.

Borrowing money from pension funds or other sources to finance deficits, the governments of Greece and Yugoslavia absorb savings from the economy that could be used for capital formation. In such cases, borrowing carried out by enterprises and individuals becomes more difficult and expensive as interest rates are driven upward, unless new money is printed to finance such deficits. In these cases, prices keep moving upward as long as the increase in money supply rises to a level higher than the increase in real production and the velocity of money is not declining. Then further inflationary expectations persist, which in turn, tend to push up interest rates and distort the efficient allocation of resources.

Another element contributing to budgetary deficits in both countries is the rush to spend near the end of the fiscal year by a number of ministries and other government agencies that happen to have unspent allotments. Such a bureaucratic waste may take place not only to avoid future cuts but also to increase the possibility of additional procurements in later fiscal years. As a result of "spend it or lose it" philosophy, many public agencies are busy spending on activities and projects of dubious importance, such as buying unnecessary furniture or employing contractors and consultants to advise them how to spend or to prepare studies for future projects that may never be implemented.

Such excessive end-of-the-year spending may cease when proper incentives are provided for responsible managers who are left with unspent appropriated funds. One possibility is the assurance that monies unspent at the end of the fiscal year can be used partially or totally toward expenses of the following year. The permission to carry forward unspent money would eliminate penalties for having failed to spend allocated public funds. Moreover, such savings should not be used as a guide to budgetary cuts in the agencies concerned during later years. Instead, appropriate rewards should be introduced to encourage savings toward the end of each fiscal year, which may lead to a reduction in taxation or/and a decrease in inflation.

A multivariate analysis of changes in inflation (consumer price index, CPI) on both contemporaneous and lagged (by one year) changes in money supply for Greece and Yugoslavia during the postwar years indicates a close relationship between these variables ($R^2 > 0.975$). For Greece, an increase in current money supply (Mt) by 10 percent was associated with an increase in inflation by 2 percent; an increase in the previous year's money supply ($Mt-1$) by 10 percent was associated with 1.3 percent increase in inflation. For Yugoslovia the figures were 1.2 and 1.7 respectively.(23) These relatively low regression coefficients were due to the fact that the growth of money supply was also responsible for financing real economic growth, which was impressive in both countries during the postwar years.

Consumer prices in Greece increased 5.9 times from 1950 to 1980, and in Yugoslavia 13.5 times (1951-1980). On an average annual basis for Greece, the consumer price index increased by 5.9 percent in 1951-60, 2.1 percent in 1961-70, and

14.6 percent in 1971-80. For Yugoslavia it increased by 5.2 percent in 1953-60, 12.6 in 1961-70 and 19.0 percent in 1971-80. In 1981-83, the consumer price index increased by 22 percent annually in Greece and 36 percent in Yugoslavia.(24)

The average annual increase in money supply in 1971-80, which was primarly responsible for inflation, was about 20 percent in Greece, and 32 percent in Yugoslavia, compared to 14.2 percent in France, 9.8 percent in West Germany, 14.6 percent in the United Kingdom, and 13.0 percent in the United States. Income velocity of money, on the other hand, remained fairly constant and close to 5.3 for Greece, and it declined from 4.8 to 3.5 for Yugoslavia during the same period.

Another serious source of inflation in both countries, in addition to excess money supply, is change in import prices. Ceteris paribus, a rise in the price of imported commodities will raise the cost of products for which imported inputs are used. Moreover, it will enable domestic producers to increase prices for their import substitute goods. The policy of more or less fixed exchange rates, practiced by both countries up to 1974, suppressed, to some extent, imported inflation at the expense of a deteriorating balance of trade. After that time, exchange rates fluctuated and moved against the drachma and the dinar, especially in dollar terms. The gradual devaluation of these currencies affected the balance of payments favorably but, at the same time, fueled more inflation domestically because of the rapid increase in import prices in terms of domestic currencies. Oil price rises, excess world demand (induced by a liquidity explosion), and a decline in the world supply of some tradables may be considered responsible for high import prices.

A multiple regression of the consumer price index on the money supply and import prices during tthe last two decades indicates that both independent variables used had about the same effect on the dependent variable for Greece. For Yugoslavia, however, money supply was a more important variable than import prices in their relationship to the consumer price index.(25)

SELF-MANAGEMENT AND ECONOMIC SOCIALIZATION: ORGANIZATIONAL AND FINANCIAL PROBLEMS

In recent decades, a remarkable development in industrial

organization has been introduced in a number of countries. Gradually and quietly, workplace communities have come to play a significant role in enterprise decision making, concerning wages, working conditions, investment, and similar matters. Such work groups have been developing not only in planned economies but also in market economies including the EEC countries and the United States. In cooperation with capital or under a system of worker self-management they aim at stimulating incentives and improving productivity and welfare. Although they grow at the expense of the traditional labor unions, they do not seem to raise questions of replacing the authority of owners of property and capital. In a number of instances, corporate management encourages labor representation in enterprise decision making so that strikes and other union opposition may be avoided as workers become responsible for company decisions affecting them. Moreover, when enterprises are not profitable or approach bankruptcy, employees are asked and frequently agree to take over management to keep the firm in operation and preserve their jobs.

In prosperous times, a competitive labor market permits some degree of worker control over employers and wage improvement because of the increase in demand for labor relative to supply. But increase in wages and improvement in working conditions may be achieved under the system of industrial democracy as well as or better than through the countervailing power of labor unions versus management in market economies. However, in times of severe recession and automation, unemployment increases and workers and unions (with dwindling power) are unable to protect their jobs, let alone to keep constant or improve real wages, as was evidenced during recent recessions in Western economies.

It may be possible for incentives for participation in a democratized workplace somehow to replace conventional incentives (pay, promotion, discharge) in market economies and authoritative work instructions in planned economies. Industrial democracy may strengthen and stimulate production. This is important in modern societies because of growing specialization, which makes a person stupid and ignorant according to Adam Smith, and increases nervousness and rivalry among workmates. Inventiveness and accomplishment, affection, relief, and happiness in the workplace may

require replacement of hierarchical and authoritarian structures in enterprises, whether based on private property or
not. Along these lines, John Stuart Mill and Jean Jacques
Rousseau believed that collective decisions and participatory
democracies advance human intellect, reduce bureaucracy,
and increase efficiency.(26) However, care should be taken
through employee training to make participation workable
and practical, otherwise there is the danger of frustration
and inefficiency, which may promote totalitarianism. A
frantic participation or apathy and too great a public preoc-
cupation with politics may make the system unworkable and
inefficient or may lead to the creation of a professional elite
in place of an old bureaucracy.

As the arguments go, self-management might be the
answer to the problems of capitalism and communism. This
would be the result of the spread of the democratic ideals in
the masses and widespread educational improvement in the
future. People would learn to put their efforts in decision
making and productive cooperation together for the better-
ment of society.(27) This might be an effective way for
people to increase their incentives to work and release their
talents for better achievements and higher productivity.
They would stop worshipping the state or being directed or
pressed by the authorities in their activities. On the other
hand, they would resent the practice of being exploited by
other people or adhere to the myths of the economically
powerful who are presented as the exclusive magicians of
economic decision making. From that point of view, state
bureaucratic socialism as well as exploitative capitalism may
not be accepted. Even the Yugoslav model of self-
management, with a good part of state control, might not be
advisable on these grounds.

The self-management or the labor-capital cosharing
system, wisely managed, can probably be made more efficient for attaining economic ends than any alternative yet
in sight. The main problem is to work out a social organization that will be efficient in achieving the best results with
the least possible costs, without offending people's notions of
a satisfactory way of life.

The main question is how to attain acceptable material
goals while preserving freedom and moral values. Rapid
economic development and removal of market imperfections
call for some form of planning. Moreover, efficient alloca-

tion of resources and exploitation of external economies may require departure from the strictures of the competitive market when this becomes necessary.

A proper measure to stimulate productivity and keep production costs relatively low might be to pay bonuses to employees instead of increasing wages. Such bonuses would depend on the profitability of each enterprise and should be equal for all workers of a given age and rank. This flexible system of remuneration, which has been successfully introduced in Japan, has the advantage of reducing the fixed labor costs significantly. Moreover, paying as much as one-third or one-fourth of workers' compensation in the form of periodic bonuses has the financial advantage of providing the enterprise with added working capital for several months. Part of these bonuses may remain with a special fund for additional pension or for extra payment after a number of years of work.

The gradual economic unification of Europe and a flexible practice of self-management seem to provide mutual support to each other. Europe then might prove to be the testing ground of self-management together with the process of economic integration.

In a number of enterprises in Greece and other market economies, workers may face the choice of either losing their jobs to a plant closing or buying and controlling the plant. In the United States, for example, the United Automobile Workers Local 736 agreed with the General Motors Company to purchase its manufacturing plant in Clark, New Jersey, to save more than 1000 jobs. Also, workers at the huge Weirton Works of the National Steel Corporation, based in Pittsburgh, bought the plant for 66 million dollars.(28) In such cases, unions may agree to certain pay reductions and work rules modifications, but they may negotiate both profit sharing and productivity bonuses in the future to offset wage reductions. On the other hand, they may agree to elect a portion of the board of directors initially, with the provision to elect more later.

Some 40,000 employees of Conrail, a huge freight-carrying railroad in the United States, are negotiating the purchase of the enterprise. If concluded, it would be the largest denationalization of government-owned assets in the United States. It is expected that the workers would buy the firm for $2 billion and sell 20 percent of the stock to the public while keeping the remaining 80 percent to themselves.

Replacement of management by labor representatives should be gradual because of the need to keep experienced personnel to share their traditional management experience with the workers. Although some operational problems may remain, such bold experiments in worker ownership and workplace democracy may prove to be successful through high productivity and improvement in the quality of products. In periods of management failures and union weaknesses, such measures are needed to avoid unemployment and all the accompanying social side effects.(29) It should be pointed out, however, that the chances for worker control are, in many cases, handicapped by the existing problems of the failing enterprises.

As happens in other countries, excessive intervention in the market processes by the Greek and, more so, the Yugoslav governments, through regulations and controls, may alter entrepreneurial investment decisions and, ceteris paribus, retard growth.(30) Thus environment and health/safety regulations may require investment that might otherwise be used in plant and equipment. They may also require manpower to operate needed control equipment and administer legal activities and office work without adding to salable outputs. However, public regulations are expected to yield contributions to total welfare of these countries, such as improvement in health and safety, which are difficult to measure and cannot be fully reflected in reported output. Thus further research and more efficient measurement of the economic impacts of public regulations on a society are needed to determine if their total beneficial effects outweigh their detrimental effects on productivity.

The system of worker self-management, seeds of which can be found in the Commune of Paris (1870s), is in operation in Yugoslavia, while a new system of employee participation in enterprise management is under consideration or partial implementation in other countries as well. Such a system of decentralized initiatives, instead of the existing centralized monopolistic direction or imposed coordination, may democratize further the political and economic life of nations. It is an emerging global system that reflects an adaptation to present economic and social conditions.

In Yugoslavia, as in China and perhaps in the United States and other countries, there is an organized system of large, medium, and small enterprises, with much of the technology and marketing coming from large enterprises, in which cases the related responsibilities and risks are reduced considerably. Sometimes certain transitional enterprises may be not economically efficient but may be kept in operation to create an experienced work force.

It seems that the Yugoslav economy is the nearest empirical approximation to the theoretical model of self-management and as such it invites a deeper analysis. Through modification and further democratization it may provide a promise of man's economic and political liberation from capitalist exploitation or bureaucratic oppression by the state. With proper adjustment, it can be implemented by other nations. Implementation or movement toward industrial or participatory democracy is slowly developing also in Tanzania (ujamma cooperatives), Israel (kibbutzim), the Soviet Union (Zlobin's method of autonomous economic units), China (communes), the European Economic Community, and to a limited extent in the United States (mainly plants in bankruptcy).(31) Indeed, the survival of the system for a relatively long period of time, in spite of all its difficulties, suggests that workers' alienation can be reduced and cooperation and work incentives for high productivity can be stimulated. However, the right form of participation in each case and in each nation should be provided so that efficiency can be preserved. Otherwise, too many cooks may spoil the broth, or, as the Chinese say, "Where there are too many hens, there are no eggs; while there are too many people, there is disorder."(32)

THE YUGOSLAV EXPERIENCE

After Tito broke with the Soviet Union in mid-1948, Yugoslavia changed economic policy toward more decentralization. The Soviet model of centralized planning and monocentric "state capitalism" was replaced with a polycentric "social" or "indicative" planning, which is characterized by worker-managed enterprises and market-incentive socialism. In this new form of socialism, the property of the enterprises is not owned by the state or individuals, but is held in trust for society. Small firms with fewer than five employees are primarily run by the workers themselves on an equal-shares basis, so that "exploitation of man by man" can be avoided.

The spirit of decentralization, social ownership, and labor management predominates in the 1974 constitution and in all the postwar development plans, particularly in the Ten-Year Plan of 1976-85.

The system of socialist self-management in Yugoslavia means the change in the nature of ownership of the means of production and the ensuing "disempowering" of the state. The workers perform direct management, while ownership belongs to society. Self-management in enterprises is one element in an integral system of social self-government. This is considered to be the system for withering away the state as Claude Henride Saint-Simon and later Friedrich Engels argued. In practice, however, many problems remain unresolved, and this socioeconomic laboratory of self-management is bound to remain active until more concrete results are produced.(33)

The unique system of self-management and social ownership in Yugoslavia needs a thorough review because of its gradual application or expected implementation in other countries, which belong to different economic systems. The Yugoslav economy then may be considered as a laboratory of experience from which other countries can learn and benefit. Of course there are serious difficulties in the system's implementation, but, as Professor Jaroslav Vanek argues, they may be considered in part as the unavoidable birth pains of this unique experiment.

However, in many instances, managers and workers are not interested in long-term investment in the enterprises they work in, but rather in short-term revenue to be used for higher wages and personal consumption. Moreover, there may be inconsistencies in the choice of investment, so that various parts of the economy may not fit together and major bottlenecks may appear. On the other hand, coordination by related commune committees or the League of Communists may not be effective because of lack of knowledge and experience or because of the prevalence of political influence on business decisions. The introduction of some kind of planning of saving and investment (programmed accumulation) may be considered as no better than state capitalism or state socialism. To avoid faulty investment and encourage incentive reforms, it would be advisable to induce workers to act as long-term owners of the enterprises. This could probably be achieved through a system of tenure and training of the workers in the enterprises they work in similar to that in Japan.

There are arguments that worker self-management in Yugoslavia is artificial and that in reality the whole process is part of the Communist party's political activity, part of the ruling structure, and that as such it cannot be very efficient. The party, the argument goes, as a privileged elite (a new class), is more interested in perpetuating its own power than establishing a classless society through self-management and social ownership.(34)

In Yugoslavia, enterprises employing more than five persons are socially owned and placed in the custody of the employees. For small firms, all employees are members of the workers' council of the enterprise in which they work. However, there are questions of whether the employees exercise authority in enterprises where party and union controls are present. To choose competent rather than indulgent managers, workers' councils look for professional and experienced persons because their own wages depend on the manager's performance. Nevertheless, managers and their staffs, armed with technical knowledge, may reduce the workers' councils to rubber stamps and render self-management and employee control in large part an aspiration. Also, there may be problems of lack of discipline, waste of labor, and excessive salaries or profit sharing above a minimum wage, which may be detrimental to long-term capital formation and growth of the related enterprises. Employees do not have a share to hold or to sell on leaving the firm.

Coordination of thousands of independent production units in a self-managed system is a serious problem, especially in Yugoslavia with its great historical, ethnic, and cultural divisions. To have a discretionary central authority to supervise the decentralized units may perpetuate hierarchy and bureaucracy, showing ordinary citizens away from participation. To have the market system rather than a central authority coordinate independent enterprises, as the Yugoslavs have perceived in their experimentation, may gradually lead to a form of capitalism with private enterprise and profit making. Already, large numbers of illegal private enterprises operate in Yugoslavia openly in trucking, construction, restaurants, inns, and other small-scale industries. Probably, a coordinating body with rotating members elected periodically by decentralized enterprises should coordinate the economy, effectively preserving at the same time the principle of democratic participation in economic decision making. Agriculture, which now in large part (80-85 percent) belongs to a private sector, is expected to turn eventually to self-management and collectivization, particularly as a result of the more efficient large-scale farm mechanization.(35) To cope with workers' control groups that may divide the economy into islands of inefficient monopolies, the Yugoslav government encourages free trade by removing import restrictions and constructing joint ventures with partial private ownership by foreign corporations and employee self-management practices. From that point of view, Yugoslavia may have set the world on a new economic course.

Yugoslavia has found that profit maximization or maximum growth of individual enterprises is an efficient tool of operation for the "free public enterprises." However, the fear is that recrudescence of the profit motive may lead to the reconstitution of capitalism. Although the opposing argument of the Yugoslav theoreticians is that the workers' councils are empowered with rights over the managers, day-to-day problems of production and distribution suggest that in many cases Yugoslav socialism still has to make its peace either with the market system or with centralized control. It would seem that the Yugoslav social ownership of the means of production is not by itself sufficient to establish an ideal socialist system. Instead, there are indications that a capitalist spirit is rising in many segments of the economy. Probably, after a long period of trial and error, the Yugoslav self-management system will show more clearly its economic and social advantages and disadvantages.

As mentioned previously, there is a trend toward adopting a version of this system in other planned economies, such as China, Poland, and Romania, as well as in market economies, through capital-labor comanagement, notably in West Germany and other EEC countries. This indicates that the system of industrial democracy deserves careful consideration. It may be the new international economic system of the future.

On the political front, although there seem to be changes in policies from time to time, the overall climate becomes more flexible toward freedom of expression and criticism. Thus seven professors critical of Yugoslavia's economic problems were fired at the beginning of 1981. But they were rehired later to work in the newly established Institute of Social Research. Moreover, they were permitted to publish their journal Praxis, which was prohibited five years ago. Such flexible policies are the result of pressures from a number of young intellectuals inside and outside the government who accept the basic principles of socialism and self-management but advocate a flexible policy toward review and criticism of the existing social and economic problems of the system.

Participatory democracy is the raison d'etre behind the Yugoslav self-management. However, in the decision-making process, there is an oligarchic type of influence similar to business firms under capitalism. Executives have greater influence than workers in critical decisions. Moreover, workers of age 30 to 45 and educated and skilled personnel participate more than women, unskilled, and very young and very old workers. Only in limited cases is there a polyarchic participation in decision making.

On many occasions, hiring decisions by Yugoslav firms have a countercyclical character. In an upswing stage of the economy, the capital-labor ratio would be increased, while in a downswing stage, it would be decreased to absorb more workers. Employment policies seem to follow the Japanese experience of providing permanent jobs, so that the "Illyrian firms" may have great similarities with the "Nipponese firms." Such a policy also resembles the tenure provisions in American universities.

Communes (obstinas), with administrative and economic powers similar to those of the individual states in the United States have been established throughout Yugoslavia. Each commune, which has wider socioeconomic functions than the local community in Western countries, is in charge of public order, health services, education, and welfare and supervises the legal and some economic activities of the enterprises in its region. Through this type of communalization and decentralization the Yugoslav policymakers expect that the state will "wither away," as Karl Marx proclaimed, not at some remote time but in the near future.

The basic organs of worker self-management are the Basic Organizations of Associated Labor (BOALs), which, before 1974, were known as work units, plants, or departments. A BOAL is a part of an enterprise the product of which can be measured and exchanged inside the enterprise or in the market. Associations of BOALs, which approve decisions on investment, income distribution, and related matters, may delegate certain powers to the self-management body (workers' council) or management board (executive committee of 3 to 11 members). Members of a workers' council or an executive committee may not be elected for more than two years or for more than two consecutive terms. Members of the executive committee may be relieved at any time by the workers' council.

However, there are problems of representative elections and management. Much of the labor force consists of recently urbanized peasants with limited education, especially when they come from less developed regions. Moreover, fusing managerial and labor-supply functions is another problem. Thus workers acting as managers may face conflicts of interest as they wear two hats at the same time. As suppliers of labor, they are interested in maximizing short-term wages and benefits. As managers, they are under pressure by banks and local and central authorities to maximize returns on equity and achieve a good long-run standing for the enterprise they manage. Also, there are questions whether workers' interests are better served through bargaining, forcing management to accept their demands, or through participation in decision making, in which case they become their own supervisors. However, in cases of recessions and widespread lay-offs, workers' demands through bargaining may be ineffective, as it has been proved in market or capitalist economies, while under self-management workers largely hold on to their jobs.(36) Moreover, such a system of industrial democracy may gradually reduce the gap between economic power and political freedom.

On many occasions, a manager in Yugoslavia has to be first a skilled politician on good terms with government authorities and the party brass and then an efficient technocrat. This seems to create a new influential and affluent class of managers, which, under the umbrella of worker management, enjoys extra salaries and other benefits, in the form of profit sharing or otherwise, over and above the normal wage provided for all workers.

In order to encourage competition, Article 30 of the Yugoslav Constitution prohibits associations that prevent free trade, or practice discrimination and promote inequality.

However, mergers may be permitted if they contribute to better organization and higher productivity, particularly in exporting enterprises. As a result, strong pressures toward monopolistic structures exist. Thus in the last two decades many mergers occurred, especially in mining and manufacturing where some 70 enterprises account for more than 50 percent of the sales.(37)

Workers usually prefer activities with a quick payoff, but good management prefers to reinvest profits to increase future productivity. When workers leave an enterprise they do not have any ownership rights to capital accumulated through underpaid labor. Worker-managed enterprises can buy and sell capital goods, but they are responsible for maintaining the book value of the assets through reinvestment. Directors of firms, who have little security of tenure usually approve wage increases at the request of workers, a fact that leads to cost-push inflation. On the other hand, worker-entrepreneurs do not have unique claims to the residuals generated by their innovative activities. This may result in low incentives and inefficient factor allocation. From that point of view, workers and managers in efficient enterprises are reluctant to change jobs, and labor mobility is low (about 1 percent of the labor force). As a result, unemployment remains high (8-10 percent), mainly because of the barriers to new entrants. Some people blame Tito's administration for misdirecting domestic and foreign investments to industrial plants that were not very useful.

The sharing by workers in enterprises also means participation in losses, that is, acceptance of lower wages in recessions and business slumps. Such sharing in the profits and losses of enterprises make the workers feel that they are the owners and they belong for life to the enterprises in which they work. Therefore strikes, boycotts, or other labor disturbances are avoided and incentives for high productivity increase, in a way similar to that of the Japanese system.

DECENTRALIZATION AND WORKER MANAGEMENT IN GREECE

Until recent years, labor's share in enterprise decision making and cooperative activities was weak or nonexistent in Greece. As mentioned previously an outstanding example of handicraft cooperatives was that of Ambelakia, founded in 1795 in Mount Ossa in Thessaly, which manufactured textiles. Similar shipping industries had operated along cooperative lines with seamen, captains, and lumber merchants, during the Turkish occupation and afterwards.(38)

After the introduction of a special law in 1911, councils of economic and social policy were established. They included representatives of labor, management, and the state. During the interwar period, particularly between 1928 and 1936, labor-management councils were introduced, primarily in the tobacco and shoe industries. From time to time, some public or semipublic enterprises implemented the principle of workers' sharing in decision making. They included the Piraeus Port Authority, the Greek National Railways, the National Bank of Greece, and the Bank of Greece. More recently, the Macedonian Bank and two shipping companies in Crete and one in Lesbos started their operations on the basis of equal or social ownership. Furthermore, in order to stimulate work incentives and higher productivity, some firms, such as Petzetakis Company, Piraiki-Patraiki, Lavreotiki Company, and the Commercial Bank of Greece have introduced some form of profit sharing by employees. Because of the encouragement of labor comanagement by the EEC, Greece is expected to apply this principle on a large scale in the foreseeable future. Enterprises wishing to be incorporated as European rather than national firms are required by the EEC to place workers on their management boards.

At present Greece is implementing an extensive program of decentralization of administrative and economic functions from the central government to the municipalities and communities. The goal is to give more authority to towns and villages, as well as the cooperatives, and through the participation of the local people in decision making to achieve a gradual socialization in the process of production and primarily in the distribution network. Through this process it is expected that the large difference between cost and price, which the middleman used to reap for decades in Greece (and which at times reached 3/4 of the price), will be reduced or eliminated. However, intensive training of the persons involved is needed, particularly for the highly individualistic Greek people in the countryside, to familiarize them with collective decision making.

In Greece, where there seems to be strong individualism and a form of worship of the state, it will be difficult to implement quick decentralization and self-management. This individualism seems not to be the result not of a deep-rooted sense of freedom but rather of the aversion or disdain of the Greek citizen to collectivism or common life with others. Such a psychology is probably the result of long occupations and oppression, which led some people to betray others, thereby feeding mistrust and suspicion among them.

Greece's new Five-Year plan (1983-1987) calls for decentralized reform programs that are expected to generate a process of democratic participation in economic policymaking. Such programs are based on voluntary agricultural cooperatives and the socialization of some sectors of industry in a way that decisions and controls would be invested in boards composed of workers, consumers' representatives, and government officials.

For wider participation of farmers and shepherds in these cooperatives, a number of incentives are provided by the government. They include price support, storage and distribution facilities, favorable loans, and investment grants. Thus grants of up to 50 percent of the amount of investment are given to such cooperatives by the Greek government. Moreover, voting for the appointment of managers and other decisions is based on simple membership and not on capital sharing as before. Such voting was enacted for the first time on October 30, 1982.

In recent years, a number of private companies borrowed from Greek banks large amounts of money that transformed into luxurious spending or into outflowing foreign currency by the individual owners of these companies. As a result, these companies appeared to be poor and ready for bankruptcy while their owners became rich. Part of the government's decentralization scheme was to purchase controlling shares in the troubled industries through conversion of debts owed to the already nationalized banks, with managing control transferred to representatives of the aforementioned social groups, which would be coordinated by national planning. However, the democratization of the workplace and the implementation of social control in the economy may be delayed because of the pressing need for technical expertise and the restraints imposed by international pressures for higher productivity and competitiveness. However, at the local level, in the growing participatory, decentralized movement, with mayoralties and communities acquiring more economic and political power, there are signs of socialization's success.

Industrialists and property owners in Greece and elsewhere may see democracy in industry as more threatening than democracy in government because constitutional orders protect property ownership or challenge its prerogatives marginally in such polyarchal states. By contrast, democratization of industry immediately and directly challenges them in a serious and permanent way. In cases of recession and depression, therefore, when enterprise losses and bankruptcies occur, worker and employee ownership and controls may have a good chance of implementation. However, in the immediate future the system of capital-labor comanagement may be practical and successful for the mixed Greek economy, which needs experienced managers and entrepreneurs.

A large number of private enterprises, with heavy debts to the banks, are near bankruptcy. In a number of cases the government turns the debts into equity and buys 51 percent of the shares.(39) Although this process of buying debts presents serious financial and budgetary deficit problems, it provides a good opportunity for the implementation of self-management and worker participation in these enterprises.

Vested interests, short-sighted government policy, and lopsided economic development combined to stifle growth in competition and effective industrialization in past years. Old industrial monopolies and large state-controlled banks entered into collusive credit agreements depriving potential competitors of needed financial sources. Conditions deteriorated further when bank credit was channeled into purchasing real estate and buildings, which amounted to more than 30 percent of all investment during the last two decades.

To increase work incentives, profit-sharing plans or related pension plans are used or contemplated by a number of enterprises in Greece. Pension plans have the advantage of being planned in advance and many variations can be available to the principal beneficiaries. Moreover, accumulated savings of such pension plans can be used productively by financing capital formation, while profit sharing may be used to discourage wasteful consumption.

In Greece, almost the whole banking system (95 percent) is owned by the state. Private enterprise shows a pathological and in many cases unhealthy dependency on the state, the money-lending institutions, and foreign capital. This dependency leads to the gradual transfer of nonprofitable firms to the state.(40) In such cases, the state is obliged to absorb unemployment and generate investment. It is estimated that about 800 small firms and 10-20 large ones are bankrupt and many more have great difficulty repaying loans. It would seem that improper use of loans and mismanagement of funds are responsible for this situation, in which the businesses go bankrupt and the businessmen get rich. One of the main concerns of the Greek government in the near future will be how to change this trend and revitalize the debt-ridden yet potentially viable enterprises. Greece recently introduced legislation toward socialization in all public and semipublic enterprises and the banks. However, the unions oppose strike restrictions incorporated in the related legislation.(41)

It is expected that decentralization in Greece will be organized and promoted through the formulation and implementation of national development plans, which are by and large indicative, that is, guiding rather than constraining. To overcome the economy's peripheral nature and its extensive foreign dependence, emphasis is placed on a self-sustained structure of the economy. Implementation of democratic planning, in the formulation of which all affected social groups are involved, is based primarily on agro-industrial cooperatives, with the active participation of local governments. For the success of such a socialized sector of the economy, properly coordinated with the private sector, appropriate research and training of the needed personnel are required. It should be mentioned that socialization does not mean nationalization. It means the formation of cooperatives and the management of enterprises by the workers and employees as well as the representatives of local or central governments, depending on the monopolistic power and the importance of the socialized firms.(42) Such socialized and decentralized units would participate in the supply of social or public goods and insurance programs, in a somewhat similar way to the Yugoslav communes and cooperatives, ensuring also more employment in less developed regions.

To survive competition from more advanced countries, small and medium-sized Greek enterprises should be grouped or merged into large and more efficient firms or cooperatives. In some enterprises, some form of capital-labor comanagement, similar to that in West Germany and other western countries, might be applied. Monetary and fiscal measures could be used as the main tools to facilitate such an organizational structure of the economy. The use of progressive income taxes and, more importantly, value added taxes, would be of particular importance for the accumulation of savings to finance social investment. At the same time, price controls and/or subsidies for basic consumption commodities and "shadow prices" for the products and services of the socialized enterprises could be used in coordination with the market prices for most of the commodities of private consumption.

Another form of socialized investment in Greece may be the establishment of hotels, motels, shopping centers, parking facilities, and similar projects with partial financing by local municipalities or communities and proportional share in the returns. In return for aiding developers with licensing and financing such projects, cities and towns may demand a proportion of rents and growth in the projects' values. For example, in such a venture the municipalities might get 50 percent of cash flow (after the developer gets 15 percent return on his equity) and 50 percent future appreciation in return for aiding with the financing of the project. In such projects, which are being developed in other countries including the United States, municipalities or governments might demand first mortgage and provide certain certain tax breaks or other subsidies. Union pension funds might be also used to finance common projects which, in addition to primary benefits to the participants, usually provide secondary benefits or have developmental social side effects to the community.

NOTES

1. In the United States, for example, each percentage point rise in average interest rates, because of inflation, boosts government interest payments by $2 to $3 billion, and each percentage point rise in unemployment automatically increases the budget deficit by more than $25 billion. Peter Peterson, "Spending Limits," New York Times, July 23, 1981.

2. Total deficits in the enterprises amounted to about 50 billion drachmas in 1981 and 77 billion in 1982. The

largest deficits come from the Institution of Social Insurance or IKA (26.2 billion drachmas in 1982), the Organization of Agricultural Insurance or OGA (19.5 billion drachmas), the Organization of Urban Transportation or OAS (13.7), the Greek Airlines Industry or EAB (7.8 billion drachmas), the Organization of Railways of Greece or OSE (7.7 billion drachmas), and the Olympic Airlines or OA (5.5 billion drachmas). Oikonomikos Tahydromos, Athens, November 25, 1982, pp. 53-54.

3. For arguments against protection in developing countries see Barend de Vries "Public Policy and the Private Sector," Finance and Development (September 1981), 11-15.

4. Organization for Economic Cooperation and Development (OECD), National Accounts, various issues.

5. Larger parts of total deficits of the public sector come from public corporations. OECD, Greece: Economic Survey 1981-1982, p. 37; and D. Karageorgas, Oi Dimosionomikoi Thesmoi (The Structure of Public Finance), (Athens: Papazisis, 1981), p. 31. More statistical data are presented in later section.

6. It was estimated by Professors W. Ellis and R. Bacon that each five-point increase in disposable income taken by government consumption lowers national income by one point. For this and similar estimates see R. Hershey, Jr., "Europeans Losing Faith in Public Spending?" New York Times: International Economic Survey, February 4, 1979.

7. At the end of 1982 there were 3.59 million working people and 1.34 million pensioners (a ratio of about 1/3). Nikitos Orfanidis, "Kammia Syntaksi Kato Apo ta 55," (No pension under 55). To Vima, Athens, January 9, 1983.

8. OECD, Yugoslavia: Economic Surveys (Paris, 1981), p. 33; and Martin Schrenik et al., Yugoslavia: Self-Management Socialism and the Challenges of Development (Baltimore: John Hopkins University Press, 1979), p. 124.

9. General government expenditures were 36 percent of GDP in Canada, 32 percent in the United States, and 30 percent in Australia in 1980. OECD, National Accounts, various issues.

10. Schrenk et al., Yugoslavia, p. 124.

11. N. Gianaris, "Indirect Taxes: A Comparative Study of Greece and the EEC," European Economic Review 15 (1981), 115.

12. Greek Government, Statistical Yearbook of Greece; United Nations, Statistical Yearbook, (for Greece),

and International Monetary Fund (IMF), International Financial Statistics, (for Yugoslavia), various issues.

13. The central bureaucracy, which is stifling the economy, has increased the number of civil servants on its payroll by 5 percent annually since 1975. There are some 500,000 (about 3/4 permanent) employees in the central government (60 percent in Athens) and about 200,000 civil servants on pension. OECD, Economic Surveys, 1981-82 (Paris: 1982), p. 43. For the structure and the role of the civil service, see Spyrus Zevgaridis, "The Characteristics Required for Tomorrow's Greek Public Servants," Spoudai, Piraeus, April-June 1982, pp. 301-22.

14. Nicholas Gianaris and Stergios Mourgos, "Centralization and Decentralization Trends: The Evidence for Greece and the EEC." Greek Review of Social Research, 41 (1981), pp. 20-25. See also Constantine Tsoukalas, Koinoniki Anaptyski Kai Kratos (Social Development and the State), (Athens: Themeolio, 1983), chap. 11.

15. The decentralization law (1235/1982) provides for the division of Athens into seven departments, with a mayor for each, and further parcelation into smaller blocks, depending on population. Discussion of these matters took place at the annual meeting of the Allied Social Science Association (URPE) by a panel that included the author of this book, primarily on the paper of Nick A. Papandreou, "Decentralization in Greece" (unpublished) in New York, December 28, 1982.

16. To increase devolution and stimulate investment in the countryside, state grants to the provincial councils were doubled in 1982 and increased by another 40 percent in 1983. These grants amount now to 0.8 percent of GNP, compared to 0.3 percent before 1982. The Economist, May 14, 1983, pp. 71-72.

17. Papandreou, "Decentralization in Greece" pp. 22-23.

18. For arguments about the effects on the Greek economy during the postwar period, see R. Bacon and H. Karayiannis-Bacon, "The Growth of the Non-Market Sector in a Newly Industrialized Country: The Case of Greece," Greek Economic Review, April 1980, pp. 44-64; and G. Hadjimatheou and A. Skouras, "The Growth of the Non-Market Sector and the Greek Economy," Greek Economic Review, August 1980, pp. 174-79.

19. N. Gianaris, "Ta Ellimmata tou Dimosiou Trofodotoun fon Plithorismo" (Public Deficits Feed Inflation), Oikonomikos Tahydromos, Athens, August 4, 1983; IMF, International Financial Statistics, various issues. For the real rates of economic growth in postwar years, see Chapter 4.

20. Pavlos Klavdianos, "Dramatiki E. Katastasi Stis Dimosies Epihiris" (Dramatic Situation in Public Enterprises) Oikonomikos Tahydromos, Athens, November 25, 1982, p. 53.

21. Real rates of economic growth are presented in Chapter 4.

22. Although the cost of holding money increases with ongoing inflation, expectations of further price rises stimulate speculative demand for money (loans) to buy assets for future gains. Ceteris paribus, this practice fuels more inflation. For related comments, see G. Brennan and J. Buchanan, "Revenue Implication of Money creation under Leviathan," American Economic Review, May 1981, pp. 347-51. For problems of the banking system in Greece, see G. Dertilis, To zitima ton Trapezon, 1871-1973 (The Issue of the Banks), (Athens: Cultural Institute of the National Bank, 1980). Also G. Kalamoutousakis, "Restructuring the Greek Monetary and Credit System," The Banker, January 1981, pp. 93-99.

23. The regression equations (1958-80) were:
Greece:
$$\log CPI_t = 0.283 + 0.192 \log Mt + 0.132 \log Mt\text{-}1; R^2 = 0.980$$
$$D{=}W = 1.013$$

Yugoslavia:
$$\log CPI_t = 1.277 + 0.121 \log Mt + 0.169 \log Mt\text{-}1; R^2 = 0.994$$
$$D{=}W = 2.180$$

24. Increases in the average price index per year in 1970-80 were: 9.6 for France, 5.2 for West Germany, 14 for the United Kingdom, and 7.0 for the United States. IMF, International Financial Statistics, various issues.

25. Thus for Greece:

$$1958\text{-}80 \log Pt = 0.3 + 0.40 \log M_{t-1} + 0.47 \log IM_{ti}; R^{-2} = 0.991$$
$$D.W. = 2.40$$

For Yugoslavia:

$$1958\text{-}80 \log Pt = -0.9 + 0.65 \log M_{t-1} + 0.41 \log IM_{ti}; R^{-2} = 0.989$$
$$D.W. = 2.03$$

Where P is the consumer price index (CPI), M money supply (currency plus demand deposits or M_1) and IM import price index in domestic currency. For international comparisons see, George Karantzas, "Inflationary Forces in Fifty-Four Countries in the Past Decade: An Analysis," Economia Internationali, July-August 1981, pp. 322-55.

26. Adam Smith, The Wealth of Nations (Chicago: Irwin, 1962), 284; John Stuart Mill, Considerations on Representative Government (London: Routledge and Son, 1905), p. 114; Charles Lindblom, Politics and Markets (New York: Basic Books, 1977), Chap. 24. Difficulties related to the bourgeois stock are presented by Joseph Schumpeter, Capitalism, Socialism, and Democracy, 3d ed. (New York: Harper Colophon Books, 1975), p. 205.

27. J. Corby-Hall, Worker Participation in Europe (London: Croom Helm, 1977), chap. 3; G. Garson, ed., Worker Self-Management in Industry: The West European Experience (New York: Praeger, 1977), chap. 1-5; and G. Hunnius and others, eds., Workers Control (New York: Random House, 1973).

28. The price of this plant, which produces tin plate for beverage and food containers, rolled steel for automobiles and household appliances, represents 20 percent of the book value of $322 million to be paid in 15 years. Some 7,000 workers and employees agreed to take pay cuts of 32 percent or more to avoid 3,100 layoffs. William Serrin, "Employees to Buy Huge Steel Works in $66 Million Pact." New York Times, March 14, 1983. Bethlehem Steel Corporation faces similar problems, also.

29. Empirical research indicates that 1 percent unemployment means an increase in suicides (4.1 percent), imprisonment (5 percent), homicides (5.7 percent), admissions to mental hospitals (3.4 percent), and infant mortality (5-6 percent). "Factors in Increasing Risks," Newsday, December 6, 1982.

30. It was estimated that federal regulations in the United States were responsible for 12-21 percent of the slowdown in the growth of labor productivity in manufacturing during the 1973-77 as compared to 1958-65; while reductions in the ratio of capital to labor are responsible for 15 percent, and the average cyclical impact 0-15 percent. E. Denison, "Explanations of Declining Productivity Growth,"

Survey of Current Business part II, 59 August 1979: 1-24. G. Christiansen and R. Haveman, "Public Regulations and the Slowdown in Productivity Growth," American Economic Review, Proceedings, May 1981, pp. 320-25.

31. For implementation trends of self-management in Kenya, Zambia, Algeria, India, and Chile, see Hans Seibel and Ukandi Damachi, Self-management in Yugoslavia (New York: St. Martin's Press, 1982). Other third world countries, being disenchanted with both capitalism and communism, may follow similar trends.

32. Jan Prybyla, Issues in Socialist Economic Modernization (New York: Praeger, 1980), p. 89. For a comprehensive analysis of labor management, see Joroslav Vanek, Self Management: Economic Liberation of Man (Harmondsworth, England: Penguin, 1975). Also, his Participatory Economy (Ithaca, N.Y.: Cornell University Press, 1971); and The General Theory of Labor-Managed Market Economies (Ithaca, N.Y.: Cornell University Press, 1970).

33. Further comments on self-management and reforms may be found in R. Stojanovic, ed., Functioning of the Yugoslav Economy (New York: M. E. Sharpe, 1982) chaps. 1,3; L. Sirc, The Yugoslav Economy under Self-Management (London: Macmillan, 1979), chap. 8; and R. Bicanic, Economic Policy in Socialist Yugoslavia (London: Cambridge University Press, 1973), chap. 4.

34. Thomas Bray, "A Conversation with Yugoslavia's Milovan Djilas," Wall Street Journal, October 20, 1982. Also, Lgubo Sirc, "The Yugoslav Debt and Socialist 'Self-Management,'" Wall Street Journal, October 13, 1982.

35. Further review in T. Wall and J. Lischeron, Worker Participation (New York: McGraw-Hill, 1977), chaps. 5, 6; Ellen Comisso, Worker's Control Under Plan and Market: Implications of Yugoslav Self-Management (New Haven: Yale University Press, 1979), chaps. 3-6, 8; and her "Yugoslavia in the 1970s: Self-Management and Bargaining," Journal of Comparative Economics, June 1980, pp. 192-208; Martin Browning, "Cooperation in a Fixed-Membership Labor-Managed Enterprise," Journal of Comparative Economics, September 1982, pp. 235-247; and Nicos Zafiris, "Appropriability Rules, Capital Maintenance and the Efficiency of Cooperative Investment," Journal of Comparative Economics, March 1982, pp. 55-74.

36. Jaroslav Vanek suggests that the participatory economy is superior to other systems. See his Participatory

Economy, pp. 21-38. Also J. Shuckleton, "Is Workers' Self-Management the Answer?" National Westminster Bank Quarterly Review, February 1974, pp. 45-47, reprinted in Morris Bornstein, Comparative Economic Systems: Models and Cases (Homewood, Ill.: Irwin, 1979), pp. 141-53; and World Bank, Yugoslavia: Development with Decentralization (Baltimore, Md.: Johns Hopkins University Press for the World Bank, 1975), pp. 29-52.

37. Jan Prybyla, Issues in Socialist Economic Modernization, pp. 100-104. Other economic data in J. Kregci, National Income and Outlay in Czechoslovakia, Poland, and Yugoslavia (New York: St. Martin's, 1982).

38. For more details, see related discussion in Chapter 2.

39. For instance, Softex, a tissue manufacturing firm; Ladopoulos, a paper company, and Velka, a textile company, have large unpaid debt. Over 50 percent of industry owes over 75 percent of its capital to the state. Anna Grant-Magrioti, "Half of Industry in Debt," Epsilon, August 1982 (in Greek); and Nick Papandreou, "Decentralization in Greece," p. 14. Also, D. Halikias, Money and Credit in a Developing Economy (New York: New York University Press, 1981). More than 40 "problematic", mostly textile, firms have a debt of about $500 million with the National Bank of Greece. "40 Disekatommyria stin Ethniki Ofiloun 40 Provlinatikes" (40 Billion Drachmas Owed to the National Bank by 40 Problematic Firms," To Vima, Athens, January 9, 1983.

40. The state owns shares in some 200 concerns, worth of about $1 billion, in 47 of which it is a majority owner. Costas Vergopoulos, Transition to Socialism: The Dimensions of Structural Change (Athens: Aletri, 1981), (in Greek); for structural problems, see Maria Negreponte-Delivanis, Analysis of the Greek Economy, 2d ed. (Athens: Papazisis, 1981), (in Greek); and Constantinos Tsoucalas, The Development of Society and the State: The Concentration of the Public Sector in Greece (Athens: Themelios, 1981), (in Greek).

41. "Dekapeute Gnomodotikes Epitropes Epihiriseou Pou Koinouikopiounte" (Fifteen Advisory Councils of Socialized Enterprises), Eleftherotypia, Athens, July 23, 1983 and M. Howe, "Parliament in Greece Enacts Contested Labor Bill," New York Times, June 3, 1983.

42. Present decentralization measures introduce self-management in public enterprises but only coordinating or

advisory councils for whole industries in the public sector. Such councils are severely criticized by industrialists and entrepreneurs because they stifle economic activities and discourage investment incentives, acting as "godfathers" upon production initiatives, as long as the Ministry or the party in power excercises effective control (Law 1365/1983). Some 15 large public or semipublic enterprises are under this law. Eleftherotypia, Athens, July 23, 1983.

PART II
DOMESTIC ASPECTS OF DEVELOPMENT

Part II deals with natural and human resources, fiscal and monetary policies for higher productivity, public finance, decentralization policies, inflation, and resource allocation on the sectoral and regional levels. All these topics look at the domestic aspects of the development of Greece and Yugoslavia, while Part III surveys the international economic position of these two neighboring nations.

The geographical location of these Balkan countries in southeastern Europe plays an important role in their economic relations with central Europe and the Middle East. Also, it has a profound influence upon the socioeconomic activities of the population as well as upon the sectoral and regional development of the area.

Both countries channeled large amounts of investment into the economy and achieved high rates of growth during the postwar years. However, Greece emphasized more the services and housing sectors, at the neglect of the manufacturing and, to some extent, agricultural sectors, while Yugoslavia pursued a policy of rapid industrialization, as other planned economies did. Transportation, a key sector in the region, deserves high priority in the development process of both countries so that commodities can be easily transferred to the marketplaces of Europe and the Middle East. From that point of view, common investment ventures are needed not only for the improvement of their transportation network but also for the development of related industries such as mining, manufacturing, and energy.

Both countries face serious problems of inflation, which stem primarily from large deficits in the budgets of the central and local governments and/or the budgets of public and semipublic enterprises. To reduce inflation and stimulate productivity, fiscal and monetary measures are taken and tax incentives and subsidies are provided to encourage investment by agro-industrial cooperatives, local communities and

individuals. Moreover, intensive measures of decentralization and eventual socialization of the economy are taken to
increase work incentives and improve income distribution.

4

RESOURCES
AND PRODUCTIVITY

NATURAL RESOURCES

Greece is in the south and Yugoslavia in the west of the
Balkan Peninsula. To the west, the Adriatic Sea separates
them from Italy. To the east the Aegean Sea and the borders
of eastern Thrace separate Greece from Turkey. To the
north, Greece borders on Albania, Yugoslavia, and Bulgaria.
Yugoslavia borders Italy (near Trieste, an Italian port with a
Slavic flavor), and Hungary to the north and Romania and
Bulgaria to the east. Both countries are located in a
primarily rugged and mountainous area that extends from
Central Europe to the Mediterranean Sea.

The major river is the Danube, which runs from central
Europe to Yugoslavia via Belgrade and along the borders of
Bulgaria and Romania, and reaches the Black Sea. There are
also the rivers Tisza and Drava in northern and the Morava in
central Yugoslavia, all tributaries of the Danube, as well as
the Neretva in western Yugoslavia. In Greece there are the
Evros (Maritsa) River on the Greek-Turkish border, the
Nestos, the Strimon (Struma), and the Axios (Vardar) rivers,
all in Macedonia, the Acheloos in western Greece, the Pineios
in Thessaly, and the Alpheios in Peloponnesus. Two large

lakes, Ohrid and Prespa, are located on the borders of Greece, Yugoslavia, and Albania. A number of fertile plains are located in northern and southern Yugoslavia and in northern and central Greece. The principal ports are Rijeka, Sibenik, Split, and Dubrovnik in Yugoslavia; and Kavalla, Salonika, Piraeus, Patras, and Herakleion in Greece.

The geographical location of Greece has been an important factor in both its past and its present. Its mainland is an integral part of Europe that juts out from the Balkans into the Mediterranean. A rugged and harsh land of some 132,000 square kilometers, it is surrounded by countless islands (some 2,800) in the Aegean and Ionian seas. The islands constitute about a quarter of the land area of the country. The mainland is composed of varying mountains (the largest range is the Pintos in northwestern Greece), hills, and plains. It differs from the islands, which also differ greatly among themselves.

Homer's description of the island of Ithaca--no meadows but highland, goat land--is true for most parts of Greece.

The islands in the Aegean appear as high mountain peaks and plateaus of an area sunk into the sea many centuries ago. Plato's reference to Atlantis, a lost continent, may be related to such a sunken area in the Aegean and eastern Mediterranean. Numerous gulfs and bays with valuable harbors are located along the Greek coastline, which is the longest in Europe.

The Yugoslav terrain of 256,000 square kilometers is mostly mountain and rolling hills. It includes the Julian-Dinaric Alps, parallel to the Adriatic Sea, the Shar and the Carpatho-Balkan mountains. The Danube River facilitates trade to and from the Black Sea, while the Morava-Vardar trade route provides an outlet from the Pannonian region to the port of Salonika and vice versa.

Although mining occupies a relatively small place in the economies of Greece and Yugoslavia, contributing less than 5 percent to the value of total production, prospects are growing that this sector will be of vital importance in the near future. The increase in world demand for metal and subsoil resources will eventually make many of the rocky places of these two countries valuable.

Central Greece, Macedonia, and, to a lesser extent, the Aegean Islands are the primary regions of mining production.

Lignite, metallic and nonmetallic minerals, clay, sand, and stone quarrying are the main mining industries in Greece. Brown coal and lignite are produced primarily in Yugoslavia (about 40 million metric tons annually) and Greece (some 25 million metric tons).

Table 4.1 shows the main mining and quarrying products of both countries. Greece and Yugoslavia are the leading countries in the production of bauxite in Western Europe, with an annual production of about 3 million tons per year each. Both countries produce iron ore (around 1,000 kilograms per capita annually) and aluminum (15 kilos per capita for Greece and 10 kilos per capita for Yugoslavia). Other metals produced are gold primarily in Yugoslavia (about 5,000 kilograms annually), as well as copper, chromite, and nickel in both countries. In Yugoslavia, uranium reserves are about 4,500 metric tons.

At present there is no significant petroleum production in Greece and Yugoslavia. The only production is in Thasos, an island near the port of Kavalla, where 30,000 barrels of crude oil per day are produced. Annual production of crude petroleum in Yugoslavia amounts to 4.2 million metric tons. Crude petroleum reserves are estimated at 20 metric tons for Greece and 45 metric tons in Yugoslavia. Some exploration for petroleum in the island of Zakynthos, known since the times of Herodotos, and elsewhere is being carried out at present but with limited results as yet. Neither country produces nuclear energy as yet, as neighboring Bulgaria and other European countries do.

There are fairly large deposits of lignite in Ptolemaida in western Macedonia and in Euboia near Aliverion, where thermal power plants have been built. Water power is a promising energy resource for both Greece and Yugoslavia because of the favorable natural terrain in the area. Hydroelectric dams in addition to those of the Acheloos River in western Greece and the Ladon in Peloponnesus, which have been operating for years, are considered for construction in a number of locations.

Energy consumption per capita is far larger in central Greece than elsewhere in the country. In Greater Athens alone energy consumption is about eight times that of the rest of Greece. Because the Aspropyrgos oil refinery is located near Athens, oil is cheaper and the cost of electric power for industrial users is lower than in the area. Simi-

Table 4.1.   Mining and Quarrying Products (thousand metric tons)

	Greece			Yugoslavia		
	1960	1970	1980	1960	1970	1980
Brown coal & lignite	2,551	8,081	21,667	21,430	27,779	39,238
Crude petroleum	n.a.	n.a.	n.a.	944	2,851	4,143
Natural gas (Teracalories)	n.a.	n.a.	n.a.	n.a.	9,391	18,369
Iron ore	149	380	725	788	1,301	1,621
Bauxite	884	2,283	2,630	1,025	2,098	2,565
Chromium ore	21	19	16	25	15	1
Copper	n.a.	n.a.	n.a.	33	91	123
Gold (kilograms)	90	n.a.	n.a.	2,044	3,025	4,323
Lead ore	9	9.6	17	91	127	124
Manganese	14	3	4	4	5	10
Mercuri (m.t.)	n.a.	n.a.	n.a.	458	533	108
Nickel ore (m.t.)	370	8,600	14,888	n.a.	n.a.	n.a.
Silver (m.t.)	3	13	9	94	106	159
Zinc	14	9	22	56	101	104
Salt	97	113	191	151	170	298

n.a. = not available.
Note: In a few cases earlier years' data were available.
Source: United Nations, Statistical Yearbook, various issues.

larly, the Esso-Pappas refinery, which is being considered for purchase, by the government, provides oil and energy in Salonika at a comparatively competitive price.

HUMAN RESOURCES

Hellenes (Greeks) live in the southern part of the Balkan Peninsula and Yugoslavs or South Slavs live primarily in the central and northwestern part of the peninsula (Serbs, Slovenes, Croats). There are about 500,000 Germans and an equal number of Hungarians in Yugoslavia, and of Italians, Romanians, and Albanians (mainly in Kosovo) as well as Moslems (about 10 percent). Greek minorities exist in Turkey, Albania, and Yugoslavia; Slavs are near the northern borders, and Moslems on the eastern borders, of Greece. Small minorities of shepherd Vlachs (from dispersed ancient Thracians) and Gypsies are scattered in Greece and Yugoslavia. Most of the people of both countries belong to the Greek Orthodox Church, while groups of Roman Catholics can be found in eastern and northern Yugoslavia. After World War II religious practices became less important, particularly in Yugoslavia, where they are discouraged by state policy.

The total population of Greece is close to 10 million (9.7 million in 1982), compared with 8.0 million in 1950 and 7.0 million in 1937; that of Yugoslavia is 23 million, compared with 16.1 million in 1950 and 15.2 million in 1937. Population growth is relatively small in both countries (around 0.8 percent per year), with a birth rate of 15-18 per 1,000 and a death rate around 10 per 1,000. Population density is 76 per square kilometer for Greece and 90 per square kilometer for Yugoslavia. Life expectancy at birth is 74 years for Greece and 70 for Yugoslavia.

Historically, crude birth rates per 1,000 inhabitants in Greece varied from 21 in 1921-25 to 19.6 during the occupation years 1941-45, and 19 in 1950-80; while death rates varied from 15-16 per 1,000 in 1921-40 to 17.3 in 1941-45 and started declining to 10.8 in 1946-50 and 10 in 1950-80. In Yugoslavia, crude birth rates per 1,000 inhabitants varied from 39 in 1906-10 to 28 in 1936-40 and 28.5 in 1946-55; death rates varied from 24.7 per 1,000 in 1906-10 to 17 per 1,000 in 1936-40 and 13 per 1,000 in 1948-55.(1) In 1970-80, net average annual increase in population was 9 per 1,000.

In 1961, 49.4 percent of the Yugoslav population, or 9,169,764 persons, remained in agriculture compared to 59.6 percent, or 10,105,587 persons, in 1953. Of those, 4,674,856 were active in 1961, compared to 5,182,521 in 1953. In industry, there were 11.8 percent of population or 2,191,256 persons (993,175) in 1961 and 6.7 percent or 1,140,606 persons (512,702) in 1953. The rest of the population was distributed among handicrafts (4.5 percent), construction (4.5 percent), transportation (3.7 percent), trade (2.6 percent), mining (2.4 percent), and other services, during 1961. In 1980, total civilian employment in Yugoslavia (in both private and socialized sectors) was 9.7 million persons, 36 percent of whom were in services, 35 percent in industry, and the rest in agriculture.(2) Of the total number of civilians employed in Greece (3.35 million in 1980), close to 30 percent were in agriculture, another 30 percent in industry (manufacturing, mining, construction, and utilities) and the remaining 40 percent in services.(3)

Registered unemployment (4.8 percent in Greece and 8.3 percent in Yugoslavia in 1981 and around 7-9 percent in both countries in 1983-84) needs some adjustment in both countries. Thus in Greece, to be eligible to register as unemployed workers must have been employed for over 80 days in the previous 3 years. After 5 months, unemployment benefits expire and some people are no longer on record. Moreover, some people do not register with the authorities when they work in order to avoid paying income taxes and social security contributions, so that they are excluded from unemployment records when they lose their jobs. In Yugoslavia, however, unemployment is lower by about one-fifth because the record includes some people who are working but want to change jobs. Female unemployment seems always to be higher in both countries.(4)

During the postwar years, large numbers of people migrated from rural areas to urban centers, particularly to Athens and Salonika in Greece. In Yugoslavia the main urban centers that absorbed large amounts of population were Titograd, Pristina, Banja Luka, Sarajevo, Nis, Split, Zagreb, Ljubljana, and Skopje.(5) Large proportions of migrants in the cities, especially in Athens and Salonika, work in small trade and other shops, primarily as self-employed persons. Such small-scale middlemen or shopkeepers enjoy some degree of monopoly because of location and contribute to inflation by raising prices arbitrarily to make profit.

Greece is among the countries that lose large numbers of professionals and scientists, mainly to the United States, the United Kingdom, Canada, France, and West Germany. This is so because political affiliations and nepotism rather than merit and achievement determine advancement in Greece, while "brain gaining" countries offer favorable conditions and appreciate the work of the scientists. To reverse the trend of "brain drain" and to encourage repatriation of scientists, Greece is introducing overdue reforms in education and research and offers seminars and other exchange programs.

In both countries, open unemployment is not high, mainly because of extensive emigration of about one-third of the labor force (about 1 million in Greece and 1.5 million in Yugoslavia) primarily to West Germany.(6) Such emigration helped mitigate the problem of surplus labor and disrupted what John Kenneth Galbraith calls the poverty equilibrium in the poor sectors of the economy. Moreover, government offices and public enterprises have padded employment rosters and swollen payrolls to accommodate unemployed persons. Such a practice may reduce unemployment but it also feeds bureaucracy, inefficiency, and inflation.

In both countries there are laws and regulations that prohibit or discourage layoffs. Such laws are strictly applied in periods of rising unemployment, particularly by public or semipublic and self-managed enterprises. In periods of recession and economic slumps, employed people are seldom dismissed but new recruiting is reduced and profits decline. However, there is strong social and political pressure on enterprises to increase employment, while central and local governments provide subsidies and employment incentives to avoid high rates of unemployment.

Investment in human beings or education is directly related to the economic development of the countries considered and brings high rates of returns, in addition to its sociocultural side effects. It frees the student from a life of drudgery on the farm or in the factory and provides better opportunities for economic and social advancement. Although free primary education is provided in both countries, there is still a bloc of 5-10 percent illiterates. Public expenditure on education is about 5 percent of GMP for Yugoslavia and around 2 percent of GNP for Greece. Yugoslavia has around 20 students per teacher and Greece 30. In higher education the percentage (of those age 20-24) is around 20 for both countries.

There is no coordination between university graduates and job opportunities, and Greece continues to follow the twentieth-century Balkan tradition of giving education to more people than can find employment in a number of fields. Up to the 1970s, a proper degree of literacy to qualify for a job largely meant a good knowledge of and the ability to write the deliberately archaizing Katharevousa, which had limited use, if any among the masses of the population. Only recently Dimotiki, the popular language, was introduced at all levels of education and among the employees of government bureaucracies.

There seem to be no serious class or caste barriers to advancement in Greece as in other countries. Family relations remain strong. When members of a family move to the cities or other countries ties with those remaining in the villages persist. Important family decisions on education, property, and occupation are taken jointly, while periodic visits back to the villages take place frequently. The intensity of family loyalty may hinder efforts for business partnerships and the formation and efficient operation of impersonal organizations requiring collective action outside the family structure. However, it has some advantages from the viewpoint of social and psychological stability. Nevertheless, it may be partially responsible for the perpetuation of personality-dominated cliques in the political and social life of Greece, where family connections and bureaucratic patrons tend to play a significant role in appointments, promotions, and sociopolitical advancement. However, aggressive nouveaux groups appear to challenge the socioeconomic elite of Greece, which desperately tries to keep its position.

Similar trends could be observed, more or less, in Yugoslavia up to the late 1940s, when dramatic sociopolitical and economic changes occurred. Mutatis mutandis, significant changes in these matters are expected to take place in Greece in the late 1980s as a result of the changes in the sociopolitical environment and the gradual improvement of the economic conditions of the country.

Along with centralization in public administration goes the inefficient operation of higher education, which is considered, together with that of Italy the worst in Europe.

Students frequently resort to strikes for educational improvements and sometimes for political reasons, while professors are more devoted to their perquisites than to the quality of instruction. Professors are usually busy searching for additional jobs and advisory councils to amass incomes that sometimes amount to six or more times their normal pay, or more than the salary of a prime minister. Their teaching duties are normally delegated to assistants while rarely can they be found in their university offices or in other public offices they occupy for pay. On the other hand, Greek parents want their children to pursue higher education and get a diploma to secure a prestigious or permanent job, probably in the civil service. However, for a number of professions the economy is unable to absorb the annual crop of graduates, and social pressures persist. The introduction of two-year colleges and reforms emphasizing technical education might mitigate such pressures in higher education. The level of higher education is expected to be improved after the new drastic changes, introduced recently, are implemented.

Industrialization requires improvement in education with emphasis on professional and technical training, particularly for people in the harsh and isolated mountains who are dour and rough compared to more outgoing and industrious people of the low and sloping shores of these two countries. However, there are complaints that students from the countryside find it hard to get into universities because of the strict examination requirements, which the urban intelligentsia can meet but not the children of peasants and workers.

On the other hand, women enjoy less power in society and fewer opportunities for work and managerial advancement. Limited education and lower average salaries for women prevail even in socialist countries. However, intensive efforts are being made now in both countries, particularly in Greece, to raise their social and economic status, and the results are encouraging. At present, the percentage of women participating in the overall labor force is comparatively low, particularly in industry, where the active female population is about 20-30 percent in both countries.

Population per physician is 450 in Greece and 760 in Yugoslavia, while the number of patients per hospital bed is 150-160 for both countries.

ECONOMIC GROWTH

Both countries performed well in terms of economic growth during the postwar years, ranking among the good growth performers such as Japan, Korea, Israel, Mexico, Venzuela, the Soviet Union, and other Eastern European countries.(7) Only in the early 1980s was there a slow-down of real growth, particularly in the industry sector, mainly because of domestic anti-inflationary policies, the downward trend of investment in physical plant, and the international recessionary trends.

The major factor shaping the remarkable economic growth that Greece and Yugoslavia experienced since 1949 has been the availability of a large supply of labor, a good part of which was transferred from agriculture to industry and services. On the other hand, emigration of unemployed or underemployed workers to the northwestern European countries helped to increase labor productivity in these two countries and benefited the economies of the host countries, particularly West Germany.

The structural shortcomings of the Greek economy, with an overemphasized services sector and a neglected industrial sector, started to affect the overall growth performance in recent years. Moreover, the lack of effective planning to coordinate public and private activities proved to be detrimental for the industrial sector, which failed to keep up with modern technological achievements. On the other hand, overinvestment in the housing sector helped preserve high rates of economic growth during the postwar years. For the last few years, however, the decline in construction led to the downturn of the rate of economic growth for the whole economy.

In the recent Greek Five-Year Plans, efforts have been made to close some of the loopholes and structural shortcomings in the economy and to proceed toward introducing new technology. The hope is to correct inherent weaknesses in the economy and to adopt up-to-date innovations immediately in order to make up for lost opportunities in the past. The guidelines for the development programs include: decentralization of economic activities with emphasis on regional development, stimulation of private initiative for increased productivity and employment, encouragement of vertical integration of industrial production and support for the exporting sector, a better distribution of income, and improvement in health and education services.

To broaden the industrial base, both countries emphasize the importance of investment, especially in manufacturing. This is particularly so for Yugoslovia, where the share of total fixed investment averages about 30 percent of GDP. However, high levels of investment in Yugoslavia are associated with high incremental capital-output ratios (ICORs or investment over changes in output) and, possibly, lower capital efficiency in the long run.

In Greece overall investment as a percentage of total production, averaging about 20 percent annually, has slowed down in recent years. Investment by the public sector and semipublic enterprises particularly declined considerably. The same thing happened also in the private sector, where investment in manufacturing, and more so in housing, declined significantly. For that reason, the socialist government of Greece, and those of France, Italy, Spain, and Portugal, resorted to capitalist measures to stimulate productive investment and reduce unemployment.

As Table 4.2 shows, the annual growth of GDP in Greece was 6.0 percent on the average during the postwar years. GDP per capita grew by about 4 to 5 percent. The labor force increased by 1.0 percent, with a labor productivity of 4.0 percent per year, which was about the same as that of the average in the four large EEC countries. Average gross investment as a ratio to GDP was about 19 percent annually and the incremental capital output ratio 3.9 during the period 1950-90. For Yugoslavia the average annual growth of GDP was 6.9 percent, in 1950-80, while the rate of investment to GDP was around 32 percent per year. Per capita GDP in 1981 was U.S. $4,420 for Greece and U.S. $2,790 for Yugoslavia.(8)

As happened in other countries, a gradual transfer of resources from agriculture to industry and services took place also in Greece and Yugoslavia during the postwar years. Thus the agricultural share of GDP in Greece declined from 34 percent to 1950 to 16 percent in 1980 while for industry it increased from 20 to 32 percent, and for services from 32 to 52 percent. For Yugoslavia, the agricultural share of GDP declined from 32 percent in 1950 to 12 percent in 1980, that of industry remained almost the same (42-45 percent), and that of services increased from 14 to 45 percent. From the

Table 4.2. Economic Growth and Investment in Greece and Yugoslavia, Constant Prices: 1950-81.

	Greece			Yugoslavia		
	1950-60	1960-70	1970-81	1950-60	1960-70	1970-81
Average annual growth of GDP (%)	6.0	6.9	4.4	9.2	5.8	5.7
Agriculture	4.4	3.5	1.7	5.6	3.3	2.6
Industry	7.8	9.4	4.5	10.7	6.2	6.8
Transportation	5.7	8.6	7.1	8.4	6.4	4.7
Construction	10.2	7.5	-0.4	6.5	7.8	5.6
Services	5.3	7.1	5.2	9.5	6.9	5.6
Investment (GFCF) as percentage of GDP	16.0	21.3	19.0	33.0	31.5	31.7
National ICORs (GFCF/ GDP)	3.2	3.4	5.2	3.8	5.2	5.7
Agriculture		1.9	4.1		1.0	1.0
Manufacturing		2.0	3.0		2.4	1.6
Transportation		9.2	9.9		4.3	2.3
Housing		14.9	14.8		4.0	4.4
Services		1.9	3.1		1.6	1.4

Note: For some cases fewer years' data were available. Sectoral ICORs 1955-70, instead of 1960-70.
Sources: World Bank, World Development Report, various issues; United Nations, Statistical Yearbook and Yearbook of National Accounts Statistics, various issues; OECD, National Accounts; and OECD, Country Surveys, various issues.

point of view of employment and income, expansion in industry and services is important because of their forward or backward linkages in the economy. However, care should be taken to complement such expansion with higher agricultural productivity, so that needed raw materials can be supplied, and to avoid extensive backwash effects upon traditional small crafts.

The weak trend of productive investment, particularly in Greece, and slower productivity gains and increasing inflationary pressures are responsible for lower overall and per capita GDP growth in recent years. High rates of emigration up to the middle 1970s created strains on these economies, while the lower recent movement of surplus labor to the cities reduced productivity rates. Overinvestment in housing has used up excessive resources with simultaneous shortages in urban infrastructure and environmental deterioration, particularly in Athens. Thus, 50 percent of Greece's population and 80 percent of its industrial activity have been concentrated on 3 percent of its soil. Such a housebuilding boom stimulated the economy in past decades because of the high labor content and small import linkage associated with housing. However, the shift of economic policy away from the housing sector in the early 1980s resulted in a marked deceleration in the overall growth of the economy.(9)

Yugoslavia, on the other hand, has to reconcile the economic objectives of each republic and province and ensure high rates of self-sustained growth for the national economy. However, investment distortions and some duplication of plants lead to significant waste of capital and other resources. Such duplications include five plants producing cars and five refineries operating at about half of capacity. That is why potential investors must notify the government in advance to assess the economic validity of the projects, so that duplication and undue distortion may be avoided.

Concerning the relationship of capital to output or production, the overall or national ICORs were higher in Yugoslavia than in Greece during the last three decades. This means that less capital per unit of output was used in Greece than in Yugoslavia. This, in turn, does not mean that capital is more productive in Greece than in Yugoslavia. In order to determine in which country or sector the productivity of capital, or the rate of return of capital, is higher, the relative share of other factors, mainly labor, must be considered along with the ICOR. To increase output by a given amount in Greece might require comparatively less capital than in Yugoslavia, but it might require more labor.(10)

Multiplying the relatively constant ICOR slope by the GDP for a year, we can estimate the capital stock of the countries considered. Thus for Greece is was $157.6 billion (3.9 X 40.4) and for Yugoslavia $275.4 billion (4.9 X 56.2) in 1980. Dividing the capital stock by the labor force we find that the capital/labor ratio (capital per worker) was $46,400 (157.6/3.4) for Greece and $28,400 (275.4/9.7) for Yugoslavia in 1980.

Average productivity of labor, that is, the ratio of output to labor input, was $11,882 for Greece (40.4/3.4) and $5,794 for Yugoslavia (56.2/9.7) in 1980. For Greece, the annual increase in output per worker, that is, the rate of productivity growth, was 8.8 percent in the 1960s and 3.5 percent in the 1970s; for Yugoslavia it was 4.0 percent and 1.7 percent, respectively.(11) In the early 1980s, however, labor productivity declined because of the worldwide recession. If emigration had not taken place, productivity rates would have been lower in both countries during the last two decades. Usually unskilled and less productive workers emigrate. In such a case, the reduction in output is proportionally less than labor. To increase productivity, which is important for the increase in real wages, additional investment and technological innovations are needed. However, in the public sector of Greece and Yugoslavia, where civil servants cannot be dismissed or demoted without serious cause, productivity is low while payrolls remain swollen. The same thing can be said for inefficient "sunset" semipublic or private industries.

As Adam Smith pointed out, to increase labor productivity new capital investment is required to facilitate division of labor. However, investment in new machinery and equipment requires, in turn, a satisfactory rate of return of capital. Macroeconomically, we can measure the productivity or the rate of return of investment with the efficiency of investment ratio adjusted for labor changes. For Greece, the labor adjusted investment/efficiency ratio was 31 percent in the 1960s and 14 percent in the 1970s. For Yugoslavia, it was 15 percent and 5 percent respectively.(12) Again, because of higher rates of emigration during the 1960s, these investment efficiency ratios were higher than during the decade of the 1970s, and they are expected to be lower in the future.

In order to see the relationship between GDP and investment a regression analysis was used. As Table A.1 of the Appendix shows, for Greece the regression coefficient was 3.6, and for Yugoslavia it was 2.2 during the postwar period (1958-80). This coefficient, which is a notion of the multiplier, indicates that an increase in investment of 1 unit was related to 3.6 units of increase in output or production in Greece and 2.9 units in Yugoslavia. A multiregression analysis of GDP on investment and exports shows that for Greece exports are a better explanatory variable of changes in GDP than is investment, while for Yugoslavia the opposite is true.(13)

As a result of the austerity measures introduced by the rotating government of Mrs. Milka Plainits and Peter Stambolits (chairman of the 9-member presidency, 1982-83) to reduce inflation, which runs at about 30 percent annually, and total foreign debt of some $20 billion, real income is expected to decline by as much as 7.5 percent in the coming year, after its decline of about 15 percent over the last three years.(14) Many Yugoslavs accept that they lived for many years beyond their resources and productivity and that it is time now to slow down and adjust their living standards. For the stabilization and revival of the economy (stabilizacisa) certain restrictive rules have been introduced. They include the limitation of only 9 gallons of gasoline per month per car and a deposit of $80 per trip abroad with a Yugoslav bank. Also, at times severe shortages appear in such basic consumer products as coffee, soap, and olive oil.

More emphasis is placed now on cost accountability and market incentives. On the other hand, Yugoslavia's highly praised industrial self-management system is criticized as fragmenting the economy in lean times and complicating the relationship of supply and demand. However, the decline in oil prices and the beginning of the recovery in the international markets, together with austerity measures at home, helped to slow inflation, increase exports, and reduce imports, thereby narrowing the deficit in the country's balance of payments.

NOTES

1. W. W. Rostow, The World Economy: History and Prospect, (Austin: University of Texas Press, 1978), pp. 14-15.

2. M. G. Zaninovich, The Development of Socialist Yugoslavia, (Baltimore: Johns Hopkins Press, 1968), p. 174; and Organization for Economic Cooperation and Development, Yugoslavia: Economic Surveys, various issues.

3. Increase in Greek employment during the last decade took place primarily in services and manufacturing. Thus in Athens employment in services increased by 164 percent and in manufacturing by 59 percent in 1971-81. Small-scale firms in manufacturing accounted for most of the increase in employment. Thus the average number of persons per plant in Greece was 5.25 in 1978. Out of a total of 129,000 plants only 751 (or less than 1 percent) had 100 workers or more, and 26 had more than 1,000 workers; while 90 percent had less than 10 workers. OECD, Economic Surveys and World Bank, World Development Report, various issues.

4. OECD, Yugoslavia: Economic Surveys, various issues; and OECD, Economic Outlook, July 1983, p. 45.

5. Colin Thomas, "Migration and Urban Growth in Yugoslavia," East European Quarterly, June 1982, pp. 199-216.

6. About half a million Greeks (200,000 in Melbourne alone) are in Australia. Also, large numbers of Greek immigrants live in West Germany, Canada, and the United States. Richard Bernstein, "Sundry Newcomers Change the Face of Australia", New York Times, March 24, 1983.

7. To be comparable with indexes used in Greece and in other Western market-oriented economies, Yugoslav data ought to be recast. Thus John Moore finds that the Yugoslav rate of industrial growth ran about 8 percent instead of the official 10 percent for the period 1952-75. See his Growth with Self-Management: Yugoslav Industrialization in 1952-75 (Stanford, Calif.: Hoover Institution Press, 1980), pp. 50-56.

8. Rostow, The World Economy, p. 265; Frederick Singleton, OECD, Country Surveys, various surveys. For some pessimistic views, see George Krimpas, "The Greek Economy in Crisis," in Ralt Dochvendorf, ed., Europe's Economy in Crisis (London: Weidenfeld and Nicholson, 1982).

9. In Greece, there is an important number of self-employed persons and employees working on a seasonal or part-time basis who do not appear in any register, making service growth management difficult. The fact that 44 percent of some 1.2 emigrants were 20-30 years old and 27 percent of age 30-40, shows the long-run loss to the economy in terms of productive human resources. This led to an inflow of unskilled workers in the 1970s, mainly from Pakistan and Egypt. Statistical Yearbook of Greece, various issues.

10. Further analysis in Nicholas Gianaris, "International Differences in Capital Output Ratios," American Economic Review, June 1970, pp. 465-77; and his "Projecting Capital Requirements in Development Planning," Socioeconomic Planning Sciences, April 1974, pp. 65-76.

11. For the calculation of labor productivity growth (q), the following equation in a logarithmic form was used:

$$\log(Q/L)_n = \log(Q/L)_o + n \log(1+q)$$

where o is output, L is labor, q is productivity growth; and n is time in years. A regression of average labor productivity (Q/L) on investment (INV) for Yugoslavia presents the following results (1958-80):

$$Q/L = a + b\ INV = 439.2 + 0.40\ INV \qquad R^2 = 0.869$$
$$(34.2) \qquad a \text{ is a constant}$$

This means that a 1-unit change in investment (INV) is associated with a change of 0.4 units of labor productivity (Q/L). Furthermore, a multiple regression analysis for Yugoslavia indicates that "exports" (EXP) is a better explanatory variable for labor productivity than is investment, while inflation (INF) is negatively related to labor productivity. Thus,

$$Q/L = 0.55 + 0.37\ EXP - 0.23\ INF + 0.20\ INV$$
$$(0.58) \qquad (-0.01) \qquad (0.22)$$
$$R^2 = 0.958, \text{ D.W.} = 1.38$$

The figures in parentheses represent the t-values.

12. For the measurement of the "labor-adjusted" investment efficiency ratio $(\Delta \dot{Q}/\Delta K)$, the following equation was used:

$$\frac{\Delta \dot{Q}}{\Delta K} = \frac{[(\Delta Q/Q) - (\Delta L/L)]Q}{\Delta K}$$

where $\Delta Q/Q$ is the growth of output (Q or GDP), $\Delta L/L$ is the growth of labor, and ΔK is additional capital or investment.

13. Thus, GDP $= a + b_1$ INV $+ b_2$ EXP. For empirical results, see correlations in the Appendix.

14. John Tagliabue, "Yugoslav Economy: A Sense of Urgency," New York Times, March 8, 1983.

5

SECTORAL AND REGIONAL RESOURCE ALLOCATION

SECTORAL DEVELOPMENT

In Yugoslavia, and more so in Greece, there has been an unbalanced sectoral growth policy during the postwar years. Yugoslavia, following the example of other planned economies, emphasized extensively the industrial sector, while Greece, consciously or unconsciously, stressed the services sector at the expense of others, primarily the manufacturing and agricultural sectors. The share of industrial production to total GDP is close to 50 percent for Yugoslavia and 32 percent for Greece, compared with 42 percent and 20 percent respectively in 1950. The share of services to GDP is around 40 percent for Yugoslavia and 55 percent for Greece, compared with 14 percent for Yugoslavia and 32 percent for Greece in 1950. On the other hand, the share of agricultural production (including cattle raising and fishing) to total GDP is 15 percent now, compared to 30 percent in 1950, for both countries.

The long-run relative decline of agriculture and the growth of industry and services is a universal economic trend, and it would be difficult for these two countries to avoid such a developmental process. However, Yugoslavia followed the usual historical trend of advancement from agriculture to industry to services, while the economy of Greece moved, to a large extent, from agriculture directly to services, neglecting industrialization. Greek policymakers, realizing that the open economy of Greece cannot catch up with the other industrial countries, started recently to emphasize technological development, primarily in microelectronics, bioengineering, aquiculture, alternative energy sources, and other scientific and high technology areas. That is why efforts are made to reverse the trend of "brain drain" toward an effective "brain gain" policy, through satisfactory remuneration and other incentives for scientists and researchers.

Unfortunately, government policies in both countries, particularly in Greece, have not done enough to discourage movement of human resources and capital from the countryside to urban centers. Moreover, foreign investments have concentrated in a few areas that have public utilities and advanced credit and market facilities. As a result of such sectoral and regional concentration, the gap between the advanced (industrial) and the subsistence (agricultural) sectors has been widening. The "backwash effects" from the poor to the rich regions have been more powerful than the "spread effects" from the advanced to the backward sectors. Therefore, income disparities persist.

At the present stage, both countries need an unbalanced growth policy in favor of decentralization to correct previous unwise policies that led to unhealthy urbanization. They would be ill advised to pursue a strategy of balanced growth, that is, a program of simultaneous investment in mutually supporting industries throughout the whole economy. Although such a policy has the advantage of making sectors and industries each other's customers, progress at snail's pace by a deliberate unbalancing of the economy would induce decision making and action through tensions and incentives for private entrepreneurs and planners at the local and national levels. Initiation of development through a chain of unbalanced growth sequences with emphasis on those sectors and industries that present maximum backward and forward linkages would, most probably, result in high and sustainable rates of growth. For Greece and Yugoslavia, manufacturing industries processing agricultural and mining products, with backward and forward linkages, seem to present good opportunities for investment and potentially high rates of productivity. What is needed mostly is transfer of technology close to the raw materials, investment financing, and improvements in the transportation network to carry the commodities produced to available and potential markets.

Investment financing is one of the weakest links in economic policy. Policymakers form development plans and, using explicitly or implicitly a version of the Harrod-Domar model, project investment requirements to achieve certain rates of economic growth. The next serious question is how to finance the required investment. Is domestic saving sufficient, and if not, are there foreign sources of financing and under what terms?

The financing of gross capital formation in Greece comes primarily from saving (64 percent of the total), consumption of fixed capital or depreciation (26 percent) and surplus or current transactions of the nation (10 percent). Higher depreciation rates can be observed in more industrialized countries, such as Britain, France, West Germany, Italy, and the United States (where they vary from 50-60 percent of total saving), primarily because of higher capital accumulation. Total saving in Greece, as a percent of disposable income, is around 20 percent annually. About 70 percent comes from households, 8-10 percent from general government, and around 10 percent from corporate and quasi-corporate enterprises.(1) In developed countries, however, corporate saving is higher. Thus for Canada it is around 55 percent, for Australia 40 percent, for the United States and Britain about 30 percent, and for West Germany 20 percent, while for India it is about 5 percent.

AGRICULTURE

From ancient times, agriculture and cattle raising were the main occupations of the people in the area. During the pre-Homeric period the diet in Greece and Yugoslavia consisted of green leaves, grass, roots, acorns, and the meat of animals that were hunted. Later, land cultivation and cattle raising were dominant. During the Roman, Venetian, and Byzantine periods, the feudalistic system of Western Europe prevailed in large parts of the two countries. Large segments of land were owned by the barons, the nobles, and the Church, primarily the Catholic church. Poor peasants (plebeians) had to work hard for their masters, who had all property rights and could even transfer the plebeians and their families to other masters.

During the Ottoman occupation, land was divided into large and small regions governed by pashas and sadjakbegs. Smaller regions were governed by other Turkish chiefs (voivodas) and local kodjabashes. The followers and collaborators of the Ottomans (mainly spahis) were rewarded with gifts of land (ziamets or smaller timars) after each military victory. The best land and even whole villages (chifliks) belonged to the Turkish local rulers (beys and agas). As mentioned earlier, heavy taxes on produce were levied every year, in addition to the taxes imposed on the Christian rayahs as a punishment for not converting into Islam (haratsi).(3) Under such conditions, many people gave their property to monasteries, which were exempt from property confiscations (vakoufia), and the previous owners cultivated the land on behalf of the Church. Large and rich farms and properties were accumulated by the monasteries (metohia), most of which were distributed back to the tillers after the liberation of Greece and Yugoslavia from the Turks.

In the postliberation years, agricultural reforms were initiated in the Balkans, including Greece and Yugoslavia. Large estates or latifundia (chifliks), particularly in fertile plains, which were unfairly acquired or inherited during Turkish domination, were distributed to the previously exploited peasant masses. Moreover, the gradual influence of western capitalism and the trend toward a market agricultural economy increased the dependency of the farmers on middlemen, loan sharks, and bank credit as well as on exports to European (mainly German) markets.(4) Such a dependency on exports of mainly raisins and tobacco from Greece and livestock and prunes from Yugoslavia to Germany was intensified before World War II. However, the distribution of land through inheritance and dowry led to its subdivision into small strips (stamps) scattered in different places. Thus the average holding in Greece was and still is less than half (9 acres) of that in Western Europe.

After World II, new reforms were introduced in Yugoslavia with the collectivization of land in a similar fashion to the Soviet kolkhoz. However, to increase incentives and to avoid shortages in consumer goods, private ownership of larger pieces of land was allowed by the Yugoslav government. On the other hand, new decentralization measures taken recently in Greece encourage voluntary collectivization and the establishment of agro-industrial cooperatives in the countryside, with the aim of organizing the unprotected farmers.

Both Greece and Yugoslavia have good subsoil but, mostly, poor soil resources. Many mountains are covered with bare rocks. Less than a third of the land is covered by forest, and the large numbers of low hills are without natural irrigation. Only about a third of the area is flat land or tillable hills. The warm, mostly dry climate promotes the production of olives, vegetables, grapes, and other fruits, especially in Greece. The temperate climate of the region and the extensive beautiful coasts attract tourists and investors.

Greece produces the largest amount of tomatoes in Western Europe (2,270,000 tons in 1981) next to Italy (4,650,000 tons). Spain produces 2,121,000 tons, France 880,000 tons, and Yugoslavia 450,000 tons. There is strong competition from Italy and Spain not only in tomatoes but in peaches, grapes, watermelons, peppers, and cucumbers. For lemons and oranges, Greece has a good market in the Eastern European countries, which absorb about 90 percent of total exports, compared to only about 3 percent by the EEC. The main importers of Greek lemons are the Soviet Union (41 percent in 1980), Poland (22 percent), Czechoslovakia (11 percent), Yugoslavia (10 percent), Romania (7 percent), Hungary (5 percent), and Bulgaria (4 percent). For Greek oranges, the main importers are Romania (30 percent), Soviet Union (23 percent), Poland (14 percent), Czechoslovokia (10 percent), Yugoslavia (7 percent), East Germany (7 percent) and Bulgaria (4 percent).

Wheat production in Greece gradually increased from 3 million bushels in 1871-80 to 7 million bushels in 1889-99, 8 million bushels in 1899-1909, and 11 million bushels in 1914-19. More or less the same increase in wheat production took place in Serbia. The most important agricultural area in the production of wheat (about half of Greece's production), cotton, tobacco, peaches, apples, and other fruits is Macedonia. Thessaly is next in the production of grain, cotton, and tree crops. Thrace produces wheat and tobacco, and Sterea Hellas, Peloponnesus, and Crete are the major regional producers of olives, grapes, and oranges. Epirus and most of the poor islands produce little aside from oranges and other fruits. In the mountainous areas of Greece agricultural and pastoral activities are dominant. However, low land productivity forced many inhabitants to leave these regions in search of a better livelihood.

The cooperative movement in Greece was closely bound up with the Agricultural Bank and its credit conditions. Its intention was primarily to provide the small farmers with marketing facilities for selling their products and buying the needed tools and materials. The government usually purchases large amounts of wheat and other products and the bank and the cooperatives are responsible for collection and warehousing.

Cooperatives deal with such products as olives and olive oil, dairy products, wine, tomatoes, and fruits (mostly peaches, oranges, and apples). However, when private merchants offer more cash down payment (around 90 percent of the price) they can break the cooperatives (which usually offer around 70 percent). The prevailing disorganized marketing for many agricultural products creates a parasitic class of a multitude of local dealers and wholesalers which raises distribution costs and inhibits effective domestic and export marketing.

In Greece, where private ownership prevails, there is extensive subdivision of land into small lots (stamps) scattered in different places. In such a division of land into small parcels, mainly because of inheritance and dowry, it is difficult to use tractors and other machines of mass production that increase land and labor productivity. However, production incentives on such privately owned lots are high, particularly for crops such as vegetables and fruits that require labor-intensive methods of cultivation and harvesting.

Large plains, which belong to cooperatives and state farms in Yugoslavia or to individual owners in Greece, are planted to wheat, corn, cotton, and other crops or are used for grazing cows. There are no fences and no parceling of land in such plains, and mass production technology can be implemented to increase land productivity. Some Greek farmers (in Styphalia, for example), realized that ownership of small, widely scattered lots is not conducive to high productivity and voluntarily agreed to exchange them and/or to form cooperatives for more efficient use. In Greece, where there are limited large grassy pastures, sheep and goats prevail, while in Yugoslavia cows and pigs are primarily raised. Hot, dry weather conditions in the south promote the production of olives, figs, raisins, tobacco, cotton, and similar products, while production of corn, wheat, potatoes, and oats prevails in the north. Production of fish is higher in Greece and that of forestry products higher in Yugoslavia.

Special agreements are enacted from time to time for the protection of the common lakes of Doirani and Prespa and their enrichment with special fish eggs. There are regulations protecting the lakes from water pollution and regulating fishing. Special provisions are made for the improvement of such types of fish as Californian trout, cyprinus caprio, and mullet.

A gradual reorientation of the Yugoslav economy away from the buildup of heavy industry to the meeting of consumers' needs took place with reasonable efficiency during the late postwar period. To increase the efficiency of the agricultural sector and to stimulate food production, investment in the rural sectors was increased and incentives to the farmers were provided. However, the size of land holdings, the maximum being 10 hectares, may not be sufficient for the use of modern technology.

In Yugoslavia, population in agriculture was reduced from 81 percent (10,494 people), in 1910 to 61 percent in 1953 and about 30 percent (6,690 people) in 1980. About 80 percent of agricultural land, 83 percent of pigs, and 97 percent of cows belong to the private sector.(5)

Greece has the same number or more sheep but far fewer cattle and pigs than Yugoslavia. In Greece milk is produced by cows, sheep, and goats by almost equal amounts, while in Yugoslavia far more milk is produced from cows than from sheep and goats. During the last two decades, the number of cattle and sheep remained constant or declined slightly while that of pigs increased in both countries. The number of horses, asses, and mules declined dramatically in Greece and more so in Yugoslavia.

Greece produces more barley, rice, tobacco, cotton, and fish than Yugoslavia, which produces more corn, wheat, potatoes, wool, and forest products. Yugoslavia has twice as many threshers and three times as many tractors as Greece, as Table 5.1 shows.

Table 5.1. Selected Agricultural Products (thousand metric tons) and Livestock (thousand head)

	Greece			Yugoslavia		
	1960	1970	1980	1960	1970	1980
Cattle	1,071	997	950	5,702	5,029	5,491
Sheep	9,353	7,680	8,000	10,823	8,974	7,354
Pigs	628	383	1,020	5,818	5,544	7,747
Horses	327	255	120	1,220	1,076	617
Asses	507	376	253	140	37	25
Mules	222	183	124	32	18	13
Milk	920	1,358	1,701	2,523	2,738	4,451
Tractors (units)	n.a.	61,945	130,000	n.a.	80,000	385,116
Threshers (units)	n.a.	4,151	5,800	n.a.	11,839	9,552
Barley	232	737	949	529	402	650
Maize (Corn)	281	511	1,223	6,160	6,933	9,106
Cotton	63	111	115	2	4	—
Eggs (hen) (thous. m.t.)	n.a.	96	137	n.a.	139	219
Ground nuts	n.a.	9	12	n.a.	1	1
Oats	149	107	87	373	309	295
Potatoes	490	756	973	3,270	2,964	2,387
Rice	54	79	78	22	32	34
Tobacco	80	95	113	28	49	56
Wheat	1,692	1,931	2,931	3,574	3,792	5,078
Wool	11	8	10	14	12	10
Forestry (roundwood) (mill. cubic meters)	3	3	3	17	17	16
Fish	82	98	106	31	46	63

n.a. = not available.
Note: In some cases earlier years' data than 1980 were available.
Source: United Nations, Statistical Yearbook, various issues.

The new law 1262/1982, concerning investment incentives for regional development and economic decentralization in Greece, encourages the formation and expansion of agricultural cooperatives. According to this law, generous grants ranging from 10 to 50 percent of the cost of investment are given to the cooperatives, which establish agricultural, manufacturing, and other productive enterprises (Article 5). Also, sizable loans with interest subsidization, tax exemptions, high depreciation allowances, and other benefits are granted for such investments by cooperatives, local government organizations, and Greeks living abroad. Even with 10 percent minimum participation such organizations and individuals may establish their own productive enterprises. Other individuals and companies may also be given generous grants of up to 50 percent of the cost of investment and other similar benefits, depending on the backwardness of the area (categories A, B, C, D) in which they invest. Such investments in agro-industrial cooperatives are encouraged by the present socialist government of Greece not only for ideological reasons but also for the expected benefits from economies of scale that result from collective action.(6) One can observe that Greek rural cooperatives increasingly integrate their operations vertically and horizontally from basic production to advanced distribution in such products as cereals, dairy products, fruits, cotton, olive oil, and other products, providing processing, storage, and marketing facilities.

INDUSTRY

Toward the end of the nineteenth century, the colonial powers of that time, primarily Britain, France, and Germany, moved with industrial capital into the Balkan area to exploit new resources and markets and to expand their military interests. Foreign capital, in the form of private or government loans and investments, was used to finance mainly the construction of highways, railways, and other infrastructural projects. One of these was the railroad connecting Belgrade with Salonika and Constantinople, which was constructed at the beginning of this century. Although the governments of Greece and Yugoslavia increased taxes and tried to stimulate exports to finance industrial investment, the flooding of their markets with western products prevented rapid industrialization. On the other hand, high tariffs on agricultural machinery and other manufactured products created a few monopolies or oligopolies and aggravated the plight of the peasants, who had to pay prices for the industrial products they purchased.

The inability of industry to absorb surplus rural labor led to extensive emigration of Greek and Yugoslav peasants, primarily to the United States, during the interwar years. However, investment in such cottage industries as flour milling, tanning, pottery, textiles, the processing of olives, grapes, and other agricultural, dairy and mineral products (bauxite, copper, iron, chrome) provided employment for some workers, particularly in Yugoslavia, where their number increased from 200,000 in 1918 to about 400,000 in 1938.(7) Many seafaring Greeks, on the other hand, were employed in vessels and steamships built mainly by wealthy emigres.

After the war, both countries were left with very limited, if any, industrial capacity. From then on, Yugoslavia paid more attention to industrialization compared to Greece, where short-run services and residential construction in large cities were emphasized. Lack of confidence and economic and political instability were responsible for the extensive channeling of Greek savings into housing and services. In addition, commercial banks lent their support to a few monopolistic or oligopolistic firms that were concentrated in large cities, primarily in the Athens-Piraeus area.(8) Because of the heavy air pollution in the industrial cities, especially in Athens, drastic measures have been taken to reverse this trend of industrial concentration. As a result of the increase in petroleum and raw material prices in the 1970s, both countries experienced a slowdown in their industrial growth in recent years.(9) Table 5.2 shows the main manufacturing products of Greece and Yugoslavia.

At present Yugoslavia produces about 50 kilos of meat, mainly pork and veal, and Greece 40 kilos per capita annually; the annual production of cheese is around 20 kilos per capita in Greece and 8 kilos in Yugoslavia. Comparatively speaking, Greece produces far larger amounts of tobacco (170,000 metric tons annually) than Yugoslavia (60,000 metric tons); Yugoslavia produces about double the amount of sugar (700,000 metric tons) and more than double amount of electricity (59,000 kilowatt-hours) than Greece (23,000 kilowatt hours). About half of the total energy production in Yugoslavia and around 15-20 percent in Greece is derived

Table 5.2. Manufacturing Products (thousand metric tons)

	Greece			Yugoslavia		
	1960	1970	1980	1960	1970	1980
Meat	139	233	359	488	809	1,119
Butter	11	6	7	22	15	12
Cheese	91	142	185	92	99	147
Salted fish	3	4	6			
Wheat flour	1,191	526	736	1,597	2,172	2,387
Sugar	3	188	354	289	385	693
Wine (thous. hecto-liters)	2,898	4,532	4,400	3,350	5,478	6,781
Beer (thous. hecto-liters)	435	777	1,380	1,630	6,665	10,005
Tobacco products (millions cigarettes)	12,359	17,029	33,307	20,100	32,072	53,738
Cotton yarn	25	42	110	51	102	118
Wool yarn	10	11	15	21	38	44
Sawn wood (thous. cubic meters)	262	272	390	2,295	3,084	4,272
Tires (thousands)	n.a.	13	14	391	2,763	8,862
Ethylene				n.a.	42	20
Phosphate fertilizers	n.a.	104	189	n.a.	233	269
Petroleum refinery capacity	n.a.	5,050	12,900	n.a.	12,000	16,400
Cement	1,649	4,848	11,436	1,967	4,399	8,698
Crude steel	n.a.	435	1,000	1,442	2,228	3,454
Aluminum	n.a.	91	146	25	48	196
Lead	3	15	21	89	97	117
Zinc	n.a.	1	0	36	65	95

n.a. = not available.
Note: In some cases earlier years' data than 1980 were available.
Source: United Nations, Statistical Yearbook, various issues.

135

from hydroelectric power. Yugoslavia has far more tractors (385,000 units) than Greece (130,000) and consumes more steel per capita (240 kilograms) compared to Greece (176 kilograms). This indicates the higher degree of industrialization in Yugoslavia than Greece. In Greece, more and more lignite and hydroelectric power and less and less petroleum is used for the production of electricity.

In Yugoslavia, the first nuclear energy unit was established in 1981 with the cooperation of Westinghouse Corporation. Its average production is estimated at 4.4 billion kilowatt-hours. The United States will provide the needed uranium for its operation until 1985. Then Yugoslavia is expected to produce enough uranium in the area of Zirovski to operate a second unit equivalent to the first. By the end of this century, it is expected that about ten nuclear energy units will be created.

Moreover, ten hydroelectric and thermal energy projects are in the process of construction. By 1986, when they are scheduled to be completed, total capacity of energy production will reach 14,000 megawatts, an increase of 8,316 megawatts or 68 percent. It should be added that Yugoslavia has large resources of coal and good potential for many more hydroelectric projects. Electricity production also proceeded vigorously over the interwar period, which led to the gradual use of electricity-consuming capital and consumer durable goods. Per capita energy consumption in Yugoslavia increased from 932 kilograms of coal equivalent in 1960 to around 2,500, at present while for Greece it increased from 407 to around 2,200 kilograms of coal equivalent over the same period.

In both countries, but primarily in Greece, industry has been concentrated in a few, mostly urban, areas, while rural areas have lagged behind in industrialization. Together with the need for emphasis on manufacturing in the countryside comes the need for the improvement in infrastructural facilities in the form of better transportation, communications, electricity, waterworks, and technical training. The establishment of small or middle-size factories in the countryside, producing flour, cloth, shoes, and pottery, and processing olives, grapes, and similar products would provide the market for each other's products in rural regions and reduce migration to urban centers or abroad. Moreover, the development of industries related to cattle raising and dairy products,

fisheries, textiles, and minerals would create additional demand and provide additional income for the underemployed
workers, which would have a multiple economic effect in
these regions. However, feasibility studies on production
possibilities and effective marketing of the related commodities and services produced will be necessary before each
investment venture is undertaken. Through trial-and-error
experience, entrepreneurs and cooperative managers could
proceed to establish first labor-intensive plants and then
concentrate on more advanced capital-intensive projects with
longer gestation periods.(10) Such industries are needed not
only to absorb disguised unemployment but also to provide
vocational and on-the-job training, so that the rural populace
can participate actively and share in the fruits of development, instead of emptying out the countryside.

Out of the 39 largest industrial firms in Greece more
than half (22) are foreign-owned. The remaining 17 Greek-
owned firms are largely subsidized. As a result, any increase
in their size leads to a decline in their rates of return.
Therefore, it seems that the policies of promoting efficiency
through size and subsidization proved to be a failure.(11) On
the contrary, such policies appeared to shield inefficiency of
such large firms, which are moving toward bankruptcy or
takeover by other EEC firms or the government and/or by
their employees and workers through self-management.
Heracles General Cement with 350 million dollars annual
sales and 13 of its executives accused of fraud and currency
smuggling is under the process of being taken over by the
government as are Peiraki-Petraiki and the pharmaceutical
industries.

There are some 13,000 industries in the Athens-Piraeus
area and their suburbs. Over 40 percent of Greece's total
population or 4,130,000, live in this area, although Athens
(the capital of the nation) around the ancient Acropolis, was
planned for about 150,000 people. Such a concentration of
industry in the area and the urban explosion over the last
three decades have made Athens the city most affected by
pollution in Western Europe, followed by Nice and Milan.
Thus a brown cloud of pollutants, called nefos, hovers over
Athens for much of the year. This nefos, which is similar to
the smog in Los Angeles, is a photochemical smoke, composed of nitrogen oxide, hydrocarbons, and peroxylacetyl
nitrate, and sometimes is formed as low as 30 yards from the

ground.(12)   The present government tries hard to reduce pollution.   However, more drastic measures are needed, although a high political price is associated with the required unpopular measures.   New decentralization measures and the air pollution in Athens are expected to lure people back to the countryside where fresh air and other rural amenities prevail.

The existing big enterprises in Greece are to a large extent family-owned oligopolies, which enjoyed protection up to the entrance of the country into the EEC. Such "sleeping" enterprises might have neglected innovative activities and have enjoyed high rates of profit under the umbrella of protection.   Under growing competitive conditions, though, they have to wake up and introduce more efficient methods of production in order to survive.

Most Greek enterprises are small or middle-size firms. About 90 percent of them employ 10 persons or fewer and are primarily in the food, canning, fats, shoes, ceramic, and cosmetics industries.   They depend primarily on overworked family members and hesitate to group themselves into large economic units in order to be able to implement modern technology and methods of mass production and achieve economies of scale.   To overcome this hestitation and to encourage the establishment of modern production units with high efficiency, the Greek government provides investment and tax incentives for the establishment of agro-industrial cooperatives that are somewhat more generous than those in the centrally planned economies.

Regarding the housing industry or construction, large numbers of housing units in Greece and Yugoslavia were lost through total and partial destruction or damage during the war.   As a result, a large number of housing units were overcrowded, unhealthy and unsafe. These conditions led to high demand for housing, which was intensified by the coming to maturity of those born in the surge of births after World War I, as well as by the high level of marriages during the immediate post-World War II years.   With the end of World War II hostilities, there was a general tendency for the marriage rate to rise and housing demand to increase, especially on the part of young couples who migrated and wanted to set up new households in urban centers. This led to slums. However, a number of slums were gradually eliminated through new housing construction under the aegis of public authorities in both Greece and Yugoslavia.

As a result of profiteering and speculation, shore land prices in Greece mounted rapidly during the post war years, particularly in areas close to the large cities. In order to pay a small transfer tax and circumvent prohibitive law provisions, buyers and sellers form various types of organizations and enter into dummy and secret transactions.(13)

Although there is a tax on income from property, there are no capital gains taxes and limited property taxes in Greece. As will be mentioned later, urban property transactions are subject only to a transfer tax (about 11 percent) applicable to all or most real estate transactions. It seems that profits coming from unearned increments in the value of shore land constitute a rational and equitable basis for taxation. Taxation on capital gains from urban and shore land sales would revoke what may be considered as a subsidy for speculation by the present tax policy, reduce speculation, and mitigate maldistribution of wealth. On the other hand, transfer taxes in rural, denuded, backward areas should be reduced to perhaps less than 1 percent (adequate to maintain the land records) so that land transactions and investment be encouraged. Such a tax policy would reduce the high prices of shore lands and increase the low prices in poor rural areas, thereby improving the decentralization process.

TOURISM AND OTHER SERVICES

The pleasant climate and the natural beauties of Greece and Yugoslavia continue to attract large numbers of foreign tourists. The picturesque beaches, the dry climate, and the rich history of both countries, as well as the innumerable archaeological monuments in Greece, make the area one of the most popular destinations for international tourists. With the winter Olympic Games of 1984 scheduled to be held at Sarajevo, Yugoslav tourism is expected to be enhanced. Moreover, if the Olympic Games were held at their birthplace (Olympia) in Peloponnesus on a permanent basis, as is contemplated, the Greek economy and tourism in particular would be greatly stimulated.

For both countries, tourism continues to be a vital and growing sector of the economy. Thus for both Greece and

Yugoslavia the number of tourists increased from 2 million in 1974 to more than 6 million per year at present. As a consequence, revenue from tourism decreased dramatically, accounting for more than one billion dollars per year for both countries. At present the largest number of tourists in Greece comes from the United States, Yugoslavia, West Germany, Austria, Italy, and France. Recent large devaluations of the drachma and the dinar aim to attract tourism, in addition to the beneficial effects on the balance of trade through cheaper exports and more expensive imports. More than half a million Yugoslav tourists come to Greece and about 150,000 Greek tourists go to Yugoslavia every year. However, recent restrictions imposed by Yugoslavia on its citizens traveling abroad have had negative effects on Greek tourism, particularly in Salonika. In order to save foreign currency and increase deposits, the Yugoslav government requires that each traveler deposits in a bank 5,000 dinars for the first trip and 2,000 more dinars for each additional trip.(14)

Following the example of the other EEC countries in upgrading technological resources and stemming the drain of talent, Greece established a new cabinet department, the Ministry of Research and Technology, with high expectations for transferring and introducing modern technology. In addition to the development of alternate energy sources, such as solar, wind, and geothermal energy, where Greece has a comparative advantage, computer and information technology, aquiculture, earthquake engineering, and biotechnology are considered for improvement. Through biotechnology, the structuring of the protein DNA for developing self-fertilizing plants can be used for the advancement of the pharmaceutical and agricultural sectors, so much needed in Greece and Yugoslavia.

The introduction of new technology and especially the use of computers in such services as communications, transportation, office work, banking, and the medical and other professions would help to increase the productivity of the service sector, which is lower than that of the manufacturing and other sectors. Moreover, the rapid spread of supermarkets and self-service stores, which can be observed in both countries, is expected to increase output per unit of time and make this sector as productive as or more productive than other sectors.

Also, further improvement in the efficiency of the service sector could be achieved through the use of telecommunications, passenger cars, and a wider spread of mass media via television, radio and printed material. Both countries have about 1 passenger car per 10 persons, while Greece has around 25 and Yugoslavia 7 telephones per 1000 inhabitants. This is not a satisfactory ratio as yet. There are also about 300 radios and 130 television receivers per 1,000 persons in Greece and 210 radios and 160 televisions per 1,000 persons in Yugoslavia.

Film festivals, such as those at Ljubljana (1980) and Athens (1981), athletic meetings (at times with other Balkan groups, known as Balkaniads) and theatrical and other joint performances help to improve the economic and cultural relations between the two nations. Also, annual international fairs, such as that at Salonika, and other trade and cultural activities attract a growing number of participants every year.

TRANSPORTATION

Greece and Yugoslavia inherited a backward Balkan transportation system, aside from their natural endowments of excellent ports. The railway system is old and inadequate, partly because of the rough terrain and partly because of neglect due mainly to the rapid development of automobile, sea and air transportation. Much of the rail equipment is obsolete and the cost of operation is high. The main line runs from central Europe to northern Yugoslavia (through the Alps) to Belgrade. From Belgrade it continues south down the Vardar (Axios) valley to Salonika and through Thessaly to Athens. This line and most of the other rail lines in the two countries have standard track gauges. However, there exist a number of narrow-gauge lines such as that of Volos-Kalabaka and those in Peloponnesus. There is also a small and mainly tourist line (22.5 kilometers) that climbs up the mountains with gears and through tunnels from the seashore town of Diakopto to the mountainous town of Kalavryta. The narrow-gauge lines, particularly the Patras-Athens line, present problems in transferring loads to standard gauge freight cars and locomotives.

The expansion of railroad mileage occurred primarily during the 1880s. Specifically, railroad mileage increased from 10 miles in 1880 to 370 miles in 1888 for Greece, and from 100 to 340 miles for Yugoslavia. At present total railway trackage in Greece is about 3,000 kilometers. In addition to Athens, Salonika is also a major freight entrepot in the railroad network of the nation.

The use of automobiles brought many changes in Greece and Yugoslavia during the interwar years and afterward. It stimulated road building, it provided transport for agricultural products, and it accelerated the relocation of urban population in the industrial centers. Commercial vehicles increased in Yugoslavia from 1 per 10,000 inhabitants in 1922 to 10 in 1950 and about 850 in 1980, and passenger cars increased to 85 per 1,000 inhabitants.(15)

Considerable efforts have been made to improve the road systems in both countries. Except for the national roads, running primarily through the middle of Yugoslavia down to Salonika, Athens, and Patras, many regional and local roads have been developed. However, in the effort to link even small villages with national or central roads, particularly in the mountainous western parts of Greece and Yugoslavia, many of these roads were badly constructed and are not much used.

The Danube and its tributaries in northern Yugoslavia near Belgrade and the Vardar (Axios) river, which flows in southern Yugoslavia and northern Greece to the Aegean Sea near Salonika, are important waterways helping navigation and trade transportation in the area. If the Morava and the Vardar rivers are connected, as expected, through the construction of a navigable canal (400 miles long), with partial financing by the United Nations Development Program, the new waterway from the Danube to the Aegean Sea would greatly facilitate transportation not only between Greece and Yugoslavia but between them and other European countries, particularly Austria, Czechoslovakia, and West Germany. Such a waterway would reduce the present distance from Europe to Port Said, via the Adriatic Sea or the Dardanelles, by one third, to 2,000 kilometers. As a result, transportation cost between Belgrade and Salonika would be greatly reduced, while the annual traffic of goods would increase by more than fifteen times (from 3 to 50 million tons). Cities along the Morava River, such as Skopje, Kumanovo, and Nis, would receive economic benefits from this waterway of some 650 kilometers (575 in Yugoslavia and the rest in Greece).

The ports of Salonika and Kavalla in Greece are important junctions for the transportation of petroleum to Yugoslavia by freight trains as well as trucks (some 35,000 annually).(16) However, to avoid high transport cost and pollution, an oil pipeline via Salonika or Kavalla may be preferable. The creation of new routes and the improvement of old ones are of vital importance to the area so that traffic congestion and the system of issuing "transit cards" by Yugoslavia can be eliminated. Also, traffic from the Balkans to the Middle East through Turkey will be relieved and transport costs and tolls will be reduced. From that point of view, joint ventures between Greece and Yugoslavia and possibly with other neighboring countries are of great importance.

While the importance of foreign trade has long been recognized, that of transportation and particularly port economics has received much less attention. In both countries, and especially in Greece, with its extensive shores, sea transportation is vital and port services important. However, aside from the natural endowment of excellent harbors in both countries, some ports often become the bottlenecks or the white elephants of economic development. Since demand for port services is quite inelastic (around 0.1), it is expected that ports can generate enough revenue to cover their costs and to create surpluses for further investment.

Regarding revenues from port services, higher prices are supposed to be charged in times of traffic congestion and lower prices in times of port underutilization. Although there are economies of scale, particularly in large ports such as those of Piraues, Salonika, Patras, and Kavalla in Greece and Rijeka, Split, and Dubrovnik in Yugoslavia, it is difficult to measure them in order to optimize port operations. On the other hand, costs may increase because of frequent scarcity of appropriate land space and limited berths, in which case diseconomies of scale set in. Appropriate price distinctions between port congestion and port underutilization would improve allocative efficiency and allow many ports to replace public subsidies with port-generated revenue. Otherwise, vessel owners using the port facilities would surely apply their own congestion charges to cargo and shipping rates. Other operational devices such as annual lease arrangements for a pier or annual fees to enter the ports should be considered for revenue maximization or cost minimization.

Although each port enjoys a considerable degree of local monopoly, some degree of competition among ports might exist. Different port managers in the same country or in other neighboring Balkan countries might try to draw some more traffic to generate more revenue. However, utilization of countervailing market power by shipping enterprises might suggest some form of cartelization or coordination of related policies on port services and prices. Development policies on port facilities should be coordinated with similar policies on inland transportation so that the uninterrupted flow of imported and exported commodities may be secured. This is particularly so for Greece and Yugoslavia, which constitute a natural gateway for central Europe to the countries of eastern Europe and the Middle East. From that point of view improvement of the Free Trade Zone of the port of Salonika for transit operations of Yugoslav goods should be considered.

To relieve the heavy traffic through Piraeus and Salonika, other Greek ports are being developed. They include Kavalla, Corfu, Preveza, Patras, Herakleion, Rhodos, and primarily Volos. In the port of Volos alone more than 5,000 vehicles and 6 million tons of cargo, primarily from central Europe, are loaded every year for the Middle East countries, while the ferries from Volos to Tartus and Latakia, Syria handle about 2,700 trailer trucks per month. Also, ships that carry trucks with merchandise travel from Patras and, to a lesser extent, Messologhi, Preveza, and Igoumenitsa northward to Dubrovnik, Split, Rijeka, and other ports of Yugoslavia.

For the improvement of transportation between the EEC and the Middle East countries, Greece and Italy agreed to collaborate on the construction of a 220-mile road linking the Greek ports of Igoumenitsa in the west to Volos in the east and to modernize these two ports. The EEC will finance 80 percent of the work, which will start next year.

Eleusina, one of the important ports of Greater Athens (less than ten miles to the west of the city) is used primarily for tankers, while the ports of Patras, Corfu, Rhodos, and Herakleion are largely used for passenger shipping. Because of the long coastlines and the large number of inhabited islands, coastal shipping continues to be an important means of transporting goods internally in Greece.(17)

However, because of its international nature, shipping is very sensitive to economic slowdowns and worldwide recessions. Thus during periods of slump (such as that of the early 1980s) the shipping industry is caught in a severe squeeze as too many ships chase too few customers. Under such conditions many tankers, bulk cargo vessels, and container ships, which belong mostly to small independent Greek shipowners, are laid up in berths, primarily in Eleusina and Piraeus, or in scrap yards for dismantling. As a result, freight rates drop and the value of ships declines, while loans using ships as collateral are rolled back or go unpaid.(18) Hellenic Lines Ltd., the largest container ship company in Greece and one of the world's largest privately owned ship companies, failed to pay 2.4 million dollars interest on 83 million dollars debt and 17 out of its 28 vessels were seized.

As Greece is interested in transporting goods from Europe through Yugoslavia, so is Yugoslavia in transporting goods through Greece to and from the Middle East. That is why Yugoslav cooperation committees press for improvement and expansion of the facilities of the ports of Salonika and Volos. Moreover, they express interest in sharing in the modernization of the related highways and bus and car transportation as well as the Idomeni-Salonika railway, which is expected to be electrified.(19) Other agreements and suggestions deal with sea and air transportation and improvement of communications. Greece, on the other hand, asks for more transit permits (30,000 instead of 26,000 in 1982) for transporting goods to and from the EEC.

REGIONAL DECENTRALIZATION

In Yugoslavia, and more so in Greece, regional concentration has been extensive during the postwar years. Actually government policies, directly or indirectly, encouraged the movement of labor and other resources to urban centers, through credit offerings, infrastructural and educational facilities, and other public services. Thus rural regions gradually lost the most talented and progressive persons to the advanced industrial areas. The long neglect of the countryside led to dualistic rigidities and distortion in the allocation of resources, particularly in Greece. As a result, the gap between the advanced and the subsistence regions became larger and rural areas remained backward compared to industrial centers.

In both countries regional development policy may be considered responsible for the maldistribution of income and wealth. It would seem that the gap in per capita income among regions widened during the postwar period. Despite favorable policy pronouncements, there was poor performance in the less developed regions of these countries in both industrial and overall growth.(20)

In Yugoslavia this may be due to the system of property rights under self-management and other indirect restraints imposed on the economy, which constrained rapid industrialization in poor regions. In Greece, on the other hand, the lack of proper regional planning and the conscious or unconscious political emphasis of urban centralism may be responsible for such a widening regional gap.

To eliminate interregional differences, the government can provide additional incentives such as tax concessions, generous depreciation allowances and even labor subsidies. Such a policy can be used as a development model, a paradigm, for each country or even a group of countries such as the EEC. Investment incentives may also be provided by local authorities to cooperatives and private enterprises. They may include capital grants, community development projects, and possibly subsidies for development in disparate regions.

Moreover, foreign investment, along with domestic investment, has been concentrated in limited areas, such as Athens-Piraeus and Salonika in Greece and Belgrade, Ljubljana, and Split in Yugoslavia, introducing advanced technology and large-scale industries. These developmental trends created, in many cases, economic enclaves that proved to be detrimental to regional industrialization.

Development planning should encourage entreprenurial activity in poor regions, promote agriculturally based small industry for absorption of disguised unemployment, improve technical education, provide credit to local college industries, and solve regional inequalities in income distribution, so that the rural populace can participate actively and share in the fruits of development.(21)

Yugoslavia presents a wide range of regions, with an advanced north, an intermediate center, and quite a poor south. Greece also has a variety of regions that belong to different stages of development. Epirus, central Peloponnesus and nonirrigated islands are classic examples of less developed regions.

Both countries provide subsidies, credit facilities, and tax benefits to investors in poor regions. For example, Greece provides generous rewards to employment-creating investment in backward areas (Laws 1116/1980 and 1262/ 1982). The whole country is divided into four regional categories: that is, developed (A), intermediate (B), and backward (C), and frontier (D) regions. Depending on the classification, the incentives provided vary from region to region. Thus investors may receive grants of from 20 to 50 percent of their investment, plus interest subsidies of from 30 to 50 percent on the money they may borrow (up to 30 percent of total investment). The investor then can invest in poor regions (C) using only about 25 percent of his or her own capital. Regions characterized as the poorest (C category) include parts of northwestern Greece (Epirus), central Peloponnesus (Arcadia, Kalavryta), parts of Crete, and similar mountainous and deprived areas on the mainland and the islands. Moreover, from 20 to 30 percent of ploughback (undistributed) profits may be exempted from taxation as long as they remain with the enterprises for reinvestment in these poor areas. Generous depreciation allowances, 25 to 150 percent higher than the normal depreciation rates, and subsidies for professional training are also provided. More benefits have been introduced for investment in areas near the borders of Greece (Laws 289/1976 and 1262/1982) which include elimination of property transaction taxes, reduction in turnover taxes, elimination of social security payments, and subsidies for construction investment.

Greek shore land, 15,000 kilometers long (11,000 on the islands and 4,000 on the mainland), is a unique and valuable resource for domestic and foreign tourism because of its esthetic and recreational importance. To preserve its beauty and accessibility, measures with noneconomic objectives may be needed. About 73 percent of the shore land is separated by sea from the great majority of the Greek people. Accessibility by automobile or by regular boat service is limited by barren rocks and cliffs, which give much of the picturesque shore land kind of wild and craggy beauty. Furthermore, acquisitions of shore lands by domestic and foreign speculators tend to monopolize the most desirable areas. Although the beaches up to the high-water mark are by law the property of the Greek people, access by land is limited.(22) Foreigners tend to buy valuable shore lands from the poor peasants and erect barriers, excluding other people from the beaches and often tending to treat the landless peasants as servants. In addition, there are comments that this type of "invasion", particularly from EEC investors, leads to a demeaning shock, cultural demoralization, and abuse of the legendary Greek hospitality (or philotimo).

From a regional point of view, central Greece (in which Attica is included) and Macedonia are the most prosperous regions, with substantial industry and a prosperous agriculture. Thessaly, coastal Peloponnesus, Thrace, and, to some extent, Crete produce substantial amounts of agricultural products, mainly wheat, grapes, olives, cotton, and tobacco. Epirus, the Aegean and the Ionian islands, and western, central and eastern Peloponnesus (with the exception of the plains of Corinth and Argos) are poor, in both industrial and agricultural production. At present the concentration in the Greater Athens area is very striking, and Herculean efforts are needed to alleviate the serious illness created by such unhealthy urbanization. As Hippocrates once pointed out centuries ago, serious sickness requires strong medicine. In the case of Greece today, however, such a policy of quick decentralization is associated with high political cost.

About half of Greece's manufacturing and more than half of the national employment are concentrated in the area of Athens. This is true for almost all industrial products, except beverages, for which Macedonia holds the lead. The dominance of Athens is obvious even in resource-oriented industries such as food, tobacco, textiles, leather and its products, chemicals, rubber, wood and cork, paper and its products, and basic metals. Only in small-scale handicraft employment mainly in footware, textiles, and wood working, is Athens' role smaller compared to other areas, particularly Macedonia. On a per capita basis, such handicrafts are widely dispersed in the country. One of the main reasons for concentration in Athens is the convenience of the place for raw material imports. Other reasons are the existence of high power capacity, which is needed for modern factories, and, for skilled workers, the significantly higher wages in the area compared to other cities and areas. Although wages for the unskilled and the newly arrived workers are relatively low, they are still higher on the average in Athens, while work opportunities are far better than in the countryside. This is so because previous capital investment was largely concentrated in the area. However, the cost of living, especially that of housing, is higher in Athens than in the rest of the country. This, together with the recent problems of pollution and urban congestion, may lead to a gradual reverse movement from Athens back to the countryside.

NOTES

1. United Nations, Yearbook of National Account Statistics, various issues. For ways of financing investment in Yugoslavia, see Branko Horvat, The Yugoslav Economic System (White Plains, N.Y.: IASP, 1976), chap. 6.
2. Pausanias, Ellados, Periigisseos, H'Arcadika, Vol. 13, section 6; with an English translation by W. Jones, Pausanias, Description of Greece, (Cambridge, Mass.: Harvard University Press, 1933), pp. 347-359; and N. Giannaris, The Province of Kalavryta: A Historical and Socioeconomic Review, pp. 19, 63.
3. John Lampe and Marvin Jackson, Balkan Economic History, 1550-1950 (Indiana: Indiana University Press, 1982).
4. The Greek peasants remained unorganized during that time, while those in Yugoslavia and in other Balkan countries were politically organized and achieved more effective agrarian reforms. See Nicos Mouzelis, Modern Greece: Facts of Underdevelopment (London: Macmillan Press, 1978), chap. 4.
5. A deeper review is V. Stipetic, "The Development of the Peasant Economy in Socialist Yugoslavia," in Radmila Stojanovic, ed., The Functioning fo the Yugoslav Economy (New York: M. Sharpe, 1982). More on agriculture in Branko Horvat, The Yugoslav Economic System (White Plains, N.Y.: IASP, 1976), chap. 3; F. Hamilton, Yugoslavia: Patterns of Economic Activity (New York: Praeger, 1968), chap. 9; and Karl-Eugen Wadekin, Agrarian Policies in Communist Europe: A Critical Introduction (Totowa, N.J.: Allunheld, Osmun,

1982), pp. 85-87. Also, P. Milenkovic, Agrocoop, translated from Greek by J. Tsiampas (Athens: Aihme, 1983), Part 2.

6. For similar results in other countries, see T. Turfoinen and J. Von Pischke, "The Financing of Agricultural Cooperatives," Finance and Development, September 1982, pp. 18-21.

7. J. Tomasevich, Peasants, Politics and Economic Change in Yugoslavia (Stanford, Calif.: Stanford University Press, 1955), p. 638; and Mouzelis, Modern Greece, chaps. 5,6.

8. In many enterprises there is only about 20 percent equity and 80 percent loans. Moreover, there is no effective capital market in Greece to finance business investment.

9. For estimates that reduce Yugoslavia's industrial growth rate by 10-15 percent from the official estimate of 10 percent per annum, see John Moore, Growth with Self-Management: Yugoslav Industrialization, 1952-1975 (Stanford, Calif.: Hoover Institution Press, 1980). Also, L. Sirc, The Yugoslav Economy Under Self-Management (London; Macmillan Press, 1979), chap. 11; and L. Tyson, The Yugoslav Economic System and Its Performance in the1970's (Berkeley: Institute of International Studies, University of California Press, 1980).

10. For some problems in Yugoslavia enterprises, see Stephen Sacks, "Divisionalization in Large Yugoslav Enterprises," Journal of Comparative Economics, June 1980, pp. 209-25.

11. Howard Ross and Stavros Thomadakis, "Rate of Return, Firm Size and Development Subsidies," Journal of Development Economics, 12 (1983), 5-18. Also Paul Lewis, "Pressure on Greek Industry," New York Times, November 28, 1983.

12. M. Howe, "Now it's official: Athens' smog is Europe's worst," New York Times, May 12, 1983.

13. To avoid severe penalties applied to under-statements of prices, a common practice (encouraged by some notaries) is to understate prices by about 49 percent. In such transactions, selective enforcement, favoritism, and bribery may come into play; while the legal system, lagging far behind economic development, leads to law evasion, corruption, and widespread cynicism.

14. The National Tourist Organization of Greece asked Yugoslavia to exclude Greece from such restrictions, especially from the prohibition of more than one trip abroad.

15. Between 1963 and 1972 private motor vehicles in use in Yugoslavia increased at an average rate of 27 percent, compared with only 7 percent in neighboring Romania and 9 percent (1963-69) in the Soviet Union. W. W. Rostow, The World Economy: History and Prospect (Austin: University of Texas Press, 1978), pp. 211-15, 281. Also, Organization for Economic Cooperation and Development, Economic Surveys: Yugoslavia, various issues.

16. For more details, see N. Gianaris, The Economies of the Balkan Countries: Albania, Bulgaria, Greece, Romania, Turkey, and Yugoslavia, p. 121.

17. Greece with 34 million gross tons of merchant ships, holds first place in Europe compared with 31 million for the United Kingdom, 26 million for Norway, 22 million for the Soviet Union, 16 million for the United States, and only 2.4 million for Yugoslavia. I. Tzoannou, Elliniki Emporiki Naftilia Kaieok (Athens: Institute of Economic and Industrial Studies, 1977), chaps. 1, 3.

18. It was established that the size of the shipping portfolios was about $100 billion at the beginning of 1983. Colonial Bank and Citibank have large loans tied up in shipping, primarily to Greek shipowners. K. Gilpin, "Global Slump Idles Word Cargo Fleets." Also, M. Howe, "Mood Glum for Greek Shipping Industry," New York Times, December 19, 1983.

19. There are reports that the highway connecting Western Europe with the Middle East through Yugoslavia, Greece and Turkey is used as an important drug traffic route, primarily for heroin smuggling, as is the road passing through Bulgaria. Nathan Adams, "Drugs for Guns: The Bulgarian Connection," Reader's Digest, November 1983, pp. 86-98.

20. For regional indicators of underdevelopment in Yugoslavia, see Fred Singleton and Bernard Carter, The Economy of Yugoslavia, chap. 17.

21. For alternative financing programs in Greece, see A. Papandreou, A Strategy for Greek Economic Development (Athens: Center of Economic Research, 1962), chap. 4.

22. For such provisions of Law 3250/1924, as subsequently amended, see I. Merryman, Some Problems of Greek Shoreland Development (Athens: Center of Planning and Economic Research, 1965), pp. 22, 32, 73; and Monthly Statistical Bulletin for Public Economies. Out of 26,689 stremmata conveyed to foreigners (from January 1960 to May

1964) 25,282 <u>stremmata</u> or 95 percent was shore land. (A <u>stremma</u> is 1,000 square meters.)

6

TAX STRUCTURE
AND TRENDS

INTRODUCTION

With an ever-growing public sector in Greece and an already
large one in Yugoslavia, the subject of public finance for both
countries acquires great importance not only on matters of
financing government expenditures but also on matters of
countercyclical policy. Since these two countries are currently facing relatively high rates of inflation and, at times,
high unemployment rates, policymakers have a rough time
implementing public policies to correct undesirable trends.
Although it is difficult to curb inflation and increase employment with fiscal measures alone, government policies on
taxes and expenditures, nevertheless, play a vital role in
these matters.

Differences in tax structures and government expenditures between the two countries are of great importance in
determining economic policies on income and wealth distribution, investment allocation, and growth performance. Recent policies, emphasizing reduction in inflation and an
increase in factor productivity, have generated more attention regarding the use of public finances for achieving these
goals. Such policies aim at stimulating saving and investment
even at a sacrifice of vital social programs.

Moreover, the phenomenon of a growing proportion of older people in the population presents new problems of financing social security and transfer payments in both Greece and Yugoslavia, regardless of their economic philosophy. Furthermore, the market economy of Greece moves gradually toward a larger public sector, mainly because of flaws emanating from the marketplace. On the other hand, the primarily planned economy of Yugoslavia moves more and more toward decentralization, mostly as a result of bureaucratic inefficiencies. These elements indicate that there is a notable drift toward structural similarities in the fiscal systems of the two countries.

While much attention has been devoted to the ways of financing investment for higher economic growth, not much attention has been paid to ways of financing growing government expenditures. The financing of growing government services requires ever larger amounts of revenue in the form of indirect and direct taxes.

From that point of view, structural changes and reforms seem to be needed in the public sector to raise more revenue through higher productivity. This is particularly so for Greece and Yugoslavia with an overburdened bureaucracy and a complicated tax system. Furthermore, recent inflationary pressures have led to significant distortions in the tax systems of many economies, including those of Greece and Yugoslavia. As a result, the public sector absorbs large amounts of national income mainly in the form of direct and indirect taxes, despite criticisms of misallocations and low performance by this sector. For that reason arguments for public spending reduction, tax indexing, and decontrolling the economy are put forward.

The main questions to be considered in this chapter are: What are the main differences in public finance between Greece and Yugoslavia? What types of taxes prevail in these two countries? How do taxes affect productivity? What are the main variables affecting indirect and direct taxes?

TAX STRUCTURE

As countries move to higher levels of development and higher per capita income, it is to be expected that direct taxes or taxes on personal income and profits will acquire more importance than indirect taxes, that is, taxes on goods and services. Indeed a more open policy toward foreign trade, higher urbanization, and monetization of the economies of Greece and Yugoslavia and the relative growth of salaried workers will create a favorable climate for structural changes in taxation toward higher income (direct) taxes.(1)

The gradual transfer of resources, primarily labor, from the agricultural to the more money-using industrial and services sectors, which can be observed in these two countries, as in almost all other countries of the world, is also favorable toward an increase in overall income taxes. The same thing can be said for government policies toward more employment and a more equitable income distribution. Such policies expand the tax base and, together with increases in nominal incomes because of inflation, and increases in real incomes because of productivity growth, offer fertile ground for further expansion in direct taxes compared to indirect taxes.

Average taxes, that is, general government revenue over national income, increased in Greece from 20 percent in the 1950s to 26 percent in the 1960s and 30 percent in the 1970s; in the case of the consolidated public sector of Yugoslavia, revenue changed from 34 percent of national income in 1966 to 38 percent in 1970, and 36 percent in 1980.(2) A similar pattern of change can be observed in marginal taxes during the postwar years. For Greece, marginal taxes increased from 29 percent in 1950-60 to 31 percent in 1960-70 and 33 percent in 1970-80, while for Yugoslavia, they were 44 percent in 1966-70 and 39 percent for 1970-80. Such positive marginal tax rates indicate that the tax structures in both countries have built-in flexibility; that is, independently of any relative decision, taxes change automatically with changes in national income.

The percentage increase in tax revenue over the percentage increase in national income (income elasticity of taxation) was positive and higher than one for Greece (1.35) during the three postwar decades, while for Yugoslavia it was positive and higher than one in the last two decades (1.30 in the 1960s and 1.04 in 1970s).(3) These results indicate that taxes increased proportionally more than national income during the postwar years in both Greece and Yugoslavia.

Such growing proportions of taxation, which were needed to finance ever-increasing public expenditures, support the Wagner hypothesis, which postulates that the share or ratio of public spending and taxes to national product increases with the growth of per capita income in industrializing nations.

It should be mentioned, though, that total taxes or consolidated revenues of the public sector in Yugoslavia include a number of taxes collected by special funds, such as "interest on funds for productive activities," "public roads," "waterworks," "joint enterprises," "funds for the reconstruction of Skopje and Basanska Krajina," and similar other public activities. Moreover, as a result of the decentralization policy, particularly after the economic reforms of 1965, an ever greater emphasis has been given to the "communities of interest" or state and local authorities rather than to the federal government.

Indirect taxes are transaction-based taxes levied on national product, while direct taxes are person-based levies on national income. Indirect taxes are usually shifted forward and push prices up, especially in Greece; direct taxes, that is, personal income, payroll, property, and corporate income taxes, tend to press prices downward and encourage leisure.

The structure of the Greek tax system has not changed much during the postwar years. Direct taxes are a small proportion of total taxes. They absorb only 5 percent of GDP compared to 16 percent absorbed by indirect taxes.(4)

In Yugoslavia, total direct taxes collected by the public sector absorb about 22 percent of national income compared to 14 percent absorbed by indirect taxes.(5)

Table 6.1 shows central government revenue as a percentage of national income for Greece. For Yugoslavia, similar data are covered, which include "budgetary revenue" of combined authorities (federal, republic, and local but not communities of interest and special funds). It also shows the subdivision of these revenues into direct and indirect taxes. For Greece, the portion of national income absorbed by central government taxes increased during the postwar years, as did direct taxes. The ratio of direct to indirect taxes increased from 22 percent in 1960 to 24 percent in 1970 and 31 percent in 1980. However, compared to other developed countries, this ratio remains very low. Greece's tax distributional effects are also largely ineffective.(6)

For Yugoslavia, the revenues of the combined public authorities (federal, republic, and local), as percentages of

Table 6.1. Central Government Revenues as Percentages of National Income, and Direct and Indirect Taxes as Percentages of Central Government Revenue (current prices)

	Budget Revenue			Direct Taxes			Indirect Taxes			Ratio of Direct/ Indirect Taxes		
	1960	1970	1980	1960	1970	1980	1960	1970	1980	1960	1970	1980
Greece	13.2	16.8	19.5	16.7	18.3	23.1	76.3	77.2	74.4	21.9	23.7	31.0
Yugoslavia	27.2	15.4	17.8	27.3	23.0	11.1	65.8	69.0	72.5	41.5	33.3	15.5

Note: For Yugoslavia budget accounts of combined public authorities (federal, republic, and local budgets).

Source: OECD, National Accounts, various issues; and United Nations, Statistical Yearbook, various issues.

national income declined at first from 27 percent in 1960 to 15 percent in 1970 and then increased to 18 percent in 1980. For these authorities, direct taxes as a proportion of the total budget revenue, declined from 27 percent in 1960 to 11 percent in 1980, while indirect taxes increased from 66 percent to 72 percent. As a result, the ratios of direct/ indirect taxes declined from 41 percent to 15 percent.(7) Although overall direct taxes (including those of other government bodies and various "self-managed" communities of interest, mentioned earlier) increased, those of the combined (federal, republic, and local) budgets declined, as did their total revenues as a portion of national income. This may be construed as the main result of the decentralization policy of the Yugoslav government in the 1960s and 1970s. (Simple and multiple regressions of total taxes on private consumption, imports, and inflation are presented in Table 1 of the Appendix.)

MAIN CHARACTERISTICS OF TAXATION IN GREECE

An important question of government economic policy in Greece, as well as in other countries, is how to finance government services in such a way that additional expenditures (marginal costs) for each public purpose will equal additional or marginal benefits. Although there is strong criticism of the public sector in Greece, which may be justified on grounds of bureaucracy and inefficiency, government expenditures and taxation continue to increase proportionally more than national income. This is so despite the fact that private industry spends a great deal on advertising in order to create new and more intense wants for private goods. If there is a deficiency in the quantity and quality of government services and public administration, this will have an adverse effect on the private sector and the economy as a whole.

Considering the three main alternative means of financing public expenditures, that is, taxation, issuance of government securities, and creation of money, it would seem that the first alternative is the most anti-inflationary for the Greek and Yugoslav economies. Money creation on the other hand is clearly inflationary when it exceeds the real rate of economic growth, given that income velocity of money is currently constant. The issuance of government bonds is not widespread in these economies.

It seems that public finance plays a significant role in investment policies, inflationary trends, and income distribution, especially in Greece. The occasional and temporary nature of governmental economic policy during the postwar years, similar to that housing policy of Athens, created a serious structural problem in the Greek economy. Such a policy, affected by the sociopolitical instability of the country, led to a swollen tertiary sector at the expense of neglecting the secondary sector (especially manufacturing) and, to some extent, the primary sector as well. As a result, a large class of middlemen and self-employed persons in services was created. Their average income is almost double that of salaried persons and farmers. These high incomes result primarily from high profits realized by oligopolistic or local monopolistic distributors and traders, who, in turn, spend the bulk of their earnings in unproductive, quick-profit ventures, such as speculation on urban lots or apartments, and imported luxury goods, which, in turn, feed the rate of inflation. These high profits are also used to increase the demand mainly for consumer goods, pulling prices up without offering much to improve productivity. Moreover, employment in many tertiary services, such as tourism and trade, is of seasonal and occasional nature.

Local Taxes

As in any other country, there are municipal and community authorities in Greece, with their own budgets, in addition to that of the central government. There are no separate states or republics like those in Yugoslavia or the United States. There are, though, 55 prefectures (regional administrative units) under the authority of the central government. Serious efforts are being made to decentralize central government bureaucracy in favor of these prefectures and local authorities.

In Greece, local government receipts, mainly those of municipalities and communities, account for only about 13 percent of the total (general government) taxes, compared to more than 60 percent of those of central government. They arise primarily as a result of transfers from other subsectors of the general government and the quasi-corporate government enterprises, primarily the Public Power Corporation.

State and local receipts kept declining continuously during the postwar years, as did state and local expenditure. They declined from 19 percent of total or general government receipts in 1960 to 15 percent in 1970 and 13 percent in 1980.(8) This means that, from the point of view of public finance, Greece had a centralized system during the postwar years, which continued to become even more centralized from year to year. Such a high degree of centralization in the public sector may be responsible for the high degree of bureaucracy that prevailed in the country.

On the contrary, state and local receipts in most developed countries absorb high proportions of general government revenues. For example, they absorb around 15 percent of total taxes in Italy, 29 percent in Britain, 34 percent in West Germany, 43 percent in the United States, 47 percent in Australia, 48 percent in Japan, and as much as 64 percent in Canada.

A useful form of local taxation levied from time to time in small communities in Greece was the exacting of a few days' labor per year--say 10 days--to be devoted to community development works; alternatively, an individual could pay a specified poll tax in cash. Morever, there is a 3 percent agricultural sales tax paid on wholesale purchases. Two-thirds of the yield from this tax goes to the Organization of Agricultural Insurance and the rest to the municipalities and rural police. However, revenues from this tax are limited because many such transactions remain undetected and escape payment of taxes.

Land Taxes

It is argued that a land tax is a good source of revenue for municipalities and communities. Such a tax has the advantage of eliminating the holding of idle land for social prestige or speculation, while providing, at the same time, a degree of financial independence for local authorities. Moreover, it increases the incentives to transfer ownership of land from those who left the rural sector to the remaining farmers. It exercises pressure to broaden cultivation and stimulates agricultural production.(9) The land tax then may help reduce the denudation of the countryside of its labor and other valuable resources. Therefore, a land tax, which may be progressive, can raise substantial amounts of revenue with low tax rates. This is so because it has a large base and there is not much evasion since land cannot be easily concealed and may be used as a security for tax payment. Particularly in Greece, a land tax in the countryside may prove to be beneficial not only for purposes of revenue collection but, more importantly, to force the reconstitution of small pieces of land, scattered about in different places, into larger and more efficient forms.

Because of the nonexistence of land taxation, many people use their money to buy land located near or inside the large cities, where its value increases rapidly. In Athens, for example, the average price of land increased by more than 1,000 times during the last two decades. Given that there are no taxes on capital gains in Greece, this type of riskless investment and speculation has been greatly advanced to include land speculation near seashores, highways, and other tourist places. A land or real estate tax on assessed property values would help reduce heavy concentration of population in urban centers, especially in Athens, where life has become unbearable because of pollution, traffic congestion, and other city disamenities.(10) At the same time, large amounts of revenue would be collected by municipalities and communities for financing projects of local importance. Such a real estate tax, although politically unpopular when introduced, could be considered an effective way to reduce or reverse the tendency toward the unbalanced regional growth of the past, which has resulted in denudation of the poorer areas of the countryside.

Greece has a tax on real estate sales or transfers, particularly in the urban areas, the rate being 11 percent or higher, depending on the value of the land or building sold. Such taxation, in addition to providing revenue, has the advantage of reducing land and building speculation, which is pervasive in Greece. Although speculation in land can help to ensure that land develops at an optimal rate over time, postwar instability and inflation in Greece have created a speculative psychology difficult to mitigate with other policy measures. Otherwise, such a tax does not eliminate speculation, but rather reduces it to socially acceptable levels. What these levels should be is largely a political decision for the local authority or government unit in control. For purposes of reducing congestion and environmental deterioration in such cities as Athens and Salonika, tax discrimination in favor of rural as opposed to urban areas, together with building code restrictions and proper zoning, seem to be appropriate.

Excises

Greece, along with neighboring Italy, has the most extensive system of excise taxes in Europe, with more than 30 commodity groups being covered. This excise system includes, in addition to the traditional excise goods (motor vehicles, petroleum products, tobacco products, and alcoholic beverages), such products as electrical appliances, radios, television sets, cosmetics, and other luxury items. However, as the Greek economy grows more complex, the excise system becomes more cumbersome, because enforcement relies, to a great extent, on physical controls. This excise tax process impedes the free and smooth functioning of business and trade and retards economic growth. Probably, a broadly based sales tax, similar to that in France and the United States, would be the appropriate alternative to the prevailing extensive excise system, which may be confined only to traditional excise goods and probably to entertainment services. However, Greece, with a relatively small manufacturing sector would probably have difficulty in collecting sufficient revenue in the replacing of excise taxes with a broad-based sales tax. It seems, though, that reforms in its tax structure, as a result of its membership agreement with the EEC, would also force changes in excise tax schedules in the near future.

In Greece, as in many other countries, excise taxes are levied on commodities at different rates. However, there is a current movement to reduce differential rates by introducing a value added tax. This system of indirect taxation with uniformity of tax rates discriminates less between different goods and services and increases efficiency by reducing the effects of distortion on the economy. Moreover, its administrative simplicity reduces the cost of tax collection and increases the welfare gain of the country.

For purposes of tax harmonization with EEC standards, as Articles 95-99 of the initial EEC Treaty of Rome provide,

Greek tax policy must consider a relative increase in direct taxes and a decrease or no increase in indirect taxes. Since direct taxes are paid primarily by high-income people and indirect taxes by low-income people, such a policy would not increasingly damage the welfare of low-income classes. The gradual reduction of tariffs on imports from third countries to the same level as those levied by the EEC, and on imports from the EEC, during the transitional period of accession (until their final elimination), is expected to decrease the relative share of excises and other indirect taxes. Then Greece will be forced to increase other taxes to provide needed governmental revenue.

It is obvious that the Greek economy needs structural changes toward industrialization and improvement in the public sector, particularly in its tax system. The country's accession to the EEC is expected to speed up such structural changes and bring some limitations on matters of policy-making, not only on tariffs and foreign trade in general, but also on a number of domestic economic policies, such as adjustment of taxes, elimination of export subsidies, budgetary appropriations, exchange rate fluctuations, and the like.(11) The value added tax, in place of the turnover tax, is a case in point. Given that the laws and regulations of the community must be observed by member nations, Greek laws on taxation and related matters will have to be adjusted to those of the EEC.

Value Added Taxes

The value added tax (VAT), which was first introduced by France and later by the other EEC countries and is expected to be adopted by Greece, is defined as a tax upon the difference between the total value of output minus the value of purchased material inputs and is collectible at each stage of production. It taxes all factors of production, including labor, and encourages the transfer of capital from declining industries to the successful sectors and enterprises. Moreover, without distorting the efficient allocation of resources, it helps policymakers determine whether demand for consumer goods is growing in an inflationary way or not. However, additional value added taxes themselves would, more likely, be passed on to consumers through rising prices.

From that point of view, exceptions may be needed in food and housing in order to soften the impact of VAT on poor families.

The VAT, or consumption tax, as it may be called, was adopted by the First and Second Directives of the EEC in 1967 and was implemented by the member nations. Also, the Sixth Directive of 1977, as modified by the Ninth Directive of 1978 and later directives, aims at the improvement and simplification of the VAT throughout the European Economic Community.

Greece, being already a member of the EEC, has started contemplating the implementation of the VAT and modifying its tax system in accordance with EEC policies.(12) To spur production incentives and expand supply, there is a need for a reduction in regulations, the introduction of tax reforms, and the implementation of policies intended to reduce consumption and stimulate investment. With the enactment of such policies, total demand would not be diminished but the mix would be changed toward a greater replacement of consumption by investment. By taxing wasteful spending and even replacing personal income taxes with sales or VAT taxes, saving and investment would be encouraged and work incentives toward higher productivity would be stimulated. The implementation of the VAT may also help reduce bureaucracy by simplifying the tax system. Although it may increase inflation when first introduced, to the extent that it does not replace turnover and other taxes, it will, in the long run, replace many other tax regulations that are so complicated and confusing in Greece.

With the tax system being adjusted to EEC standards, taxes upon imports and domestic commodities will become the same. Moreover, vertical monopolization, which was encouraged by the previous turnover taxes, and the movement of capital and companies into countries with low taxes will be avoided. There are considerable delays, though, in the harmonization process of special consumption taxes on certain Greek products, especially wine, despite the fact that considerable progress has been made in introducing common taxes on manufactured tobacco, mineral oil, alcohol, and beer.

However, the member nations, including Greece, are permitted enough flexibility to apply their own policies on matters of incentives for investment and the development of a tax system that would stimulate productivity and reduce inflation. In the unique case of Greece a transitional period was provided for the review and application of the value added tax and other reforms, which are badly needed, independently of EEC membership. Such reforms will reduce bureaucracy, which is pervasive throughout Greece, and will also increase the productivity of the public sector. Moreover, there will be less confusion over tax legislation, which has resulted in the expansion of the legal profession of the country.

A modification and simplification of the tax system would also help small and medium-sized enterprises, since the disadvantages of the present turnover taxes, which favor vertical integration, would be eliminated. Instead, the way would be clearer for them to adjust their size in such a way that they can enjoy the best results from economies of scale and improved factor productivity. At the same time, their independence would be preserved. As a result, small, non-vertically concentrated enterprises, which are in the majority in Greece, would find themselves in a relatively more favorable competitive position. They are the ones upon which the great pressure of EEC competition will fall and that need all the support they can get.

From the point of view of tax revenue, it would seem difficult for Greece to replace the turnover and other indirect taxes with a VAT. As mentioned earlier, the VAT is collected at each stage of production and distribution, and is more successful in countries having a high level of industrialization with many intermediate stages of production. In Greece, however, the proportion of industrial to total production is relatively low and the in-between manufacturing stages are limited. For example, Greece would collect taxes at the first stage of metal production needed for cars or aluminum products, electrical equipment, and the like, but all the other stages up to the final product would take place elsewhere, so that Greece would not benefit from tax revenues from the VAT levied at each intermediate stage. Moreover, as a result of EEC membership, Greece cannot collect tariffs on imports from the EEC, which account for more than half of its total imports. Only at the final stage of sales, whether it be at the wholesaler or retailer level, would a VAT be collected. Although parts or the total amount of revenues from tariffs are or may be substituted for consumption (domestic) or other forms of taxes, there are or may be limitations to this type of tax substitution or "circumvention" of EEC regulations.

From the above analysis it becomes clear that France, for example, can afford to have low direct (personal income) taxes because of large revenue from indirect (VAT) taxes, but Greece, with a large tertiary or services sector and limited tax-levying stages of manufacturing, may not be able to collect the needed revenue from the VAT.   Under such conditions, Greece would be forced to increase income taxes or decrease public expenditures, both of which would be painful.   A more desirable and efficient way out of this dilemma seems to lie with the rapid industrialization of the country with the main emphasis on import substitution and/or export promotion.

MAIN CHARACTERISTICS OF TAXATION IN YUGOSLAVIA

In Yugoslavia, the determination of total taxes, as well as total investment and its allocation to various sectors of the economy, takes place primarily through the national plan. The investment sum is pooled in the General Investment Fund (G.I.F.) and is held at the National Bank, which allocates it to the specialized banks for loan distribution to individual enterprises.   The G.I.F. which represents about half of the country's total gross investment, is distributed among firms and within each industry in accordance with the expected rates of return on each particular project. Via its impact on such rates of return, tax policy affects the investment behavior of Yugoslav firms.

The income or net product of each firm is computed by deducting expenditures for goods and services, as well as depreciation, from total revenue. After deducting a turnover tax and rent and 6 percent tax on capital from this income, the profit of the firm is obtained. Before 1965, net profit was equal to gross profit minus a federal tax of about 15 percent. After subtracting the internal funds (working capital fund, reserve fund, and collective consumption fund) and a 20 percent tax on these internal funds to local government, the remainder amounted to the wage bill, which was then subject to a 22 percent social security contribution and a 15 percent tax to local government.   Since 1965, interest on capital and turnover taxes and other legal and contractual obligations are subtracted from net product or income to derive "profit." From that profit the wage fund and an 18 percent tax (exclusive of social security contribution), as well as the business fund and an 8 percent estimated tax are subtracted to determine the wage bill.(13)

The wage bill thus is a function of each firm's profit and as such is not included in the cost of production. Although the state guarantees about 80 percent of the hiring (basic) wages of the employees, actual wages vary according to the profits of the firm.

The Yugoslav tax policy favors investment in and production of labor-intensive goods and services because of the relative scarcity of capital and the surplus rural labor, which moves rapidly into the cities (about 100,000 workers per year) or seeks better opportunities abroad. In addition, tax incentives for labor-intensive investment help increase exports and improve the balance of trade of the country.

Taxation and Decentralization

Although independent taxing power was given to the republics, provinces, and communes as early as 1952, further decentralization in 1965 and 1974 provided for the transfer of budgetary functions from the federal level to lower self-managed communities, which are responsible for health, education, culture, and other social welfare services. As a result, the federal budget accounts for about 60 percent of total tax revenue, republican and provincial budgets for 18 percent, and city and commune budgets for the remaining 22 percent.(14) The main sources of federal revenue are customs duties, taxes on business capital, and contributions from republics and provinces. Income taxes (mainly taxes on income of enterprises, personal income from the social and private sector, and income from real estate) and turnover taxes are collected by republican, provincial, and especially commune authorities. In addition to proportional income taxes in each class, with some variation for each republic, there is a commune progressive income tax, with rates varying from 3 to 70 percent of the taxable income and an exemption of 20,000 dinars per family. In this type of income tax there is a great deal of tax evasion, mainly by professional classes.

Turnover taxes are levied at the retail or final consumption stage. The rate of the federal takeover tax is fixed at 12 percent on all commodities, except alcohol and fuel, which are subject to higher, varying rates. Food, educational equipment, children's clothing, and certain other items are exempt. Turnover tax rates for the republics (1.5 to 3 percent) and the communes (3 to 6 percent) are lower than the federal ones.(15) In contrast to what prevails in Greece and other western economies, particularly in the United States, where the federal government contributes revenues (revenue sharing) to state and local governments, the Yugoslav republics and provinces contribute a fixed portion of their turnover and excise taxes to the federal government.

Income and profit taxes, as well as subsidy revenues, are collected primarily by republics, provinces, cities, and communes. Customs duties belong exclusively to the federation. Categories of government collect turnover and excise taxes. In addition to the budgetary receipts mentioned above, which account for less than about 20 percent of gross material product, there are the "receipts of communities of interest," about 20 percent of GMP, which include revenue for education, health, pensions, child welfare, and unemployment. Moreover, there are the "receipts of special funds," which include revenue for productive activities, joint ventures of enterprises, public roads, and waterworks. The last category of revenue accounts for about 5 percent of GMP. In accordance with decentralization policies, the relative portion of budgetary receipts and that of receipts of special funds declined during the 1970s, while that of receipts of communities of interest increased.

Tax Rates and Trends

Budgetary receipts, which include the federal, republic, and local budgets, declined from 34 percent of GMP in 1953 to 32 percent in 1960, 25 percent in 1970 and about 20 percent in 1980. A more dramatic decrease took place in the budgetary direct taxes, which declined from 8 percent of GMP in 1958 to 4 percent in 1970 and to about 2 percent in 1980. At the same time, indirect taxes remained almost stationary, around 10 percent of GMP, not much different from those of Greece.(16) As was expected, the ratio of direct to indirect budgetary taxes declined, primarily because of the decline in direct taxes. This is an annual phenomenon for other countries and is mainly the result of the decentralization policy in the Yugoslav economy. This ratio was 80 percent in 1958, 38 percent in 1970 and about 20 percent in 1980.

Policymakers in Yugoslavia try to maintain balanced budgets and price stability, especially through the effects of heavy hidden turnover or sales taxes (the equivalent of value added taxes) and controls. Such taxes siphon off large amounts of income and purchasing power from the working people to finance government outlays. Despite these measures, chronic inflation is a serious drag on the economy and frequently takes the form of supply shortages, consumer lines, and even black market conditions for commodities in short supply. To deal with this problem, procurement prices are raised above what consumers pay and the difference is covered by subsidies. Therefore, large amounts of collected taxes are paid back through budget outlays to keep production of food and other necessities at proper levels.

The graduation in the scale of turnover taxes is related to the classification of a product as either "nonnecessity," "luxury," or "socially harmful." Although recent reforms tend to reproduce the fiscal role of turnover taxes in favor of new taxes on profits of enterprises, capital charges, and so forth, they still constitute about one-third or more of the budget's revenue in Yugoslavia. This is so because collection of turnover taxes is easier and manipulation by lower production units is more difficult than in the collection of profit taxes.

As a result of the gradual shift in imports away from consumer and capital goods, which carry comparatively high tariffs, rates in favor of raw material and intermediate goods, with low tariff rates, federal revenues from customs duties started to decline. Moreover, the termination of the 10 percent import duty surcharge in mid-1980 and the relative decline in the volume of imports had considerable adverse effects on revenue from tariffs. Only receipts from sales and turnover taxes grew at just about the rate of inflation (around 30 percent annually), while the revenue of the other government bodies and the various "self-managed" communities of interest grew by less than the inflationary rate.

DIRECT TAXES

Direct taxes, which are primarily income taxes collected by the governments of both countries, were an important source of public revenue also in ancient times. As was mentioned earlier, Athens (Solon's laws) and Rome relied on income taxes, progressive in character, as did medieval Europe (based on the gross product of land). However, the rise of industry and the expansion of domestic and primarily foreign trade in Greece and Yugoslavia, as in other developing nations, led to the extensive use of indirect taxes. The increasingly pecuniary nature of economic life though, and the quest for an improvement in income distribution, particularly in Greece, call for a shift to direct taxation in the form of income and/or property taxes.

Direct taxes of the central government, which normally reside at their original impact point and are not shifted forward or backward by the bearer of the burden, absorb close to one-third of total tax revenue in Greece and far less in Yugoslavia. They increased from 17 percent of total tax revenue of the central government of Greece in 1960 to 30 percent in 1981. On the contrary, they declined from 27 percent in 1960 to 12 percent in 1980 for Yugoslavia. Greece seems to follow the trend of a growing population of direct taxes that prevails in the EEC and other developed market economies. Yugoslavia, on the other hand, follows the opposite trend of relatively declining proportions of direct taxes, collected by government (federal, republics, and local) mainly because of the decentralization process from the central authorities to the local "communities of interest."

Because of the detrimental effects of highly progressive taxes on investment and production incentives, a number of countries, including Greece, are in the process of reviewing or implementing counter measures. Another reason for such measures may be the fact that high rates of taxation could lead to lower tax revenue because of the resulting disincentives for work and the expected lower levels of investment and production (supply-side arguments). Raising taxes by increasing tax rates beyond a certain point may decrease total revenue by reducing the tax base. This is analagous to the increase in prices by monopolists in order to raise profits, which may lead to a decrease in total profits because of a proportionally larger decrease in demand. However, tax incentives to producers for investment stimulation and industrial growth should not be used to shore up obsolescence and perpetuate inefficiency.

Primarily because of the impact of inflation, Greece introduced legislation in 1980 that reduced the rates of personal income taxes for all brackets.(17)   Different tax reductions were introduced for different classes, such as merchants, self-employed persons, clerks, and pensioners. As Figure 6.1 shows, the highest tax rates are applied to the incomes of merchants (varying from 3.4 percent for taxable income of 300,000 to 350,000 drachmas to 40.9 percent for income above 1,500,000 drachmas), followed by tax rates on income of professionals; while clerks and pensioners pay the lowest rates (varying from 1.9 to 32.2 percent, respectively). Taxable income is what remains from salaries after social security payments and a small contribution to the insurance of rural workers have been deducted.

Taxes on income and profits, as percentages of GDP, in Greece are less than half (4.4) of those of the EEC (11.5, average of France [7.5], Italy [13.9], West Germany [8.4], and the United Kingdom [14.8]).   As percentages of total taxation, they are (15.5) again about half of those of the EEC (30.8). Taxes on corporate income in Greece, as a percentage of GDP, are around half (1.14) of those of the EEC (2.13), while as percentages of total taxation, 4.06 compared to 5.75 for the EEC (average of the four large countries).(18)

With a recent law (1364/1982), Greece introduced a property tax similar to that of France. Thus for owners of real estate property worth more than 25 million drachmas the tax is 0.5 percent on the 10 million drachmas from 25 million to 35 million. For every additional 10 million drachmas property value, the tax rate increases progressively by 0.5 percent, but to no more than 2 percent. If the other spouse also has property, then 35 (25 + 10) million drachmas worth of property is exempted from any tax payment and the above tax rates (from 0.5 to 2 percent) start on property worth more than 35 million drachmas (or more than $350,000).(19)

This property tax is very small compared to other Western countries and regions. In New York, for example, property tax is about 9 percent of the assessed value and there are no exemptions, as there are in Greece for 25 million drachmas worth of property for a single person or 35 million for a couple when both have property. Such property

Figure 6.1. Income Taxes of Persons with Wife and Two Children in Greece (effective after 1981)

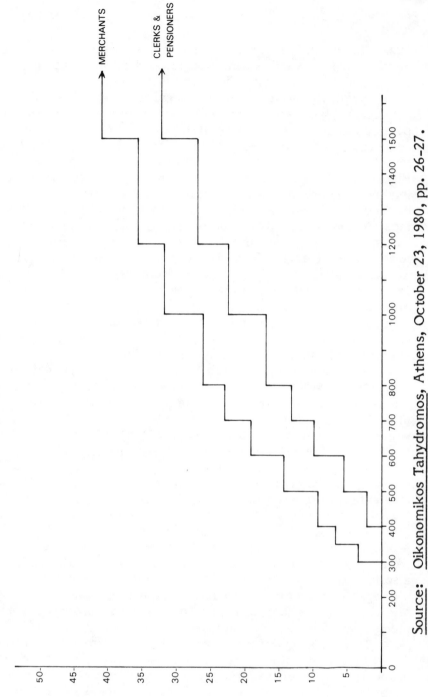

Source: Oikonomikos Tahydromos, Athens, October 23, 1980, pp. 26-27.

taxes, with even higher rates than the ones mentioned above, seem to be needed by the government not only for revenue but also for decentralizing urban centers, particularly Athens.

All forms of corporations and companies (joint stock companies, limited liability companies, and proprietorships) in Greece are liable to pay income or profit taxes (Laws 3325/1955 and 3843/1958). Taxable corporate income is determined after dividends and fees of the executives are subtracted. The latter are subject to personal income taxes and are withheld and paid by the corporations. Ploughback or undistributed profits (regular or extra) are subject to corporate income taxes. Dividends from stocks already listed on the Stock Exchange of Athens are subject to a tax rate of 38 percent if the stocks are personal and 41 percent if they are non-personal. If the stocks have not been listed on the stock exchange the rates are 43 percent and 47 percent, respectively. However, an amount of 25,000 drachmas per stockholder is deducted from the dividends of the same company and 100,000 drachmas for all dividends from different companies.

Incomes of enterprises or profits are subject to taxes after the cost of operation, donations (to public, educational, religious, and athletic institutions), and depreciation are subtracted. Rates of depreciation vary from 4 to 15 percent for machinery, 8 percent for factory structures, warehouses and hotels, 5 percent for other buildings, 20 percent for office furniture, 30 percent for hotel furniture, and 100 percent for tools and repair of instruments in operation (Decree 88/1973). Incomes from agricultural enterprises up to 1 million drachmas annually (an increase from 300,000 drachmas previously) are exempted from taxation.

The tax rate is 40 percent on the taxable income of domestic and foreign corporations. However, for domestic industrial and mining corporations whose stocks are listed on the Stock Exchange of Athens, the tax rate is 35 percent. Moreover, there is a contribution to the Organization of Agricultural Insurance for the pensions of farmers, which, added to the tax rates above, raise them to 43.40 and 38.24 respectively.(20) To avoid double taxation, taxes paid on income earned in a foreign country and taxable in Greece are deducted from the taxes due. For this reason, agreements with many countries have since been negotiated.

Net income from rent, which is subject to taxation, is gross income minus mortgage interest and a fixed amount of 25 percent deducted for depreciation, insurance, other taxes, and repairs. The deduction of 25 percent is reduced to 10 percent on rents from stores, offices, and warehouses and 5 percent on rents from open lots. On the gross income from rents (whether actual or imputed) of buildings in the Athens metropolitan area and Salonika a 3 percent special duty is imposed for waterworks.

Certain provisions arrange for the problems of over or underpricing of products and services in foreign transactions. Export incentives are provided through deductions from taxable income varying from 3 percent for industrial enterprises to 2 percent for agricultural enterprises and 1 percent for other exporting companies.

Income from interest is completely free of taxes in Greece. However, in the EEC countries such income is subject to taxes of about 35 percent. The same is true for other market economies, such as the United States, where income from interest is added and taxed together with other incomes as is income from dividends, after a deduction of certain amounts (up to 200 dollars per single taxpayer and 400 dollars for couples with joint tax returns). It would seem that, after certain exemptions, taxes on interest would encourage purchasing of more stocks and bonds and increase direct investment. From that point of view, a tax treatment of interest similar to that of dividends seems to be appropriate.

In comparison with other Western European countries, Greece has the lowest rates of income tax, followed by France. Harmonization of the tax system of Greece to that of the EEC would most probably lead to a change in the tax structure of the country toward higher proportions of direct taxes (including social security contributions) relative to total tax revenue.(21) However, social and political factors, in addition to pressures from groups of taxpayers that are powerful in Greece, may delay such structural changes in the foreseeable future.

For purposes of providing budgetary revenue and restricting personal consumption and wealth accumulation, progressive income taxes are used in both Greece and Yugoslavia. However, maximum tax limits are introduced to minimize disincentive effects on labor allocation, performance, and improvement of skills. Nevertheless, problems of tax evasion perpetrated by scientists, artists, writers, and primarily middlemen appear in both countries. To eliminate or reduce tax evasion and loopholes, both governments try from time to time to dig deeply into high incomes but it is usually said that this is "carried out with a sieve." Thus measures such as the requirement made by the Greek government recently that the origin of income be reported when property is bought or an investment is made proved not to be too effective. Instead, such measures discouraged investment and encouraged the outflow of capital abroad. In a way, the cure turned out to be more harmful than the disease itself.

A rough approximation of tax evasion can be made by comparing income tax revenues, as proportions of national income, of different countries with similar tax rates. Thus income taxes in Greece absorb about 4 percent of national income, compared with 16 percent in the United States. However, progressive tax rates in Greece start at around 4 percent of taxable income and go to 41 percent; in the United States they start at 14 percent and go to 50 percent (70 percent before 1981). Considering these differences, it can be said that tax evasion in Greece, compared to the United States tax revenues, is roughly 6 to 8 percent of national income (about 228 billion drachmas or close to 1.7 billion dollars in 1981).(22)

Tax evasion in Greece seems to be rampant, probably the highest in Europe. Payoffs by tax evaders are common. Go-betweens collect payoffs from both the individual tax evaders and the officials in the ministry who usually agree to settle for a fraction of the tax assessed. Thus in 1981 300,000 drachmas ($5,000) payoff was collected to save two million drachmas.(23) Similar payoffs take place in other ministries for other activities, primarily for import licensing. This is part of the system of rousfeti or patronage that has plagued Greek since its independence in the 1820s. Businessmen get bank loans, parents obtain jobs for their children, and civil servants get their promotions and privileges through patronage, with not much regard for merit or performance.

As mentioned earlier, both Yugoslavia and Greece have a progressive income tax system. With inflation, when money incomes rise at the same rate as prices, real income remains the same. However, under progressive taxation, after tax real incomes decline because tax rates increase as nominal or money incomes rise. Thus people find themselves sliding up the rate brackets and paying higher taxes although their real incomes remain constant or may even decline. The same thing can be said for nominal gains resulting from increases in the prices of assets because of inflation. From that point of view, the inflationary setting of the Greek and Yugoslav economies has had a major impact on income taxes. Both countries have implemented or considered measures of indexation to mitigate the taxpayer's real burden, similar to measures that have been adopted in Canada and some Western European and Latin American countries and contemplated in the United States.

Direct taxes are primarily levied on personal income and on corporate income or income of enterprises (profits). As such, their changes are affected by changes in nominal income, which, in turn, is affected by inflation. As income increases, direct taxes are expected to increase even more, as long as progressive tax system prevails. This is true for Greece, where the elasticity of direct taxes with respect to national income was higher than one (varying from 1.35 in 1950-60 to 1.25 in 1960-70 and 1.41 in 1970-80). In Yugoslavia, however, the elasticity of budgetary direct taxes remained lower than one for all three decades considered (varying from 0.81 in 1958-60 to 0.37 in 1960-70 and 0.40 in 1970-80).(24)

On the other hand, the elasticities of direct taxes with respect to total taxes (general government revenue) were 0.97 in 1950-60, 0.84 in 1960-70, and 1.18 in 1970-80 for Greece; for Yugoslavia (central government), they were 1.70 in 1958-60, 0.74 in 1960-70, and 0.35 in 1970-76. These results indicate that direct taxes grew proportionally more than total taxes in the 1970s, compared to the previous decades, for Greece and less for Yugoslavia.(25) However, as a proportion of total taxes they still remain low compared to other EEC countries.

Although personal income tax rates in Greece and Yugoslavia are not as high as in most Western developed countries, tax reductions to stimulate personal incentives to work may increase production, thereby increasing tax revenue. However, if tax cuts are not matched with more tax receipts from new work efforts and higher levels of production, budget deficits may be pushed upward. Then public finance policies may be directed to other forms of taxation, notably value added taxes, which discourage wasteful spending especially in Greece, where the propensity to consume seems to be high lately.(26)

In order to reveal the relationship between direct taxes and inflation, as well as between imports and private consumption, simple and multiple correlations have been used. In the simple correlations of Table B.2 of the Appendix, the regression coefficient of direct taxes on inflation was higher than that of private consumption, as well as that on imports, for both countries. Comparatively speaking, all coefficients in simple, as well as in multiple regressions (except for imports), were higher for Greece than for Yugoslavia. This indicates that the independent variables of inflation, imports, and private consumption were more important in determining direct taxes in Greece than in Yugoslavia. This might be due to greater rigidity in the Yugoslav tax system compared with that of Greece.

In all cases considered in Table B.2 of the Appendix the correlations were high, because the value of the corrected coefficient of determination was close to one (R   0.820), though lower in Yugoslavia than in Greece. Although the Durbin-Watson (D-W) statistics were relatively high in almost all the regressions for Greece, for Yugoslavia they were low enough to signify the existence of serial correlation.

INDIRECT TAXES

Indirect or in rem taxes, which are levied independently of the owner's ability to pay and are likely to be shiftable forward, constitute the largest part of government revenue in Greece and Yugoslavia, as they do in most developing nations. They include mainly turnover or sales taxes, excises, stamp duties, and tariffs.

As Figure 6.2 shows, in Greece the indirect taxes, as a percentage of national income, were not much different from those of Yugoslavia. On the average, they were constant and around 10 percent of national income for Yugoslavia and gradually increasing to about 15 percent for Greece. For the EEC they were constant at around 15 percent of national income.

Indirect taxes account for about 70 percent of central government revenue in both Greece and Yugoslavia. In

Figure 6.2.   Indirect Taxes as Percentages of National Income

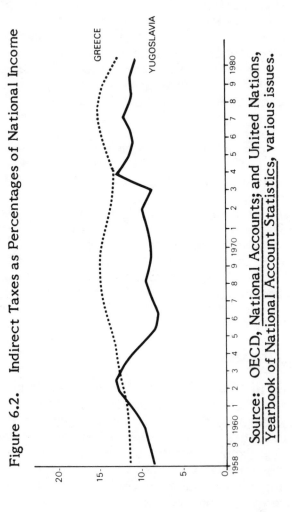

GREECE

YUGOSLAVIA

Source: OECD, National Accounts; and United Nations,
Yearbook of National Account Statistics, various issues.

178

Greece the largest proportions of such indirect taxes come from stamp duties (about 28 percent of total indirect taxes), turnover taxes (20 percent), petroleum products taxes (14 percent), tobacco taxes (9 percent), taxes on transport (6 percent), and taxes on real estate transfers (4 percent). Excises or taxes on special consumer goods, including those on petroleum, tobacco, sugar and beverages account for about 30 percent; broad-based taxes account for more than 50 percent of the total revenue raised from indirect taxes. Stamp duties are levied at 2.4 percent on invoices and 1.3 percent in other cases. Turnover taxes on domestic or imported manufactured goods are levied at 8 percent or less. Import ad valorem duties, primarily on luxuries, vary from 10 to 50 percent.

There are no general sales taxes in Greece and Yugoslavia such as one may find in many other countries, especially the developed ones. However, there are high turnover taxes, tariffs, and other forms of indirect taxes, which can be considered as expenditure or consumption taxes.

Empirically, indirect taxes, which depend more on imports than on private consumption and inflation, are higher in Greece than in the EEC. Tax harmonization with the EEC, as a result of Greece's membership, would mean a relative increase in direct taxes in Greece, as well as structural changes in both direct and indirect taxes. One can expect that the same situation will be encountered with other EEC candidates, notably Spain, Portugal, Turkey, and it is to be hoped, Yugoslavia. As mentioned earlier, a major tax reform contemplated at present for Greece is the introduction of the VAT to replace the present turnover and other complicated indirect taxes.

The VAT, as an expenditure tax, discourages consumption spending in favor of savings and investments, which, in turn, are associated with higher rates of economic growth. The use of VAT in both countries, and particularly in Greece, would simplify the tax system, decrease tax evasion, and stimulate productivity. The VAT, as an indirect proportional tax on the value of all goods and services included in a firm's invoices, reduced by the amount of previous VAT liability, is less painful and more easily collectible with low administrative costs.(27) Contrary to turnover taxes, it discourages vertical concentration of enterprises, encourages competition, and assists policymakers in adjusting demand to the conditions of supply.

Because the advantages of the VAT seem to exceed its disadvantages, it is suggested that it would be proper to shift these countries' burden away from taxes on income and profits toward a value added tax. In order to soften the impact of the VAT on low-income people, a system of gradually decreasing income tax credits can be introduced that would make this tax progressive and fair. Moreover, other fiscal policy prescriptions, in addition to the tax measures, can be used to improve distribution of income and wealth in both Greece and Yugoslavia.

The accession of Greece to the EEC, as the tenth member of the community will mean a further decline in indirect taxes collected from imports. However, the introduction of the VAT is expected to increase tax revenue and help make up for the reduction in indirect taxes arising from lower tariffs. But as long as the elasticities of total government expenditures in relation to GDP keep on growing, as they did in Greece during the postwar years, other forms of taxation, mainly higher direct income taxes, will probably be used to fill the gap.

High tariffs on imported goods (which account for about 25 percent of central government revenue) make their prices higher in Greece and Yugoslavia compared with other countries.(28) Elimination or reduction of such tariffs and excise taxes in Greece, according to the directives of the EEC, would exert pressure on domestic industries producing the same goods or close substitutes. However, such a competitive process has become necessary in order to reduce or eliminate inefficiency, despite the expected detrimental effects on employment conditions in a number of small and middle-sized enterprises.

The elasticities of indirect taxes, with respect to private consumption, imports, and gross domestic product (GDP), were higher in Greece than in Yugoslavia during the 1950s and 1960s. During the 1970s, however, these elasticities were higher in Yugoslavia than in Greece. As Table 6.2 shows, all these elasticities for Greece were higher than 1 for all three decades considered (except for the import elasticity of indirect taxes in 1970-80), while for Yugoslavia they were higher than 1 only in the 1970s. Moreover, the elasticities of indirect taxes with respect to imports and GDP were declining for Greece and growing for Yugoslavia during the postwar years.(29) Such findings support the argument that countries with comparatively low incomes rely more heavily on indirect taxes than countries with high per capita income. However, for Yugoslavia there was a surprising upward turn in all three elasticities considered in the 1970s compared to those of the two previous decades, which remained relatively constant. Thus for each 1 percent increase in private consumption there was more than 1.5 percent increase in indirect taxes in Yugoslavia, as was also the case for imports and GDP in the 1970s.

Indirect taxes are primarily consumption taxes and as such are affected by changes in private consumption, imports, and inflation. In order to examine the relationship of indirect taxes and these variables, simple and multiple regressions with statistical data for the years 1950-80 for Greece and 1953-80 for Yugoslavia were used.

Table 6.2. Elasticities of Indirect Taxes with Respect to Private Consumption (PRC), Imports (IMP), and Gross Domestic Product (GDP) (current prices)

	PRC	IMP	GDP
Greece			
1950-60	1.44	1.56	1.35
1960-70	1.74	1.22	1.41
1970-80	1.10	0.74	1.06
Yugoslavia			
1956-60	1.00	0.62	0.73
1960-70	0.80	0.66	0.91
1970-80	1.62	1.52	1.57

Source: OECD, National Accounts, various issues.

The simple regressions of Table B.3 of the Appendix indicate that for Yugoslavia inflation was a more important variable than imports in explaining changes in indirect taxes. For Greece, on the other hand, imports were a more important variable than inflation. Thus the slope of the regression line of indirect taxes on inflation was 0.68 for Yugoslavia and only 0.14 for Greece. This means that, on the average, every 1 percent change in inflation was related to a 0.68 percent change in indirect taxes in Yugoslavia and a 0.14 percent change in Greece. Imports, though, were more important in explaining changes in indirect taxes in Greece (regression coefficient 0.57) than in Yugoslavia (0.42) while the regression coefficient of indirect taxes on private consumption was in between for both countries (0.2).(30) Thus in Greece an increase in imports by 100 drachmas was accompanied by an increase in government revenue from indirect taxes by 57 drachmas, while in Yugoslavia an increase in imports by 100 dinars was related to an increase in indirect taxes by 42 dinars. In all cases the corrected coefficients of determination were 0.90 in both countries, indicating a very good fit of the regression lines.

Table B.3 of the Appendix shows the results of multiple regressions of indirect taxes on private consumption, imports, and inflation for the 1950-80 period. For both Greece and Yugoslavia the fit for the regression lines was very good. The corrected coefficient of determination was more than 0.98 in both cases. Moreover, the D-W statistic was high enough to signify the nonexistence of serial correlation. Again, the inflation coefficient was higher than the import coefficient for Yugoslavia and vice versa for Greece. This indicates that, for Yugoslavia, inflation was a more significant variable in explaining changes in indirect taxes than imports; for Greece, the imports variable was more significant than inflation. Therefore, policymakers on matters of public finance may expect (ceteris paribus) a close relationship between indirect taxes and inflation in Yugoslavia and indirect taxes and imports in Greece.

INFLATION AND TAXATION

Greece follows, more or less, the Keynesian prescription for deficit spending, as do many other market economies. Such deficit spending can be financed by either creating new money or selling bonds or other government securities to the public. In all cases, competition between the government and the private sector for scarce economic resources is intensified. Ceteris paribus, the increase in money supply leads to inflation. Deficit financing through borrowing also leads to inflation because it absorbs primarily private saving, which is used mainly for government consumption. This is the way for government to shove other borrowers aside in order to finance the deficit, while investors are crowded out of the credit markets (crowd-out effect) and interest rates tend to rise because of the growing demand for loanable funds. Inflation, in turn, poisons entrepreneurial initiatives and directs investment to short-term speculative ventures or to real estate business, which is usual in Greece.

As was explained previously, a good part of inflation may be due to monetizing central government deficits, which has become a familiar practice in recent years. While Yugoslavia's postwar central government budgets were either balanced or showed a small surplus, those of Greece showed large deficits. Thus budget deficits for Greece (administrative basis) increased from 7.25 percent of GDP in 1977 to 15 percent in 1981, while the growth of money supply was also high (more than 20 percent) in recent years.

Increases in money supply and the rates of inflation were greater in Yugoslavia compared to those of Greece during the postwar period considered. Therefore, it is expected that inflation will be a more significant variable in economic policy for Yugoslavia than for Greece.

Taxation at progressive rates allows the governments of Yugoslavia and especially of Greece to thrive on inflation while people with fixed incomes, or with incomes growing proportionally less than the increases in prices, suffer. With inflation rates higher than wage rates, their modest real incomes, provided mainly through low-paying jobs and private or public retirement systems, are either reduced or not growing. Inflation then provides for unlegislated tax increases that create a remarkable government prosperity. In such an inflationary bonanza, pay increases go to the government's treasury rather than into the employees' pockets. With every rise in income that merely keeps pace with inflation, taxpayers are forced to pay higher taxes as they are propelled into higher brackets.

Inflation is a practical way of transferring command over resources from individuals to the public sector. This can occur either when the monetary authorities issue more money to satisfy demand for higher nominal incomes because of inflation, or when tax rates are progressive.

Additional tax revenues in both countries are then provided by inflation. This takes place through increases in income and spending, pari passu with inflation, and the automatic increases in rates under the progressive tax system. These additional revenues finance additional government expenditures, which stimulate inflation (as long as they are not directed toward productive investment), and the public sector keeps on expanding. For the government, then, inflation is a wonderful tax. From that point of view, inflationary financing for the governments of Greece and Yugoslavia seems to have all the attractions of an invisible, "indirect" tax. It is a form of taxation that can easily be enforced and the public finds hard to evade. But, from the point of view of investment and growth, inflation poisons incentives and melts away savings. It gradually devalues the currency and undermines the economic system of the countries in which it occurs.

To offset or neutralize the impact of inflation on taxation, tax indexing may be suggested for Greece and Yugoslavia. If the income tax were indexed to the inflation rate tax rates would not rise unless real income also rose. However, although indexing can be expected to eliminate the tax bracket creep induced by inflation, it would reduce government revenue to lower amounts than anticipated. That is why such indexing can be rejected directly or indirectly by government officials and legislators, whose political dividends from inflation would disappear. In such a case, each time the government officials decided to raise expenditures for grandiose projects they would be forced to show a very apparent rise in taxes.(31) Inflation-generated revenue allows political leaders and elected officials to cut taxes and be generous in financing new services and facilities so they can be easily reelected. In other words, they may accommodate themselves to the inflationary spirals because they are well served by perpetuating the status quo.

With the adjustment or indexing of the tax system for inflation, as consumer prices rise, so do the standard deduction, the personal exemption, and both ends of each tax bracket. Indexing, then, would end unlegislated increases in tax revenues and would automatically limit governmental spending. However, it might lead to bigger deficits in the Greek and Yugoslav budgets if spending is not held in check. It might also limit the government's ability to use tax cuts for countercyclical purposes.

The acceleration of inflation has increased the effective rate of taxation on income in both countries, especially in Greece. Therefore, investment in income-bearing ventures, as in the case of manufacturing, for example, has been discouraged in favor of investment in owner-occupied housing, where limited or no property taxes are paid. The nonneutral effects of inflation on the Greek tax system has misdirected capital investment toward owner-occupied homes in urban areas at the expense of rapid industrialization of the country. The inflation-tax interactions were partially responsible for high investment concentration in housing in Athens, Salonika, Patras, Herakleion, and other urban centers in Greece, as well as in Belgrade, Zagreb, Ljubljana, Titograd, and Skopje in Yugoslavia. This is one of the main reasons for the high prices of houses and apartments in these cities despite the extensive capital formation in housing and the low expected rate of return on investment in this sector. The rapid increase of the housing sector and the relatively slow increase of the manufacturing sector in Greece may have a common explanation, the interaction between inflation and the tax system. Although interest income is exempt from taxation and interest rates paid by thrift institutions are relatively high, the almost nonexistent property taxes, together with inflation, increase incentives for channeling accumulated saving into housing and real estate speculation to the neglect of investment in productive ventures that would provide permanent jobs and higher incomes.

Greater emphasis on the reduction in overspending and income taxes may increase productivity, encourage exports, and combat inflation. Also, a faster rate of depreciation, that is, higher deductions from taxable income for the cost of productive assets, and low capital gains taxes, may be additional measures to stimulate investment in more efficient equipment, the creation of new jobs, and the lessening of stagflation.

To stimulate competition and encourage initial investment in productive enterprises, favorable loans and a tax structure favoring small and new, employment-creating firms should also be considered by the monetary or fiscal authorities of Greece and Yugoslavia. Perhaps the widespread practice of borrowing funds by government or other public enterprises for investment purposes should continue in these two countries because the private sector may be unable to invest in long-term infrastructural projects. However, if such borrowing takes place to finance further consumption, then the government competes with productive enterprises for a finite supply of lendable funds and inflation could be expected to increase.

As Greece and Yugoslavia are bedeviled simultaneously by inflation and unemployment, policymakers in these countries are hard put to implement proper tax measures to correct undesirable trends. Indirect taxes, which are levied against goods and services, and especially direct (income) taxes are largely affected by inflation. Indirect taxes, which include customs duties and turnover taxes, are more or less proportional to the value of goods and services on which they are levied. From that point of view, an increase in prices would bring about an increase in indirect taxes, which would, most likely offset growing government expenditures caused by inflation. Therefore, the real value of ad valorem excises, tariffs, and other indirect taxes will be largely unaffected by inflation, or affected less than that of direct progressive taxes.

In order to lighten the punitive tax burden resulting from inflation, the governments of Greece and Yugoslavia try to give a jolt to the economy by changing the tax structure and stimulating economic efficiency. Their main fiscal dilemma is how to provide sufficient tax revenue without discouraging production incentives and overburdening the low and middle-income classes.

For purposes of examining the relationship between inflation and taxation related elasticities were used. For the measurement of inflation elasticity of taxation, the percentage changes in tax revenue over the percentage changes in inflation were used. Similar formulas can be used for the calculation of elasticities of taxes with respect to private consumption and imports.

During the last decade the inflation elasticity of taxation was 9.6 for Greece and 1.6 for Yugoslavia, compared to 2.3 for the EEC, 2.7 for Japan, and 2 for the United States. Thus each 1 percent change in inflation was related to a 9.6 percent change in total taxes in Greece, 1.6 percent in Yugoslavia, 2.3 percent in the EEC, and 2 percent in the United States. Tax revenue in Greece seems to be more sensitive to inflation than that of Yugoslavia, and that of the United States a little less sensitive compared to the EEC.

During the 1970s, the elasticities of direct taxes with respect to inflation were 7.4 for Greece and 0.6 for Yugoslavia; those of indirect taxes on inflation were 5.8 for Greece and 2.7 for Yugoslavia, respectively.(32) This means that each 1 percent increase in prices was associated with a 7.4 percent increase in direct taxes and a 5.8 percent increase in indirect taxes for Greece; for Yugoslavia, it was an increase of 0.6 percent and 2.7 percent respectively. These results indicate that indirect and primarily direct taxes were more sensitive to inflation in Greece than in Yugoslavia during that period, or that there is more flexibility, with respect to inflation, in the tax system of Greece compared with that of Yugoslavia.

In addition to the elasticities of taxation with respect to inflation, simple and multiple regressions of taxes on inflation were used (see Tables B.1, B.2, B.3 of the Appendix and related analyses there). The empirical results reveal that there is a high correlation between direct taxes and inflation as well as total taxes and inflation for both Greece and Yugoslavia. With the usual caveats regarding causation, this implies that inflation is a significant variable in explaining changes in tax revenue in general and direct taxes in particular for both countries.

Such findings may be useful for proper policymaking in these two countries as well as other countries with similar problems. Although it is difficult to slay the ogre of inflation with tax measures alone, proper tax policies can have significant effects upon its behavior because of the close relationship between these two variables.

NOTES

1. For similar conclusions regarding other countries, see R. Musgrave and P. Musgrave, Public Finance in Theory and Practice, 3d ed. (New York: McGraw-Hill, 1980), pp. 322-33; A. Tait, W. Gratz, and B. Eichengreen, "International Comparisons of Taxation for Selected Developing Countries, 1972-76" IMF Staff Papers 26, (1979) 123-56.

2. Organization for Economic Cooperation and Development (OECD), Economic Surveys: Yugoslavia; and OECD, National Accounts, various issues. In developed countries, total tax revenue varies from 30 percent of national income for Japan and the United States (a sizable growth from 16 percent in 1950), 35 percent for Australia, 40

percent for Canada, 45 percent of GDP for the EEC, and 60 percent of NMP for the Soviet Union.

3. For the United States, the income elasticities of taxation were 1.4 in 1950-60, 1.2 in 1960-70, and 1.1 in 1970-80, compared to 1.0, 1.1, and 1.3 for Japan respectively. For the EEC, the GDP elasticity of taxation was 1.2 in 1970-80.

4. Direct taxes in Greece amounted to 118.1 million drachmas in 1981 (65.6 million income taxes on individuals, 17.1 million on corporations, 6.4 million property taxes, and 29 million drachmas from other sources.) Indirect taxes were 262.2 million drachmas (118.6 million in consumption taxes on domestic products, 65.5 million in consumption taxes on imported goods, 32.0 million in stamp duties, 19.6 million in custom duties, 8.7 million in real estate transaction taxes, and 18.8 million drachmas in other indirect taxes). P. Linardos-Rylmon, "Oikouomia Se Arithmus," (Economy in Numbers), Oikonomikos Tahydromos, Athens, July 22, 1982, p. 18.

5. Direct taxes for the EEC are around 14 percent of GDP, as are indirect taxes. For the United States, direct taxes are about 17 percent of national income, while indirect taxes are 10 percent.

6. A U-shaped tax rate pattern in Greece was found by D. Karageorgas. See his "Distribution of Tax Burden by Income Groups in Greece," Economic Journal 83 (1973): 436-48. However, a bell-shaped tax rate structure, which burdens upper-middle income brackets relatively more, was found for the period 1958-74 by G. Provopoulos, "The Distribution of Fiscal Burdens and Benefits by Income Groups in Greece," Greek Economic Review 1 (1979): 77-99; for the challenge of the latter results, see a related note by P. Reppas, Greek Economic Review 2 (1980), 180-87.

7. The ratio of direct/indirect taxes was 0.95 for the EEC and 1.77 for the United States in 1980. See OECD, National Accounts, various issues.

8. Greek government, Statistical Yearbook of Greece; and OECD, National Accounts, various issues.

9. For further arguments, see Gerald Meier, Leading Issues in Economic Development, 3d ed., (New York: Oxford University Press, 1976), pp. 281-84.

10. Some form of differential land tax is favored by A. Prest, The Taxation of Urban Land (Manchester, England: Manchester University Press, 1981).

11. For comments on tax harmonization and problems of substitution, see the valuable articles in C. Shoup, ed., Fiscal Harmonization in Common Markets (New York: Columbia University Press, 1967); also, N. Gianaris, "Fiscal Policy: Greece and the EEC," Spoudai 15 (January-March 1980), 1-11.

12. In accordance with the Articles 99 and 100 of the Rome Agreement, establishing the EEC in 1957, and Greece's accession agreement of 1980, Greece should introduce the VAT. E. Lozos, "O Foros tis Prostithemenis Aksias" (The Value Added Tax) Oikonomikos Tahydromos, Athens, January 13, 1983, pp. 49-50.

13. Thus, $T=0.15Pg+0.15W+0.20I$; and since $I=0.85Pg-W$, then $T=0.32Pg-0.05W$, where T is taxation on gross profits (Pg), Wages (W), and internal funds (I). For a penetrating analysis, see S. Pejovich, "Taxes and Pattern of Economic Growth: The Case of Yugoslavia," National Tax Journal, June 1964, pp. 96-110; and S. Pejovich, "The Banking System and the Investment Behavior of the Yugoslav Firm," in M. Bornstein, ed., Plan and Market: Economic Reform in Eastern Europe (New Haven: Yale University Press, 1973), pp. 289-91.

14. Total public revenue in Yugoslavia is composed of: 1) budgetary receipts (40 percent); 2) receipts of communities of interest (50 percent); and 3) receipts of special funds (10 percent). For more details, see M. Schrenk et al., Yugoslavia: Self-Managed Socialism and the Challenges of Development (Baltimore: Johns Hopkins University Press for the World Bank, 1979), pp. 122-25.

15. V. Dubey, Yugoslavia: Development with Decentralization (Baltimore: John Hopkins University Press for the World Bank, 1975), pp. 248-251.

16. These calculations were based on: International Monetary Fund (IMF), International Financial Statistics; United Nations, Yearbook of National Accounts Statistics; and United Nations, Statistical Yearbook, various issues.

17. To mitigate the impact of inflation on taxation, an income tax reduction, by 25 percent from October 1981 to July 1983, was introduced in the United States. Similar measures may be expected in other countries, such as Sweden, Denmark, and the United Kingdom, that rely heavily on progressive income taxes.

18. OECD, Revenue Statistics of the OECD Member Countries 1965-79 (Paris: 1980), pp. 45-46.

19. Further clarification is provided by Laws 1249/1982 and 1281/1982. "Pos Tha Symplirosete Sosta ti Dilosi Forou Akinitis Perirusias" (How to Fill Correctly the Declaration of Property Taxes), Oikonomikos Tahydromos, Athens, February 17, 1983, pp. 49-53. (Exchange rate at the end of 1983, $1= around 100 drachmas.)

20. George Nezi, "E Forologia Esodimatos Ton Ellinikon Anonimon Eterion Kai Allodapon Epihiriseon" (Income Taxation of Greek Joint Stock Companies and Foreign Enterprises), Oikonomikos Tahydromos, Athens, August 20, 1981, pp. 25, 16, 33 and August 27, 1981, pp. 27, 28.

21. For related discussion see, N. Gianaris, "Sygrisi Forologikon Epivarinseon Stin Ellada Kai Tis Hores Tis EOK" (Comparison of Tax Burdens in Greece and the EEC Countries) Okonomikos Tahydromos, Athens, November 22, 1979, pp. 16-17; and G. Gilbert and M. Mouillart, "H. Dynamiki Ton Forologikon Domon Etis Xores Tom OOSA," (The Dynamics of the Tax Structure in the Countries of the OECD) Oikonomia Kai Koinonia, April 1981, pp. 83-93.

22. Maria Negreponti-Delivanis, "Income Distribution, Tax Policy and the Propensity to Industrial Investment in Greece 1980-81." Report presented at the Symposium of Union of Democratic Scientists of North America (E.D.E.B.A.) in New York, April 16, 1983, p. 9 (Unpublished).

23. New York Times, October 25, 1981.

24. For the EEC, the GDP elasticities of direct taxes were 0.77 in 1950-60, 0.82 in 1960-70, and 1.31 in 1970-80; the income elasticities of direct taxes for the United States were 1.30, 0.95 and 1.14, compared to 0.70, 1.28, and 1.22 for Japan respectively.

25. However, it should be noted that these "budgetary revenues" in Yugoslavia do not include revenues of "special funds" and "communities of interest." If these revenues are included the elasticity of direct taxes with respect to total taxes would be 1.14 in 1976-80, for example.

26. The marginal propensity to consume ($\Delta C/\Delta Y$ or MPC) of the private sector in Greece was 0.65 in 1960-70 and 0.67 in 1970-80, compared to 0.58 and 0.55 in Yugoslavia respectively. If government consumption were included, MPC would be 0.79 in 1960-70 and 0.86 in 1970-80 for Greece and 0.75 and 0.74 for Yugoslavia respectively.

27. For the renewed widespread interest in consumption taxes, see articles in J. Pechman, ed., What Should Be

Taxes: Income or Expenditures? (Washington, D.C.: Brookings Institution, 1980).

28. For customs duties in different categories of imported goods in Greece see, Greek Government, Statistiki Epetipis Dimosion Oiconomikon (Statistical Yearbook of Public Finance), various issues; and Th. Georgakopoulos, Emmesi Foroi kai Viomihania eis tin Ellada (Indirect Taxes and Industry in Greece), (Athens: Institute of Economic and Industrial Research, 1977), p. 68.

29. For the EEC, all these elasticities were lower than those of Greece and declined from around one or more in 1950-60 to 0.85 for private consumption and GDP and 0.56 for imports in 1970-80.

30. Almost the same regression coefficient of indirect taxes on private consumption (0.22) was attained for the EEC; while the EEC coefficient of indirect taxes on inflation (0.15) was close to that of Greece. However, the regression of indirect taxes on imports gave a smaller coefficient for the EEC (0.45) than that of Greece. The difference may be justified because of the higher tariffs in Greece than in the EEC. N. Gianaris, "Indirect Taxes: A Comparative Study of Greece and the EEC," European Economic Review, 15 (1981), 114.

31. Tax indexing has been introduced in at least 15 countries, including Canada and France. However, in Canada it added to budget deficits instead of encouraging spending cuts or increasing taxes. Also, a similar indexing of social security benefits in the United States since 1972 has resulted in problems of large deficits for the system. In Brazil and other Latin American countries, indexing seems to be responsible for high rates at inflation (around 200 percent in Brazil). Elio Gaspari, "Origins of the Debt Crisis," New York Times, November 7, 1983.

32. For the EEC, the inflation elasticity of direct taxes was 2.7 in 1970-80, while for the United States it was 2.0 and for Japan 2.5, respectively.

PART III

INTERNATIONAL TRADE AND ECONOMIC COOPERATION

Part III deals with interregional and international trade and investment, the relationship of Greece and Yugoslavia with the EEC and COMECON, and the possibilities of closer cooperation and eventual regional integration. The geographical position of these two countries is such that they stand as a natural bridge between Europe and the Middle East, a fact that suggests closer cooperation in common investment ventures in transportation and industry.

Better investment opportunities and modern technology require large markets and big enterprises, which, in turn, point to the need for elimination of trade restrictions and improvement in economic relations between Greece and Yugoslavia as well as among all the neighboring Balkan countries. However, the fact that Greece is a member of the EEC and Yugoslavia, although closely related with special trade agreements, is not creates problems as to how far they can proceed in their economic cooperation or eventual integration.

It would seem that the need for closer economic relations between the two countries leads to mutual cooperation and development policies that tend to submerge ideological and territorial differences and prepare the ground for eventual integration. Although there may be trade and other restrictions resulting from Greece's membership in the EEC, there is enough leeway for the creation and strengthening of regional markets between the countries, especially after the recent agreements between Yugoslavia and the EEC. For many products and development projects there seems to be no contradiction with the EEC. On the contrary, the development of regional trade, on many occasions, may be considered to be complementary to that with the EEC countries.

195

7

FOREIGN TRADE
AND INVESTMENT

INTERREGIONAL TRADE

During the immediate postwar years, Greece had to trade with the West and Yugoslavia with the East, mainly because of the cold war in international relations. After the break with the Soviet Union and the East European countries (Cominform), Yugoslavia began a gradual increase in trade with Greece and other Western countries. In recent years, the increase in trade between the two countries has been remarkable, and joint investment ventures have been planned or implemented. Although historical and nationalistic factors do not seem to favor the rapid growth of trade, the geographical position of these two countries, which facilitates land transportation and joint investment ventures, favors specialization of productive factors and regional development.

Comparatively speaking, Yugoslavia is more industrialized than Greece. About half of the Yugoslav national product comes from industry compared with only about one-third for Greece. This means that Greece, with a comparatively inferior position in industrial production may face difficult problems in its efforts to speed up industrialization. The increase in imports of machinery and other industrial products by Greece from its northern neighbor would pose problems for the establishment of its own industries in such products, as well as an unfavorable balance of payments. This became obvious after the recent abolition of the system of clearings between the two countries, which was based on bilateral agreements. In this case the value of imports was equal to the value of exports and there was no need for hard currency. For less industrialized countries like Greece, such equilibrating clearings were advantageous, because agricultural products could be exchanged for machinery and other industrial products for which Yugoslavia had and still has a comparative advantage.

It would seem that clearing arrangements between Greece and Yugoslavia and other East European countries gave Greece the opportunity to sell such agricultural products as lemons, oranges, raisins, olive oil, and tobacco that cannot easily be disposed of in the free markets of West European countries. However, almost all East European countries, except Albania and Romania, stopped using clearings and seemed to favor free trade transactions. Moreover, clearings are being abolished in Greece because of its entrance into the EEC. As a result, Greek imports of industrial goods from Yugoslavia and other East European countries are expected to continue, without a proportional continuation of agricultural exports, and balance of trade deficits to grow, on top of those with EEC and other Western countries. Unless invisible receipts grow to cover the difference, this will mean deterioration of the international position of the drachma and detrimental effects on income and employment for Greece. Such conditions may adversely affect the trade balance through competition with other Mediterranean countries producing similar products that try to grab the same export markets. The net result may be reduction not only in prices but also in the quantities of exports of agricultural products, which have low income and price elasticities.

The Yugoslav economy is more controlled than the Greek economy. Therefore, Greek exports to Yugoslavia, and more so to other communist countries, may face monopolistic market conditions with possible abrupt demand changes by the Yugoslav policymakers. However, the need for trade with and transfer of technology from the EEC and the already abolished clearings may decrease noneconomic considerations in mutual transactions, thereby reducing the danger of abrupt policy changes and allowing the smooth flow of trade between two countries.

As Table 7.1 shows, Greece has had mostly large trade deficits with Yugoslavia in recent years. The same thing can be observed in the foreign trade of Greece with Bulgaria and Romania. As mentioned previously, the main reason is that Greece imports more industrial goods from its more industrialized northern neighbors. Moreover, Greece imports large amounts of veal, pork, and other kinds of meat from the other Balkan countries, particularly from Yugoslavia. Also, electricity is another commodity imported by Greece from these countries. From an economic point of view, therefore, northern Balkan countries have more interest in developing good relations with Greece, as they sell more to it than they buy from it. That is one way to save foreign currency to pay for their imports from other Western countries.

Although the present trade between Greece and Yugoslavia is a small proportion (about 5 percent) of their total foreign trade, the trend is positive and largely growing. Thus, imports by Greece from Yugoslavia increased by more than five times from 1974 to 1980. In 1981, though, a sizeable drop of such imports occurred mainly because of EEC restrictions on Greek imports of veal and other products from Yugoslavia as well as the severe recession in the area. However, Greek exports to Yugoslavia did not increase as much, especially after the abolition of clearings between the two countries on July 1, 1977. Such clearings were based on previous trade agreements of 1953 and 1966. To improve trade relations, a committee with representatives of both countries has been established. This committee, which meets at least once per year, reports to a common ministerial committee that has been operating since 1965.

Other functions of this economic committee include improvement in the relations of enterprises and organizations of the two countries, participation in world trade exhibits, arrangements for needed initial stage manufacturing for commodities in transit, exchanges in scientific and technical information, preparation for development programs concerning the two countries, and arbitration in cases of disagreements and disputes.

To facilitate seaborne trade, Greece and Yugoslavia established the Free Trade Zone of Salonika in 1923 for duty-free transit of Yugoslav goods. A new agreement in 1975

Table 7.1. Trade of Greece with Yugoslavia (million U.S. dollars, F.O.B.).

	Exports	Imports	Trade Deficit
1960	9.1	19.8	-10.7
1961	12.0	19.6	-7.6
1962	16.5	10.4	6.1
1963	10.1	20.1	-10.0
1964	11.0	16.5	-5.5
1965	13.3	24.0	-10.7
1966	21.0	26.4	-5.4
1967	27.0	30.2	-3.2
1968	22.5	42.4	-19.9
1969	38.5	29.3	9.2
1970	40.0	35.0	5.0
1971	30.0	35.4	-5.4
1972	29.2	55.4	-26.2
1973	60.0	48.0	12.0
1974	86.1	39.6	46.5
1975	70.0	25.9	44.1
1976	43.5	64.0	-20.5
1977	79.5	130.2	-50.7
1978	60.5	137.5	-77.0
1979	71.7	152.7	-81.0
1980	94.4	158.9	-64.5
1981	74.3	35.7	38.6

Source: United Nations, International Trade Statistics, various issues.

provided for a new arrangement and further expansion of the use of the Free Trade Zone for ten more years. Under the terms of this new agreement, ships that transport Yugoslav commodities can enter the eastern pier of the harbor without delay, provided that the Port of Salonika Authority has been informed in advance. Imported or exported commodities in the Free Trade Zone are free of tariff or any other duty of the Greek government or the municipality of Salonika. However, loading and unloading operations, storage facilities, and ships' accommodations are paid for by Yugoslavia.

INTERNATIONAL TRADE

A common problem for Greece and Yugoslavia is the worsening balance of trade with ever-increasing deficits. Although invisible receipts pay for large parts of trade deficits, the growing foreign debts lead to the deterioration of the credit position and the decline of the value of the currencies of these countries.(1) One of the main reasons for growing foreign debt is energy consumption, which, during the last two decades, increased about five times for Greece and three times for Yugoslavia (to more than 2,000 kilograms of coal equivalent per capita). As a result, Greece spends about 50 percent of its merchandise export earnings to pay for energy imports and Yugoslavia 25 percent.

About 50 percent of the exports of Greece and 25 percent of the exports of Yugoslavia go to the nine EEC countries; imports from the EEC account for around 40 percent of the total imports of Greece and 35 percent of those of Yugoslavia. Greek exports to Eastern Europe and the Soviet Union fluctuate around 10-12 percent of total exports but those of Yugoslavia are around 40-45 percent annually. Imports from Eastern Europe and the Soviet Union are about 6 percent for Greece and 25-30 percent for Yugoslavia. West Germany, absorbing some 20 percent of the total Greek exports and about 10 percent of Yugoslavian exports, is an important trade partner for both countries, followed by Italy (close to 10 percent), France, and the United States.

The Soviet Union is the main trade partner of Yugoslavia, at present absorbing about 30 percent of total Yugoslav exports compared with less than 15 percent in the early 1970s. The growth of Yugoslav exports to the Soviet Union, while imports remained more or less the same (around 18 percent), signifies the growing dependence of the economy of Yugoslavia on that of the Soviet Union. The recent trade agreements with the EEC will probably reverse this trend. Although there was a decline in the volume of imports of oil and gas recently, the rise in their prices kept the total value of Yugoslav imports from the Soviet Union about the same. Greek trade with the Soviet Union is small, about 3 percent or less. Japan is the second country in Greek imports (around 10 percent) after West Germany that accounts for some 15-20 percent of the imports of Greece and Yugoslavia.

Both countries appear to have growing trade with the Middle East countries, particularly Saudi Arabia, Iraq, Egypt, and Libya. Also, Greece and Yugoslavia have signed agreements with Iran and other Middle East nations to provide foodstuffs and industrial products in exchange for petroleum. Not only has annual trade increased, but also exports from both countries are picking up some of the projects abandoned by U.S. and other Middle Eastern concerns, especially in Lybia and Iran, where Yugoslavs are working the largest mine at Sar Cheshneh.

Although both countries desire closer relations with other developing nations, trade with them for both Greece and Yugoslavia is limited to around 10-15 percent. Therefore, no matter how much alliance with third world countries is pursued, economically and technologically both countries depend primarily on Europe and are expected to depend on it for many years to come.

As Tables 7.2 and 7.3 show, Greece and Yugoslavia have recorded considerable annual deficits in foreign trade (especially during the last five years), primarily because of relatively large imports to accommodate rise in consumption and expansion in productive capacity. However, substantial earnings from tourism and shipping, and emigrant remittances helped to reduce the balance of payments deficits and to service external debt.(2) In addition to these invisible receipts, foreign exchange deposits have been used to narrow the trade deficits.

Emigrant remittances and foreign exchange deposits, though, have slowed down and are expected to decline further mainly because of the reversal of population flows, especially in Greece, where repatriation accounts for about 25,000 people per annum (compared to emigration of about 70,000

Table 7.2. Exports, Imports, Balance of Trade Deficits (in billions of U.S. dollars), and Exchange Rates (drachmas per U.S. dollar; end of year) in Greece.

	Exports	Imports	Deficits(-) or Surplus	Exchange Rate
1950	.09	.43	-.34	15.00
1	.10	.40	-.30	15.00
2	.12	.35	-.23	15.00
3	.13	.27	-.14	30.00
4	.15	.33	-.18	30.00
5	.18	.38	-.20	30.00
6	.19	.46	-.27	30.00
7	.22	.52	-.30	30.00
8	.23	.56	-.33	30.00
9	.20	.57	-.37	30.00
60	.20	.70	-.50	30.00
1	.22	.71	-.49	30.00
2	.25	.70	-.45	30.00
3	.29	.80	-.51	30.00
4	.31	.88	-.57	30.00
5	.33	1.13	-.80	30.00
6	.41	1.22	-.81	30.00
7	.49	1.19	-.70	30.00
8	.47	1.39	-.92	30.00
9	.55	1.59	-1.04	30.00
70	.64	1.96	-1.32	30.00
1	.66	2.10	-.144	30.00
2	.87	2.35	-1.48	30.00
3	1.46	3.48	-2.02	29.70
4	2.03	4.38	-2.35	30.00
5	2.03	5.07	-3.04	35.65
6	2.23	5.56	-3.33	37.03
7	2.52	6.42	-3.90	35.51
8	3.00	7.34	-4.34	36.00
9	3.93	10.11	-6.18	38.28
1980	4.09	10.90	-6.81	46.53
1981	4.75	11.42	-6.67	57.63
1982	6.54	10.11	-3.57	70.57

Source: International Financial Statistics, various issues; and OECD, Economic Surveys: Greece, various issues.

Table 7.3.   Exports, Imports, Balance of Trade Deficits (in billions of U.S. dollars), and Exchange Rates (dinars per U.S. dollars), in Yugoslavia.

	Exports	Imports	Deficits(-) or Surplus	Exchange Rate
1950	.15	.23	-.08	.50
1	.18	.38	-.20	.50
2	.25	.37	-.12	3.00
3	.19	.39	-.20	3.00
4	.24	.34	-.10	3.00
5	.26	.44	-.18	3.00
6	.32	.47	-.15	3.00
7	.39	.66	-.27	3.00
8	.44	.68	-.24	3.00
9	.48	.69	-.21	3.00
60	.57	.83	-.26	3.00
1	.57	.91	-.24	7.50
2	.69	.89	-.20	7.50
3	.79	1.06	-.27	7.50
4	.89	1.32	-.43	7.50
5	1.09	1.29	-.20	7.50
6	1.22	1.57	-.35	12.50
7	1.25	1.71	-.46	12.50
8	1.26	1.80	-.54	12.50
9	1.47	2.13	-.66	12.50
70	1.68	2.87	-1.19	12.50
1	1.81	3.25	-1.44	17.00
2	2.24	3.23	-.99	17.00
3	2.85	4.51	-1.66	15.60
4	3.80	7.54	-3.74	17.05
5	4.07	7.70	-2.63	18.00
6	4.88	7.37	-2.49	18.23
7	5.25	9.63	-4.38	18.44
8	5.67	9.99	-4.32	18.61
9	6.79	14.02	-7.22	19.16
1980	8.98	15.06	-6.09	29.30
1981	10.93	15.76	-4.83	41.82
1982	6.98	8.97	-1.99	62.49

Source: International Monetary Fund, International Financial Statistics, Yearbook, 1980 pp. 64-5, 68-9, 450-1; and OECD, Economic Surveys: Yugoslavia, various issues.

per annum in 1960-75). Moreover, the rise of interest, profit, and dividend payments in recent years may be considered as part of the adverse trends in some invisible items that reflect hidden capital outflows. In the wake of high international interest rates and a considerable increase in borrowing abroad by Greece and Yugoslavia, the debt service ratio with respect to gross exports increased and official reserves fell.

The successive steep rises in oil prices in the 1970s were a severe burden on the economies of Greece and Yugoslavia. As a result, the current account deficits of these two countries increased significantly. In the early 1980s, the reduction of the external deficit received top priority in the policies of both governments. Such policies included the curbing of domestic demand (even through imposing blackouts in Yugoslavia), which was buoyant, so as to allow a transfer of resources to exports and a decrease in the growth of imports. Statistically, there seems to be a close relationship between domestic demand growth and external deficits, especially in Yugoslavia.(3)

After the considerable devaluation of both the drachma and the dinar vis-a-vis the United States dollar the bargaining power of holders of foreign exchange increased.(4) As a result, exports, tourism, and foreign capital inflow were stimulated, and a further surge is expected in the foreseeable future. Industrial exports continue to rise relatively faster than agricultural exports. Exports to the Middle East countries continue to increase rapidly for both countries. For the long-run increase in exports, however, what Greece and Yugoslavia need is a rapid progress in diversification and substantial gains in competitiveness, linked to an increase in productive investment.

In 1980, the Greek authorities aligned broadly the drachma exchange rate with the European Monetary System (EMS) currencies. As a result, the drachma follows, more or less, the fluctuations of the purchasing power of the main European currencies. However, because of the appreciation of the U.S. dollar, the drachma depreciated in effective nominal terms. In real terms though, the drachma appreciated against its main EEC partners in 1980-81 largely because of a rise of around 26 percent in unit labor costs.

Both countries export mainly primary products and import machinery and fuel. As a result, their terms of trade, that is, the price index of exports over the price index of imports, are deteriorating. Thus in 1980 the terms of trade ratio (for Greece) was 93 (1970=100) and 99 for Yugoslavia. For the terms of trade to improve and unemployment to be reduced, a higher degree of industrialization should be pursued with more intensity. Both countries are working in that direction.

The percentage share of primary commodity exports, except fuels and metals, declined from 81 in 1960 to around 30 for Greece at present, and from 45 to less than 20 for Yugoslavia. In the past, both countries seemed to suffer from "terms of trade" illusion because of their overvalued currencies, with detrimental effects on their short-run exports. Recently, though, their currencies were devalued significantly so that their exported products became relatively cheaper and the imported ones more expensive. This trend is expected to improve the balance of trade and the credit position of these countries. It will also help to reduce their foreign debt, which was 11 percent of GNP for Greece and 7 percent for Yugoslavia in 1980.(5)

Shipping and tourism allow the Greek economy to look good on the surface, although it is actually weak in its structure. Under stable international and domestic conditions, that economy can continue its good performance as long as the "invisibles," mainly from tourism and shipping, provide sufficient amounts to pay for its ever-increasing imports. In the case of disturbances, however, the reduction of invisibles would place the economy in a precarious position. On the other hand, the extensive use of foreign (mainly immigrant) deposits to finance imports of consumer goods would add another element of potential disturbance to the economy if large withdrawals were to occur. Moreover, immigrant remittances, which help stabilize the balance of payments and the credit position of the country, may exaggerate, at the same time, the inflationary nature of the economy, insofar as they are used for wasteful consumption and other unproductive urban ventures, and perpetuate the parasitic way of life in a large segment of the population.

Already, imports have increased significantly to the extent of even substituting domestic production for certain industries. And this despite the fact that the drachma has been gradually devaluated substantially. It is expected that this policy of devaluation will help tourism. It will also increase exports and decrease imports, since Greek products will be cheaper for other countries and foreign products more expensive in Greece. However, the continuous increase in imports of luxury or semiluxury products, which also push the overall price index upward (imported inflation), indicates that the economic policy of the government should turn toward increasing productivity and reducing or holding the incomes of those persons (mainly middlemen) whose spending is directed toward imports of such unnecessary consumer goods. From that point of view, Greece cannot afford to walk--she has to run in the foreseeable future.

The average annual growth rate of imports in the 1970s was around 6 percent for both countries, while the growth rate of exports was 5 percent for Yugoslavia and around 12 percent for Greece. There is a considerable improvement in the volume of exports to the Middle East and other capital-surplus oil countries, especially in textiles and other manufacturing products. However, the slackening in the growth of demand in the EEC and other Western countries recently led to deteriorating trade balances and growing foreign debt for both countries, despite their intensive efforts for more exports. It would seem that delays in decision making, government bureaucracy, lack of modern research and innovation, and inflexibility in adopting new technology, especially in Yugoslavia, are mainly responsible for the inadequate competitiveness of their exported commodities.

During the postwar years, Greece did not emphasize industrialization as much as Yugoslavia and the relative share of its manufacturing exports was comparatively less. On the other hand, Yugoslavia pursued a rapid structural transformation from agriculture to industry, away from primary and toward manufactured exports. This policy helped Yugoslavia to expand exports, which have been largely offset by import liberalization. At the same time, import substitution was deemphasized. This policy prescription was probably the cause of the higher rates of economic growth.(6) In both countries, and particularly in Greece, the present slowdown of construction and the high world prices of materials are responsible for stagnant imports of housing materials.

The main Yugoslav exports consist of transportation equipment (about 14 percent of total exports), iron and other metals (13 percent), food and live products, nonelectric machinery, electric machinery, clothing and footwear, chemicals (about 10 percent each), and wood products (5 percent).

On the other hand, the main imports consist of nonelectrical machinery (about 22 percent of total imports), petroleum and petroleum products (12 percent), iron and steel (11 percent), transportation equipment, electrical machinery, and food and live animals (6-8 percent each).(7)

The main exports of Greece, as percentages of total commodity exports, are fruits and nuts, fresh or dried, iron and steel, tobacco, aluminum, and cotton. The main imports, on the other hand, are mineral fuels, lubricants and related materials (about 23 percent of total imports), transport equipment (22 percent), machinery other than transport equipment (14 percent), manufactured goods classified chiefly by material (14 percent), and food and live animals (8 percent).(8)

The relative share of Greece in the Balkan trade is about 10 percent, while that of Yugoslavia is around 30 percent, as are those of Bulgaria and Romania. The trade of each country with the other Balkan countries is about 6 percent of world trade.

However, present efforts for the reduction of external deficits aim at the restraint of imports when exports cannot be expanded. This policy reduces the pace of investment and hinders economic growth particularly in industrial production that usually offsets swings in agricultural production. To stimulate investment, jurisdiction on foreign operations in Yugoslavia was transferred, after the act of 1977, from state organs to self-managed bodies as well as to individual republics and provinces.

Deteriorating world market conditions have forced both countries to scale down domestic growth in order to moderate their foreign indebtedness. Although net revenue from tourism remained an important source of foreign exchange, it may be expected to slow down because of strong competition from other countries in the Mediterranean area and because of increasing foreign travel by Greeks and Yugoslavs.

Greek exports cover less than half of its imports, and the trade deficit is covered mostly by "invisibles," primarily tourism and shipping (about 15 percent of total receipts each). Emigrant remittances, another important part of the invisibles, mainly from Western Europe, gradually declined in recent years. They covered 24 percent of the imports in 1970, 15 percent in 1975 and only 9 percent in 1981.

On the other hand, Yugoslav exports cover more than half of its imports, and the remaining trade deficit is covered partially by tourism and net emigrant remittances (about 13 percent of the value of imports each). Because of the EEC farm policy, British and West European imports of Yugoslav agricultural products declined rapidly. Thus, before 1970, the EEC absorbed around 40 percent of total Yugoslav exports, while at present it absorbs only about 25 percent. As a result, the trade balance of Yugoslavia with the EEC has deteriorated but that with the COMECON countries is more or less in equilibrium. Such a trend indicates that sooner or later the country may ask for closer cooperation with the EEC group and, probably, to be a full member.

In order to protect their economies from certain imported inflation, both countries try to restrain or reduce imports when exports cannot be increased. Because this policy may hinder economic growth, policymakers try to increase the pace of investment. Nevertheless, implicit or explicit controls over prices and wages, as well as subsidies, are used to keep prices low and stimulate exports. Also, fiscal buffers between the external sector and the domestic sector are used at times to avoid abrupt price changes and maintain moderate growth targets, especially in Yugoslavia.

To reduce the current external deficits, the Yugoslav authorities decided to curb imports and stimulate exports by, among other things, import controls, fiscal incentives, and steep depreciation of the dinar vis-a-vis the U.S. dollar. With the dinar depreciating continuously, especially since June 1980, Yugoslav products gained some competitiveness in foreign markets, which was lost because of high costs of oil and other raw material imports during the 1970s. To pay for oil imports from the Soviet Union and Middle East countries, the volume of Yugoslav exports to these countries has been gradually growing.

The Middle East markets are less sophisticated than those in the EEC and not much attention is paid to quality. This is an important reason for the rapid growth of Greek and Yugoslav exports in the area. However, oil imports continue to absorb large amounts of foreign currency revenue (accounting for about two-thirds of the overall trade deficit) and contribute to an ever-growing external debt, which reached $15 billion for Greece and $20 billion for Yugoslavia. To mitigate the growth of external debt, policymakers in both countries also use administrative limitations on currency allowances for imports of some consumer goods, such as coffee. Such policies lead to the gradual fall of imports, particularly from developing nations.

Another factor that influences balance of payments trends is shipping receipts. Both countries, and particularly Greece, face deceleration in transport revenue due to present poor world shipping conditions. Moreover, although tourism continues to grow rapidly in both countries, traveling abroad by Greeks and Yugoslavs also continues to grow at the expense of net tourist receipts. However, currency depreciation in both countries and the completion of the repairs following the Montenegro earthquake of 1979 in Yugoslavia are expected to further increase net receipts from tourism and relieve some of the balance of payment pressure. On the other hand, the growing attraction of holding foreign exchange with Greek and Yugoslav banks and the transfer of funds from foreign accounts may increase foreign exchange deposits. Also, more review on profit expatriation, mainly through the practice of under-or-overinvoicing, primarily in Greece, would stop the phenomenon of socializing industrial expenses and risks without discouraging outflow of industrial policies.

Yugoslav faces a heavy burden of foreign loan repayments. Interest payments alone ($2.3 billion in 1982) equal about 5 percent of gross social product. Interest and capital owed ($5.35 billion in 1982) amount to about half of the country's earnings in convertible currency. Indebtedness per head (about $1,000) is high. Serious efforts made recently to reduce deficits brought Yugoslavia high praise from the IMF, but debt servicing remains a major headache for economic policymakers. Moreover, the trade surplus that the country realized recently with socialist countries is in inconvertible currencies, which cannot be used to pay Western debts, which have to be refinanced. Further exports to the socialist countries depend to a large extent on imports of machinery and technology from the West. The same thing can be said for the production of many commodities and services used domestically.

In Greece things are not much better from the point of view of foreign debt. More than 20 percent of the foreign currency inflow must be paid back to service this debt. This percentage is above the 10-15 percent accepted internationally.

FOREIGN INVESTMENT

Competition in exported products and technological transformation and assimilation may present obstacles to closer
trade ties between Greece and Yugoslavia. Therefore, it may
be better for these countries to emphasize joint investment
ventures in competitive products and, at the same time,
proceed with closer trade cooperation in complementary
products. In the past, political, territorial, and structural
differences and suspicions have not permitted large-scale
mutual investments and joint ventures. However, gradual
liquidation of such differences has created a more favorable
enrichment for closer cooperation of these two economies in
both trade and investment. Establishment of joint investment ventures may take place for the production of bauxite,
copper, uranium, and other metals, especially in border areas.
Moreover, the construction of man-made lakes, useful for
irrigation and electricity, the planting of new forests, and the
setting up of pilot cities, so widespread in Yugoslavia, may be
some of the additional projects to be considered.

As a result, both countries encourage foreign investment in the
hope of acquiring new technology and earning hard currency
needed to service their debt. They try to attract foreign
firms to invest in poor regions and in exporting industries.
Thus, in order to attract investment from abroad, Greece
provides a number of advantages to foreign investors (Law
2687/1953). Such advantages, which are guaranteed by the
Greek Constitution, include the right of the investor to
export his capital investment in a period of ten years, a 12
percent return on his capital and 10 percent interest on loans.
Also, reduction or elimination of tariffs on imported machinery and related spare parts and tools as well as reductions in
local taxes and port duties are provided. Other privileges
introduced later (Law 4171/1961) include the hiring of foreign
personnel paid in foreign currency and a number of exemptions on stamp duties and other taxes.

As a result of the acts of 1967, which deal with foreign
investment, joint ventures may be undertaken in Yugoslavia,
particularly in industries that import new technology and
know-how. However, a foreign partner cannot have more
than 49 percent of the total value of a joint investment.
Foreign capital can be invested in manufacturing, transportation, tourism, and scientific and technical research, but not

in trade, banking, and other services. Net profits of foreign partners are taxed at a rate of 35 percent, but this tax can be progressively smaller if the profits are reinvested.(9) In each enterprise, a business committee, the composition of which is based on investment shares, with some power transferred from the workers' council, would decide on related matters. Approval of the establishment of joint business ventures is required by the Federal Committee for Energy and Technology.

However, it would seem that, in many instances, these laws promote foreign exchange exports instead of capital imports. International statistics indicate that capital repatriation to the advanced countries, in a period of 15 years, is twice as large as the initial investment. Moreover, foreign exchange outflow from direct investment may be infinite compared to loans, for example, which have a finite limit. On the other hand, foreign firms use mainly host-country sources of investment financing, thereby draining available savings from native entrepreneurs.

To some extent, the problem of importing technological know-how can be solved by buying the right to use a certain technology from other Western or Eastern countries in exchange for raw materials or other products. Furthermore, care should be taken to make sure that imported technology is suitable to the development needs of the host country, avoiding, at the same time, probable unhealthy influence upon local traditions and cultures. Such a selection of productive technology that fits the socioeconomic conditions of the countries considered may provide a viable alternative to the submission and parasitism of the peripheral economies of Greece and Yugoslavia to foreign monopolies and oligopolies. From that point of view, both countries should make every effort to avoid turning into supplements of other economies and free themselves from the belief or the myth that they cannot make it without "protectors" or "godfathers."(10)

Although foreign investment in Yugoslavia has been limited, a number of foreign enterprises have established themselves in that country. Thus the International Hotels Corporation, a subsidiary of Pan American World Airways, operates and continues to build new hotels in Zagreb and Belgrade as well as in other Balkan cities. Also, a number of joint banks, such as the French-Yugoslavian Bank, have been established to finance exports and other trade transactions.

Direct foreign investment in both countries, which has fallen off in recent years, is expected to pick up again after the world recession is over and uncertainties about economic policies are reduced. Such investment by Greeks and Yugoslavs living abroad is expected to reverse its trend from real estate purchases to individual and tourist units primarily in provincial towns and poor regions. Moreover, repatriating emigrants are expected to invest part or the whole of their accumulated capital in productive ventures and modern enterprises. As a result of the new regional incentives for decentralization, investment is anticipated in competitive import-substitution and export industries in the countryside.

The emergence and expansion of multinational corporations affect economic conditions in both countries, particularly in Greece. The monopolistic or oligopolistic giant corporations gradually take away powers from governments on matters of economic policy, and they may even create problems of political influence. Already, there is criticism that both countries make their economies too open to foreign economic and political influence. This is particularly so for Greece, where foreign investment controls about 30 percent of the total industrial assets and 60 percent of industrial exports, primarily in oil refining, chemicals, basic metals, and transportation equipment. Also, about 90 percent of the trade deficit of Greece comes from the transactions of 11 large companies in which the average share of foreign capital is 54 percent.

On many occasions cooperation between Greece and Yugoslavia, as well as among other countries, can be promoted if the governments set up common industrial policies. On the other hand, corporate policies of expansion and cooperation may nullify viable integration. Transnational corporations are there to remain and grow, often helping the shaping of markets while internally they are based on central planning. They seem not to belong to the potentially extinct species of business dinosaur. Although Article 86 of the Treaty of Rome, which established the EEC, forbids the abuse of dominant positions, especially in input tying, economic realities in Europe suggest that corporate domination increases through time.(11) In order to counteract the growing corporate power a closer regional cooperation between the policymakers of the two countries may be needed. However, business investors who transfer foreign capital and introduce modern technology should not be discouraged. They provide overhead capital, jobs, and managerial know-how, so much needed in both recipient countries, in exchange for raw materials and profitable returns. From that point of view, introduction of new technology requires big enterprises and large markets, which can be achieved by common investment policies in the area. At the same time, guarantees against arbitrary administrative controls and favorable conditions for profitable opportunities should prevail for foreign investment to flow in the region. Somehow, a balance of mutual interest should be struck between big foreign investors and the interests of the countries considered so that the economic and political influence of the corporate "beasts" may be reduced and needed capital investment and managerial expertise continue to flow into the area.

Both countries have received some form of aid, primarily from the United States, and Yugoslavia also from the Soviet Union. U.S. postwar aid (1948-71) amounted to $1.1 billion for Greece and $500 million for Yugoslavia. However, aid was gradually reduced because it was often given for political and military (strategic) reasons and hidden strings were customarily attached. It would be better for both recipient countries to ask for more trade than aid because the latter breeds unhealthy economic dependency. Transfer of technology may take place through trade and investment, which can stimulate economic development in these countries while preserving, at the same time, their economic and political independence. Moreover, loans have been provided by international institutions to Greece and Yugoslavia as well as to other Balkan countries, particularly from the World Bank, for agricultural credit and the construction of highways.(12)

Greece is in a better position than Yugoslavia regarding possession of gold reserves. She has about 4 million ounces of gold compared to about half of that for Yugoslavia. However, regarding Special Drawing Rights (SDRs), Yugoslavia is in a better position (about 100, with 35 SDRs per ounce of gold), while Greece was in a relatively better overall reserve position in the 1960s and early 1970s.

INTERREGIONAL INVESTMENT

As mentioned previously, a significant joint investment venture under serious consideration is the construction of a navigable canal between the Danube and the Agean Sea. In recent meetings of the related Joint Greek-Yugoslav Commission feasibility studies and specific engineering problems were examined. They included existing waterway designs, evolution of expected commodity flows, estimating the time required for the project's construction, and the competitive transportation networks through the Adriatic ports or other Greek ports (Volos, Kavala, etc.). Also, alternative transit routes such as that through the Constanta-Cerna Voda canal (under construction) as well as the Bulgarian and USSR ports in the Black Sea were considered, together with other land and air routes. The Danube-Morava project, construction of which is expected to begin in 1985, would benefit not only the internal ports (Kraljevo, Nis, Skopje, Yanitsa, etc.) but also neighboring regions through higher efficiency and more production of hydro power. However, needed environmental protection measures, along with expected benefits, should be considered in the final stages of projection of this important waterway.

Joint ventures are implemented or projected not only between Greece and Yugoslavia, but between them and other Balkan countries. Romania agreed to provide technical services and equipment to Greece for the planned subway network of Athens (Metro). Also, common preparation and implementation of development projects for third world countries, primarily in the Middle East, were the subject of a recent agreement (May 1982) between the two countries. Other common projects include the manufacturing or trading of buses, tractors, and other motor vehicles, food processing, as well as common enterprises in petroleum exploration, chemicals, iron, and steel products and other mineral resources. Further development of communications, transportation, and tourist and other service enterprises were also reviewed.

Moreover, modernization of the Greek railway system and the possibility of electrifying the Athens-Salonika-Idomeni lines were considered between Greece and Romania, as well as the improvement of the Athens-Bucharest highway. Also, the possibility of establishing mixed shipping companies and exchanges in science, books, and technological know-how, and improvement in cultural relations were emphasized by the Romano-Greek Ministerial Committee, which was established in 1976.

Joint investment ventures have been implemented in Yugoslavia with other neighboring countries in irrigation projects and hydroelectric dams, especially in border areas, such as Samoritz-Islaz, near the Danube, and the Iron Gate on the Yugoslav-Romania border. Similar joint ventures are under consideration in mining projects in the Greek-Yugoslav border near Florina.(13) On the other hand, further bilateral agreements between Greece and Yugoslavia are expected to be concluded for common investment in subsoil resources, transportation, electricity, manufacturing, tourism, and banking, after careful feasibility studies have been made to overcome the lack of statistical information and research in the region.

A good number of joint investment ventures have also been undertaken between Greece and other Balkan countries, particularly Bulgaria. They include: the Machine Export Industry (MEVET); the Chemiport-Bilimport Company, in which the Unifert Company of Lebanon participates, for the production of chemical products; the DKW, which cans vegetables and fruits in the region of Almyros, in which the Bulgarian Plant Export, the Greek Kanaris Company and Uink-Konk of Holland participate; the Kopelouzos-Balkan Car Impex Company, which manufactures and repairs buses; and some other ventures under implementation, dealing with the production and trade of meat products and sausages, fish products, and the manufacturing of leather products (DERAS). Moreover, the establishment of an aluminum enterprise in Greece is under consideration by Bulgaria in cooperation with the Soviet Union.

Also, commercial agreements have been concluded from Greece and the Soviet Union for the transmission of Soviet natural gas and electric power to Greece through Romania and Bulgaria, as well as agreements concerning technical, economic, industrial, and tourist cooperation. Moreover, the Soviet Union's industry has imported Greek bauxite in the past and there is another agreement for Soviet investment in a plant converting Greek bauxite into alumina, which is used for the production of aluminum.(14)

NOTES

1. The external public debt of Greece grew from $0.9 billion in 1970 to $4.5 billion in 1980, while that of Yugo-

slavia grew from $1.2 billion to $4.5 billion in 1980. Total (accumulated) foreign debt, $20 billion for Yugoslavia and $14 billion for Greece in 1982. World Bank Report 1982, p. 139 and "Sta 15 Ekatommina to Eksoteriko Hreos tis Ellados."

2. The Greek commercial fleet with 2,876 ships in 1982 (the largest in the world) and 42 million tons (next to Liberia in tonnage), is estimated to exceed 54 million tons if Greek-owned ships under foreign flags are included. Organization for Economic Cooperation and Development (OECD), Economic Surveys, 1981-82 (Paris: May 1982), p. 28.

3. OECD, Economic Surveys: Yugoslavia, various issues. Also L. Tyson, The Yugoslav Economic System and Its Performance in the 1970s (Berkeley: University of California, 1980), chap. 7.

4. The drachma vis-a-vis the U.S. dollar, was devalued from 30 drachmas per dollar in 1974 to 70.6 in 1982; while the dinar was depreciated from 17 dinars per U.S. dollar in 1974 to 62.5 in 1982. Additional devaluations pushed the exchange rates to around 100 drachmas per dollar and to 103 dinars per dollar in 1983.

5. OECD, Economic Surveys, 1981-82: Greece (Paris: 1982), p. 139. To prevent an economic and political collapse, Western countries put together an aid package to Yugoslavia in December 1982. The United States offered about $1 billion to help finance the servicing of foreign debts amounting to about $20 billion. New York Times, December 8, 1982.

6. For empirical support see Hollis Chenery "Interactions Between Industrialization and Exports" American Economic Review, May 1980, pp. 381-92. Regarding shares of export earnings, see Charles Chittle, "Foreign Exchange Distribution in Yugoslavia's New Planning System: An Input-Output Approach," Journal of Comparative Economics, March 1981, pp. 79-86.

7. A. Banks, et al. eds., Economic Handbook of the World (New York: McGraw-Hill, 1981), pp. 510-14; and D. Flaherty, "Economic Reforms and Foreign Trade in Yugoslavia," Cambridge Journal of Economics, August 1982, pp. 110-12.

8. OECD, Greece: Economic Surveys, 1981-1982 (Paris: 1982), p. 5.

9. L. Adamovic, "The Foreign Trade System of Yugoslavia," in R. Stojanovic, The Functioning of the Yugoslav Economy (New York: M. Sharpe, 1982), pp. 159-61.

10. See a related review in C. Vaitsos, Intercountry Income Distribution and Transnational Enterprises (London: Oxford University Press, 1974).

11. For the effects of growing corporate power on European integration, see articles in D. Seers and C. Vaitsos, eds., Integration and Unequal Development: The Experience of the EEC (New York: St. Martin's Press, 1980).

12. The European Investment Bank granted some $30 million (2.3 billion drachmas) in loans in 1982 to Greece, as part of the cost (13.8 billion drachmas) the construction of two hydroelectric dams of 130 megawatts capacity each.

13. Both Greece and Yugoslavia subscribe to the idea of building up a Balkans-wide network of multilateral agreements concerning trade and investment. For comments, see Mike Pournarakis, "Inter-System Development Integration: The Case of the Balkans," East European Quarterly, June 1982, pp. 231-248.

14. Some of the agreements were concluded on February 1983 when Soviet Prime Minister Nikolai Tikhonov visited Athens, returning a visit to Moscow in 1979 by the then Greek Prime Minister Constantine Caramanlis. "Soviet Premier to Visit Greece," New York Times, February 16, 1983 and M. Howe, "Greece Joins Soviets in Urging Deep Arms Cuts," New York Times, February 25, 1983.

8

ECONOMIC RELATIONS
WITH THE EEC
AND COMECON

The European Economic Community, which was established in 1957 in Rome by Belgium, France, West Germany, Italy, Luxembourg, and the Netherlands, has particular importance for Greece, which is a full member of the group, and Yugoslavia, which is related to it with special trade agreements. Because the EEC proved to be a successful group in eliminating tariffs and implementing common policies in transportation, agriculture, and other sectors, Britain, Denmark, and Ireland joined it in 1973.   Moreover, Greece became the tenth member of the EEC in 1981.

From the point of view of regional policy, the EEC, through the Competition Directorate, began to enforce ceilings on the value of regional incentives in order to prevent distortions in trade among members and to emphasize continent-wide priorities. However, its actions supplant rather than supplement national efforts. EEC policies seem to favor imports of labor-intensive goods from less developed countries and tend to defend older industries by recruiting temporarily migrant workers from less developed parts of Europe such as Yugoslavia, Greece, and Turkey.

Spain and Portugal are expected to join the Common Market in the foreseeable future. However, France seems to have strong objections to Spain's early entry because of the pressures of the producers of competitive products in southern France. The French arguments are that more time is needed for the EEC to formulate a more efficient policy on competitive Mediterranean products and that Spain should implement the value added tax before she enters the community.

To facilitate transactions among the member countries and to promote a better monetary system, the EEC put into operation, on March 13, 1979, the European Currency Unit (ECU), as Article 107 of the Treaty of Rome enunciated. This new monetary unit is defined as a weighted average of member currencies. It was also agreed that in case of fluctuations of member currencies beyond a certain margin (2.25 percent, with some exceptions) the EEC would intervene to preserve monetary stability.(1)

GREECE'S MEMBERSHIP IN THE EEC

In 1962 Greece became an associated member and in 1981 the tenth full member of the EEC. As an associated member, she was allowed to export many products to the EEC countries duty free, while gradually reducing tariffs on imports from the EEC during the transition period of association. With the membership agreement, a five-year transitional period of gradual tariff reduction (1981-85) for Greek agricultural exports in general and a seven-year period for peaches and tomatoes was provided by the EEC. Also, a seven-year transitional period was provided for the free movement of Greek workers in the EEC countries. Now, trade policy is basically dictated by articles 110-116 of the Treaty of Rome and by articles 115-117 of Greece's EEC Accession Act.

As a result of the accession, Greek agricultural products would enjoy preferential treatment compared to those of nonmember countries. The EEC would be expected to absorb surpluses at guaranteed prices, subsidize agricultural exports, and support regional development and structural adjustment in the Greek economy. However, during the initial stages of membership, the EEC imposed variable import levies upon the main agricultural products imported from Greece and did not subsidize transportation costs for exports as expected. On the contrary, it offered better preferential treatment for the Turkish products that competed with similar Greek products (Regulation 652/1981). Moreover, Greece expected the EEC to absorb surplus agricultural products but the EEC failed to do so. In addition, it obliged Greece to cover 20 percent of its needs in sugar by imports from third countries, to abolish clearings with East European countries and to modify trade policy with third countries. As a result, the main exported agricultural products, primarily peaches, oranges, lemons, tomatoes, and other fruits and vegetables, suffered extensive losses. During the initial stage of Greece's full membership in the EEC there was an upsurge in the value of Greek imports from the other countries of the EEC, whereas the value of exports remained relatively stable or declined, thereby raising the trade deficit with the EEC. To avoid further deterioration of trade, Greece asked for certain deviations from the initial agreement of accession.

The complete elimination of Greek tariffs on imports from the EEC leads not only to the reduction of customs revenue, but also to losses of income and employment. This is so because of the replacement of domestically produced industrial as well as agricultural goods (for which productivity is half or less of that in the EEC) with imported goods. From that point of view, special treatment of the Greek products, along with similar Mediterranean products seems to be needed for some time to come. In that case, the negative effects of the accession could be reduced through redistribution of taxes and EEC grants for regional and social development, especially for the poor and "problematic" areas.(2)

Greece is in the process of renegotiating some of the terms of its EEC membership in order to protect small businesses that stand to suffer from Common Market competition. The Greek government is trying to change certain provisions of the accession agreement so that Common Market policies will not run afoul of its socialization plans, particularly regarding agricultural and industrial subsidies and the retaining of some protective tariffs.

Greek agriculture is inferior to that of the other EEC countries. The average size of each farm in Greece is about 35 acres, compared with 150 acres in the other EEC nations, farms are scattered over large distances, and the level of agricultural equipment is very low. Furthermore, agricultural population is close to 30 percent, compared to less than 10 percent, on the average, for the rest of the community. As a result, farm productivity in Greece is far lower (about half) than that in the other EEC countries, and average income is even lower. The policy of the EEC, which favors large agricultural units with modern equipment, leads to higher productivity in the long run, but to more unemployment and misery for the small and medium-size farmers in the short run. Greek farmers, with limited or no proper training, may try in vain to find jobs in the industrial sector, which is already under heavy pressure from EEC competition. Therefore, pressure for migration of young farmers to European industries will continue. An agricultural policy that supports the formation of agro-industrial cooperatives and the decentralization of decision making can mitigate the seriousness of these farm problems as well as some similar problems in the industrial sector.

The transitional period for agricultural exports proved to be detrimental to the Greek economy because of the severe hardship of agricultural exports, particularly peaches, large amounts of which remained unsold and were finally buried in large ditches all over Greece. Moreover, certain protected industries producing such goods as metal products, cloth, leather, and footwear have been under heavy pressure because of the serious competition they encounter from similar EEC products. Perhaps more severe competition will come from non-EEC countries as a result of tariff reduction in harmony with those of the EEC.

The amount of economic aid Greece would receive from the EEC during the five-year transition period (about 15 billion dollars) might prove to be insufficient to cover the losses incurred from the unfavorable results of the country's membership in the long run.(3) Part of the aid is the result of relatively higher prices Greece achieved for its exported products.

From that point of view, Greece should press for a transitional period of some seven years for the protection of a few critical industries, particularly metal products, as the EEC did for some Greek agricultural exported products.

As a result of accession, Greek tariffs were cut by 20 percent and quota restrictions were abolished in the first stage. Tariffs would be gradually eliminated by 1986. However, Greece's trade deficit with the EEC continues to grow at an alarming pace. It doubled to $2.5 billion in the first two years of membership, adding to the already high overall trade deficits of the country, which amounted to some $6 billion in 1982. As expected, protected sleepy Greek firms have been caught unprepared by the imported European products that flooded the Greek markets. To everyone's surprise, not only manufactures but also food products, where Greece was expected to perform well, came under heavy competitive pressure from the EEC. Efficient production and distribution methods by other European partners manage to outsell Greek food products even in Greece. Thus, the food trade surpluses of previous years turned into deficits after accession.(4) Moreover, Greece cannot buy cheaper food from other nonmember countries because of the EEC farm policy, which asks for high import levies.

To reverse this unfavorable trend, the Greek government announced the devaluation of the drachma by 15.5 percent at the beginning of 1983. At the same time it invoked a clause in the accession agreement to restrict imports from the EEC to the 1980 levels.(5) Such a devaluation is expected also to stimulate tourism, shipping, and immigrant remittances, which dropped by about 20, 10, and 8 percent respectively in 1982.

Greece is rich in mining resources, as is Yugoslavia. Large amounts of minerals, such as bauxite, lignite, and aluminum are exported in the form of raw materials, primarily to other EEC member nations, while a good deal of ready metal products are imported from these countries. It would be proper, then, for Greece to utilize fiscal and monetary policy incentives to develop its metal industry even by using protective tariffs for a transitional period. Such a policy would help domestic employment and improve the balance of trade by substituting imports for metal products, the raw materials of which are produced in the country. Moreover, more value added taxes would be levied from the multistage process of manufacturing these products domestically.

On the one hand, Greek enterprises are largely family owned and small in size (about 90 percent of them employ fewer than 10 persons) and as such are unable to apply modern technology of mass production. On the other hand, labor cost in Greece is about half that of the EEC. This gives a comparative advantage to these small industries. It would seem that such small enterprises need to merge into larger ones to be able to implement capital-intensive production techniques and advanced managerial know-how so that they can be efficient and competitive in domestic and foreign markets.

In terms of foreign trade, it is expected that Greek exports to the other EEC countries (around $2 billion dollars annually) will rise, but not as much as imports, which are more than double exports. The increase in exports will take place primarily in agricultural products, for which EEC tariffs will gradually decline and finally be eliminated after the assigned transitional period has elapsed. However, exports of industrial products, for which EEC duties have been eliminated since 1974, are not expected to increase as much. Another reason for low expectations for increases in industrial exports is the elimination of government subsidies and other tax privileges for such products as a result of Greece's accession to the EEC. Therefore, the gap in the balance of trade should, most probably, increase for some years to come. Perhaps Greece has greater opportunities to increase exports to other neighboring Balkan and Middle East countries than to other EEC member nations. From that point of view, EEC membership should not frustrate efforts for further economic cooperation with Yugoslavia and other Mediterranean countries.

Transportation and tourism are two sectors in which the accession to the EEC should have beneficial effects. Both sectors should continue to play their traditional favorable role in the economy in general and in the country's balance of payments in particular. The Greek merchant fleet, the first in the world, with 2,876 ships in 1982 (compared with 2,512 of the Soviet Union, 1,751 of Japan, 1,100 of Britain, and 569 of the United States), should continue to transport oil and other products to and/or from the EEC. Thus Greece's wealth is expected to increase. However, earnings from shipping depend primarily on changes in world trade. Empirical research indicates that Greek shipping earnings are affected by changes in the value of world exports and, to a lesser extent, by the number of seamen.(6)

After Greece joined the EEC, the economy became more open to international or Common Market competition. This means that if Greece is unable to achieve the desired structural changes and improve her industrial position, she might be forced to specialize even more in the tertiary sector. Competition is expected to be more intensive after the complete elimination of tariffs on imports from the EEC for such protected products as clothing, footware, and metals, as well as the reduction of tariffs on similar imports from third countries to those levied by the EEC.

Consequently, the government and the financial institutions, in exercising their fiscal and credit policies, should emphasize productive investment, mainly in the manufacturing and the exporting sectors. The fact that labor is relatively cheaper in Greece than in the other EEC countries should make such investment successful in reducing inflation and improving the balance of trade. Perhaps investment in entreprenurial and technical training is the most promising endeavor to be pursued by public policy, both for long-term employment and higher productivity.

Greece has already started receiving support payments from the EEC, (Fond Europeen d'Orientation et de Garantie Agricole, or FEOGA), as a result of the implementation of Regulation 355/77, which covers one-fourth of investments in storage facilities of wheat and corn, preservation and manufacturing of fruits and vegetables, and manufacturing, standardization, and marketing of olives and olive oil. Such payments are expected to reach about 7 billion drachmas or around $115 million by 1984. Moreover, there are annual payments for the price support of olive oil, sugar, tobacco, wheat, wine, peaches, tomatoes, and other fruits and vegetables, which are estimated at a total of about $2.5 billion by 1985. As a result of these subsidies, it is estimated that the prices of these products will rise 15 to 25 percent annually during the five-year transitional period. Another 500 million drachmas or some $5 million will be received by Greece from the EEC for the development of its fishing industry.

Regarding the free movement of EEC persons among the member nations, no visa issuance or other similar written statement is required, except for the showing of a passport or identification card. However, Greece continues to require that all persons entering the country fill out a special entrance card. The responsible EEC authority protested such incidents and asked Greece to stop this police-type practice, which is a violation of the Treaty of Rome.

Greece used to be against Spain's early entrance to the EEC because of expected strong competition from such agricultural products as olive oil, wine, tomatoes, and fruits. However, she changed position after discussions with Spanish representatives. The conclusion was that the accession of Spain and Portugal would strengthen the bargaining position of the Mediterranean group of nations in the EEC for policies favorable to their products.(7)

The Treaty of Rome, establishing the EEC, required the benefits of community membership to be evenly spread among its members. In reality, however, inequalities among the regions and countries of the community are growing larger instead of diminishing, especially between the northern regions and the southern or Mediterranean regions. This trend endangers the community's cohesion and forces the EEC budgetary authorities to curtail or suspend advance export subsidy payments for various agricultural products. Such a suspension of subsidy payments occurred during the second half of the year 1983, when Greece had its first six-month term in the presidency of the EEC.

A serious problem of the Common Agricultural Policy (CAP) of the EEC is the establishment of upper limits on the production of dairy and other products and the determination of common agricultural prices, including price support of Mediterranean products through FEOGA. About 60 percent of total EEC revenue (14 billion ECUs in 1983) is spent annually for price support of agricultural products. Greece received 0.6 billion ECUs in 1982, Italy 1.5, Ireland 0.7, and so on.

About 50 percent of total EEC revenue comes from the VAT (11 billion ECUs in 1983), which is 1 percent of those collected by the member countries, 33 percent from custom duties, and 13 percent from levies on certain agricultural products, such as sugar. Since Greece has not introduced the VAT as yet, GNP is used as the basis of VAT calculation. Total budgetary receipts by Greece from the EEC were 995 million ECUs in 1982, while total payments were 359 million, giving a net gain of 636 million ECUs, compared to 1,464 million for Italy, 728 for Ireland, and 367 for the Netherlands. On the other hand, West Germany had net payments of 2,211 million ECUs and Britain 1,980, during that year. As a result of Britain's demand for 1 billion dollars budget refund and the proposed cuts in farm spending, the summit meeting of EEC leaders ended in Athens on December 6, 1983 in a deadlock, leaving the ten nation common market on the brink of bankruptcy. On the other hand, it was argued that, in terms of investment and new technology, Europe has been left far behind Japan and the United States.

YUGOSLAVIA AND THE EEC

Since 1970 a number of meetings on the EEC-Yugoslavia Joint Committee, have taken place and a number of trade agreements have been signed. The two parties have set up a number of subcommittees to deal with the development of closer cooperation and explore the areas of market improvement and investment financing.

The signing of a joint declaration of economic cooperation in Belgrade on December 2, 1976 by the President of the Council of the European Community and Yugoslavian representatives marked a turning point in EEC-Yugoslavian relations.

On December 22, 1976 the European Investment Bank was authorized by its board of governors to grant loans of $68.5 million (50 million ECUs or 1.25 billion dinars) for such projects of mutual interest as the extension of the high tension electricity network and its connection with Greece, Italy, and other European countries, as well as the construction and widening of the trans-Yugoslavian motorway, which provides a direct link between the community on the one hand and Greece, Turkey, and the Middle East on the other. This last project is particularly important for Greece, a member of the EEC, to facilitate transit traffic and foreign trade.

Yugoslavia enjoys many benefits from the community's generalized system of preferences. Some 310 agricultural products and all manufactures and semimanufactures are covered by this system, which provides complete freedom from customs duties. However, certain ceilings or quotas have been laid down for different industrial products.

The Multifibre Arrangement of 1976, which has been renewed repeatedly, provides that Yugoslavia will exercise voluntary restraint in its exports of a number of textile products, such as cotton yarn, cotton fabrics, knitted undergarments, pullovers, trousers, women's blouses, and men's shirts. Such voluntary restraints or individual quota shares, covered by tariff exemptions, depend on the degree of competitiveness of each beneficiary country. Other agreements provide for participation in meetings of the scientific and technical cooperation (COST) group and closer cooperation in the fields of telecommunication, air and water pollution, metallurgy, as well as the establishment of research programs on maize as a basic foodstuff, mineral enrichment of basic crops, and early weaning of piglets.

In the EEC-Yugoslavia cooperation agreements, provisions are made for specific tariff concessions on products of particular interest to Yugoslavia, such as morello cherries, slivovica wine, and Macedonean tobacco. Also, a special reduction of the levy on imports of baby beef, within the limits of a monthly quota of 2900 tons, is provided. For a number of industrial products, tariffs will be reduced in stages. However, Yugoslavia will be able to introduce or increase tariffs or quantitative restrictions insofar as such measures are necessary for the protection of certain industries and the workers associated with them. Special attention is given to the fields of energy, transportation, tourism, and fishing because of their importance to both parties, as well as to the field of labor, including employment conditions of Yugoslav workers in the EEC member countries. Moreover, further cooperation to promote the free trade zone established between Italy and Yugoslavia by the Osimo agreement are stipulated.

In the long run, all these economic activities aim not only at the actual increase in trade but also at closer sociocultural and political cooperation of the EEC and Yugoslavia. Furthermore, Yugoslavia, together with Greece, constitutes a natural bridge between central Europe and the oil-producing Middle East countries that is of vital importance to the EEC for its energy needs. One can speculate that even the negotiations and the timing of Greece's entrance into the EEC were affected, to a large extent, by such considerations. Therefore, EEC concessions to Yugoslavia may be justified on those grounds. In the future it would seem desirable for the EEC to admit Yugoslavia. This would not only facilitate traffic and stimulate trade, but it would also increase the EEC's political influence in the Balkan and eastern Mediterranean regions.

From the viewpoint of foreign trade, Yugoslavia depends more and more on the EEC. One-fourth of its exports go to and close to half of its imports come from the EEC.

Yugoslavia is in 12th position among community's customers and 26th among its suppliers. Yugoslav exports to the community increased 4 times from 1968 to 1980, while imports from the community increased more than 5 times during the same period. As a result, Yugoslavia's trade deficit with the EEC increased six times (from 328 million ECUs in 1968 to about 2.1 billion ECUs or $2.85 billion in 1980), which accounts for about 50 percent of its overall trade deficit. This relatively large deficit was due primarily to machinery imports to equip Yugoslav industry and to the structure of exports, approximately 30 percent of which are primary products (meat, maize, wines, etc.) However, 70 percent of its exports to the EEC are in the form of machinery, equipment, chemicals, and other manufactured products.

On April 2, 1980 Yugoslavia and the EEC signed a new agreement that permits gradual reduction of tariffs for Yugoslav exports of large quantities of wine, fruits, beef, textiles, metals, and other industrial products. Also, community loans of close to $250 million until 1985 and the immigration of Yugoslav workers to Western Europe have been arranged under this agreement.(8) Such arrangements strengthen bonds between Yugoslavia and the EEC. As a result, Yugoslavia's stake in Western Europe has become substantial, and vice versa.

As a result of her membership in the EEC, Greece should have implemented the EEC-Yugoslav trade agreement. This would have affected Yugoslav exports of veal (baby beef) to Greece. In order to protect their own exports of veal to member countries, France and Ireland expressed objections to Greece's importing any significant amount of Yugoslav veal. Greece raised objections to signing a related protocol of adjustment and, until a final arrangement is reached, she will implement either the tariff system for third countries, imposing tariffs according to General Agreement on Tariffs and Trade (GATT) standards, or the EEC-Yugoslav agreement, as the EEC committee suggests. In both cases tariffs and related subsidies are such that prices would become unacceptable to Greek consumers. The result has been that veal exports from Yugoslavia to Greece have stopped completely since the accession. However, Greece is determined to help Yugoslavia in this matter and plans to import veal from Yugoslavia, implementing the preaccession status, even if this means violation of the accession agreement and court action by the EEC. Such a policy by Greece may be viewed as a consequence of keeping and improving further economic and sociocultural relations with the neighboring Balkan countries, particulary Yugoslavia, which is so vital for the transportation of Greek exports to and imports from the EEC.

Because of the similarity of the economic systems of the Council of Mutual Economic Assistance (CMEA), popularly known as COMECON, trade between it and Yugoslavia, as well as trade among the member countries themselves, was not expanded as much as that with the EEC. Barriers to trade have been built through bilateral trade agreements. During the immediate postwar years, Yugoslavia, along with the COMECON countries, adopted an import-substitution policy for industrial products. As a result of duplication in production, it became difficult for Yugoslav manufactures to find a satisfactory market in the COMECON countries because each of these wanted to unload similar exportable products onto others. Deprived of modern technology and sheltered from pressures of competition, Yugoslav firms produced no high-quality manufactures able to compete effectively in international markets. The need for market expansion to advanced countries, especially the EEC, became obvious. Trade reorientation after the break with the COMECON countries (1948) and economic reforms in the 1960s and 1970s was aimed also at increasing economic cooperation with Western countries.

The recent sluggishness of manufacturing exports was due to the slow growth of world markets, particularly in the OECD (Organization for Economic Cooperation and Development) countries, and the investment-led expansion policy, which diverted resources from exports to the domestic market. Moreover, the development policies of the individual republics and regions have, in many cases, allowed duplication of production by a large number of enterprises without the benefits of specialization and competitiveness. Such policies have resulted in low-quality products and lower growth of exports to the highly sophisticated markets of the EEC.

There is an obvious competition between COMECON and the EEC for Yugoslav trade and economic influence. When trade with COMECON is growing rapidly the EEC offers more favorable treatments to Yugoslavia and vice versa. However, it would seem that in the long run the EEC, with more advanced technology, will probably prevail and attract Yugoslavia closer to its economic sphere. In this effort, Greece might prove to be instrumental in allowing the EEC to include the economy of Yugoslavia, although Yugoslavia tries to keep its political independence vis-a-vis the two groups.

RELATIONS WITH COMECON

The Council of Mutual Economic Assistance, or COMECON, which was established in 1949 and includes Bulgaria, Czechoslovakia, East Germany, Hungary, Poland, Romania, and the Soviet Union, has particular importance for neighboring Greece and Yugoslavia. Yugoslavia became an observer, but it seems to have closer relations with the EEC than with COMECON. On the other hand, Greece has good trade relations with the individual members of COMECON, particularly Bulgaria and Romania. Although trade among the COMECON member nations has not advanced as much as that among the EEC members, good cooperation on matters of production and long-term economic development have been achieved. Among the COMECON financial institutions, of particular importance for Yugoslavia and, to a lesser extent, for Greece is the International Bank for Economic Cooperation (IBEC), which facilitates credit among the trading nations of the region.

The need for capital and modern technology force greater cooperation of the COMECON planned economies with the EEC. From that point of view, Greece, as a member of the EEC, plays a vital role in promoting trade and investment relations between European Common Market and COMECON countries, particularly Bulgaria and Romania. The same thing can be expected with the economic relations of COMECON and Yugoslavia, which moves toward closer cooperation with the EEC. In financing more trade and eventually joint ventures among the countries of the two economic groups of Western and Eastern Europe, the World Bank, the IMF, and the IBEC (the charter of which provides for acceptance of nonsocialist countries as members in Article 43) can play an important role.

In spite of their controlled economies, centrally planned nations of COMECON have similar problems to those of the

EEC and are not fully immune to stagflation emanating from abroad. As the worldwide economic slowdown catches up with them, the rates of economic expansion are slowing and shortages of manufactured goods and food are becoming more acute. East European socialist countries, except perhaps Russia, are weighed down by a heavy burden of foreign debt, and it is difficult to continue borrowing. Although they utilize central planning and more controls than Greece and Yugoslavia, they are no better able to resist current economic trends.

To stimulate incentives and increase productivity, these countries move toward relaxing the cumbersome centralized planning, assigning a greater role to market forces and contemplating self-management and decentralization in decision making resembling, to some extent, the Yugoslav economic system. In their effort to reduce bureaucracy and maximize effectiveness, they take a less doctrinaire approach to economic policy, relaxing some of the ideological shackles that bind them. However, economic changes are so tied up with political issues that much depends on what the party leadership decides. The pressure for reforms, though, is so high that there are cases in which room has been created for private entrepreneurs and variation in wages according to productivity. This form of "new economic mechanism," which was introduced by Hungary in 1968 and is under consideration by other COMECON countries including the Soviet Union, allows bands of skilled workers to sell their services to state-owned enterprises. Also, it permits farmers to retain substantial private plots that can be sold or passed on to children, although most farm land is owned by cooperatives and profits are divided among the members. Moreover, factories are not ordered to achieve given production targets and sell their products at prices fixed by the planners, but they have more control over what to produce and how much to charge. This policy encourages them to secure cheap supplies and sell their products at the highest possible prices.(9)

As mentioned earlier, COMECON has not advanced as much as the EEC, mainly because of much duplication in industrial production among the member states. At present, efforts are being made to emphasize specialization, so that production in one state complements production in other states. This is a situation achieved, to some extent, by the

EEC through tariff reduction and expansion of multinational corporations. The chief partner of COMECON, that is, the Soviet Union, seeks more integration and less bilateral trading among the member states. However, the gradual abandonment of Russian subsidies to other COMECON countries presents problems, primarily because of high Soviet prices of energy, which are close to those of OPEC (the Organization of Petroleum Exporting Countries).

At the present stage of development, Yugoslavia seems to have a somewhat parallel economy with the other COMECON countries, producing largely competitive goods. This suggests that opportunities for substantial trade expansion between them is limited. However, Greece's trade with COMECON countries is expected to grow because of different orientations and specializations and because of the new economic conditions to be created as a result of Greece's gradual adjustment to EEC policies.

The construction of the natural gas pipeline, which is built primarily by Western European companies to link Siberia to Western Europe, is expected to reach Yugoslavia and Greece as well. Although such a link would increase the influence of COMECON, notably the Soviet Union, upon the economies of these two Balkan countries, low gas prices would relieve part of their energy and balance of trade burdens.

Additional trade agreements were made between the two countries and the Soviet Union regarding electric power, and agricultural and mining products, when Soviet Prime Minister Nikolai Tikhonov visited both countries in Feburary 1983. Thus an agreement between Greece and the Soviet Union provides for the construction of a plant with an annual capacity of 600,000 tons of alumina, the intermediate product between bauxite ore and aluminum metal. The Soviet aluminum industry would then import Greek alumina instead of bauxite ore. Also, total trade would be increased from $570 million to $1.4 billion annually.

In the ten-year program of economic cooperation between Greece and the Soviet Union, it was agreed (February 1983) that the Soviet Union would provide to the first 700 million cubic meters of natural gas annually, which would be gradually increased to 4 million by 1990. Also, some 2 million metric tons of petroleum and 300-400 million kilowatt hours of electricity would be provided per year. However, the electricity network of Yugoslavia presents technical problems for the transfer of COMECON's electricity to Greece.(10)

CUSTOMS DUTIES

Greece and Yugoslavia use tariffs or customs duties mainly for the protection of domestic enterprises and as a source of revenue. Together with the protective effect comes the employment effect. Although prices of imported commodities, as well as prices of the same or similar commodities produced domestically, are kept high as a result of tariffs, gains from employment stimulation and economic development may offset losses to the consumers due to high prices. This is particularly so for both countries, especially Yugoslavia, where unemployment may be expected to grow rapidly after the removal of the protective tariff walls. However, keeping protective tariffs for a long period may feed inefficiency and misallocation of resources. This, in turn, may lead to far higher losses in the overall welfare of the country, which will not enjoy the full benefits of comparative advantages. Only on goods that are not produced at home may tariffs have revenue effects but not protective and redistributive effects. Therefore, tariffs on such commodities can be kept or even increased without significantly affecting domestic employment.

From the viewpoint of public finance, the importance of tariffs is expressed through the amounts of revenue collected by the government. In both countries, a substantial proportion of government revenues (about one-fourth of central government's receipts) comes from customs duties. Such revenues have the advantage of low cost and administrative convenience, regardless of their effects on the principle of equity in taxation. The heavier burden of tariffs falls on consumption. Machinery and capital goods in general are exempted or pay low tariffs. Therefore low income groups, with a larger proportion of their incomes spent for consumption, bear a heavier burden of import duties.

As a result of Greece's membership in the EEC and the closer trade relations of Yugoslavia with the EEC, tariff duties will eventually be reduced. To avoid extensive revenue losses, the two countries, and especially Greece, would then attempt to substitute domestic taxes for customs duties. If such taxes are levied on domestic consumption, the distorting effects will be less because with low demand elasticity will be taxed more heavily.

In order to repeal tariffs and discard fiscal frontiers while maintaining tax neutrality, the EEC decided that value added tax rates should be made uniform across all member countries. In such a tax uniformity, all products, regardless of origin, would be subject to the same tax within the EEC. However, member countries would continue to set their own retail sales taxes, thereby taxing their own consumers but not those of other member countries.

As Greece and eventually Yugoslavia reduce tariffs on imports from the EEC, consumers in these countries will substitute imports for home products. As imports rise the prices of their currencies will decline relative to those of the other EEC countries. Then their exports will rise until new equilibrium is established at a somewhat higher level of trade with more specialization and more efficient production. However, the burden of import competition would fall on protected industries, while Greece and Yugoslavia would specialize more in the production of primary products. This may lead to deterioration of their terms of trade unless measures are taken to correct such conditions through EEC subsidies and other kinds of support for such primary products.

Government revenue from customs duties in Yugoslavia increased during the postwar years not only in absolute terms but also as a percentage of the value of imports. As Figure 8.1 shows, they increased from 7 percent in 1960 to 11 percent in 1970 and about 20 percent of the value of imports recently. At present, both Greece and Yugoslavia have about the same percentage of tariffs on imports; that is about double those of the EEC. Although Yugoslavia is not a member or even an associated member of the EEC, a number of trade agreements have been concluded between these two economies that may eventually lead to the reduction of tariffs on the Yugoslavian imports.

As a proportion of central government revenue, customs duties increased for Yugoslavia from 5 percent in 1960 to 17 percent in 1970 and 20 percent in 1980. However, for Greece they declined from 30 percent in 1960 to 27 percent in 1970 and 22 percent in 1980.

The annual increase in imports and especially the dramatic increases in the value of oil imports after 1973

Figure 8.1. Customs Duties as Percentages of Imports (current prices) for the EEC: Average of France, W. Germany, Italy, United Kingdom.

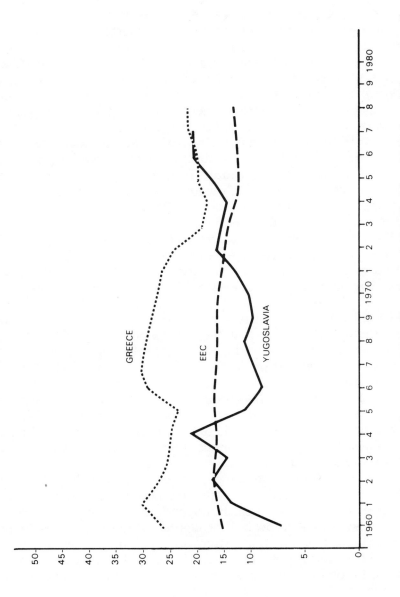

Source: United Nations, Statistical Yearbook, and Yearbook of National Accounts Statistics, various issues; OECD, National Accounts, various issues.

seem to have been responsible for such a large increase in customs duties in Yugoslavia. This proportional increase in customs duties may also be due to the relative decline of central government revenue in favor of "communities of interest" and other local activities resulted from the postwar decentralization policies of the government. Similar increases in imports and oil prices also took place in Greece, but the decrease in tariffs on imports from the EEC, as a result of the association agreement of 1961, were probably responsible for the small declines in tax revenue from customs duties relative to total government receipts.

High customs duties in Greece as compared to those of the EEC, would have serious repercussions on government revenues in the foreseeable future. As a result of Greece's accession to the EEC, customs duties or tariffs would be eliminated for imports from the EEC and would be reduced to match those of the EEC for imports from other countries. Such a tariff harmonization would mean a significant reduction of revenue for the Greek government. The fact that more than half of Greece's imports come from the EEC, for which no customs duties would be collected, would mean a great loss of government revenue. Another loss would occur from lower Greek tariffs on imports from non-EEC countries. Although a good part of the tariffs on imports from the EEC has already been reduced or eliminated as a result of Greece's association with the EEC since 1961, Greek ad valorem tariffs are still about double those of the EEC and the trend since 1974 seems to be upward. If tariff harmonization means their reduction to the same level as those of the EEC (around 10-12 percent of the value of imports), then about half the revenue from customs duties, or more than 30 billion drachmas, would be lost.

To avoid large budgetary deficits Greek policymakers may try to supplement these lost tariff revenues with other forms of taxation such as expenditure or consumption taxes on the same imported products. However, this may be considered a circumvention of the accession agreement, which requires that domestic value added taxes be the same in all member countries. Some of these lost revenues may be recovered by the value added tax that Greece is required to introduce in the near future.(11) However, as was explained previously, total revenue from this form of taxation may not be sufficient to cover the ever-growing budget deficits, and as a result inflation may continue to undermine the Greek economy. To protect domestic industry and to continue collecting tax revenue, Greece is permitted to reduce taxes gradually (regulative tax), so that by 1989 tax rates on domestic products and those imported from the EEC would be the same.

NOTES

1. More details in R. Triffin, "The European Monetary System," in D. Seers and C. Vaitsos, eds. Integration and Unequal Development: The Experience of the ECC (New York: St. Martin's Press, 1980).
2. Such a position was supported by Ernest Gleen, president of the Socialist group of the European Parliament in Athens in September 1982. The EEC recognized that Greece faces difficult problems and accepted the Greek memorandum for some changes in the accession agreement pertaining to taxation and support of certain sectors and products for a period of transition.
3. Sociopolitical and environmental aspects of the EEC are in C. Pinkele and A. Polis, eds., The Contemporary Mediterranean World (New York: Praeger, 1983), chaps. 5 and 11. Also, "Arthro ton Taims Gia Ellada-EOK," (Article of Times for Greece-EEC," Proini, New York, May 17, 1983.
4. From $140 million surplus on food trade with the EEC in 1980, Greece had some $300 million deficit in 1982. To counter higher food costs, Greece receives about $600 million a year from the EEC. See "Greece: European Tragedy," Economist, January 15, 1983, p. 74.
5. At the end of 1983, the exchange rate was around 100 drachmas per U.S. dollar, after another devaluation of about 10 percent in August 1983 and the subsequent floating of the drachma vis-a-vis the dollar.
6. For comparative statistics, see G. Karatzos. "Greek Earnings from Ocean Transportation in 1960-77: An Analysis," International Review at Economics and Business (forthcoming): I. Tzoannou, Elliniki Emporiki Naftilia kai EOK (Greek Merchant Shipping and the EEC) (Athens: Institute of Economic and Industrial Studies, 1977), chaps. 1,3; J. Carr "New Trade Horizons: Greece Could Strengthen Ties Between East and West," Europe, January-February 1981, pp. 10-13; "Proti Ston Kosmo E Elliniki Naftilia Me, 2,876 Plia," (First

in the world the Greek fleet with 2,876 ships); and To Vima, Athens, August 8, 1982.

7. More discussion on the expected enlargement of the EEC in Loukas Tsoukalas, The European Community and Its Mediterranean Enlargement (London: Allen and Unwin, 1981), chap. 1.

8. EEC Regulation 1272/80 of the Council, Gazeta of European Communities, N. 130/1,5/25/80; and David Binder, "After Tito: European Community Helps Provide a Safety Net," Europe, May-June 1980, pp. 10-13.

9. J. Van Brabant, Socialist Economic Integration (New York: Cambridge University Press, 1980), chap. 5. On Yugoslavia's relations with COMECON and other countries, see L. Tyson, The Yugoslav Economic System and Its Performance in the 1970s (Berkeley: University of California Press, 1980), chap. 7.

10. "Fthinotero Petreleo Mos Dini E ESSD," (Cheaper Petroleum from USSR), Ta Nea, Athens, February 19, 1983; and Marvine Howe, "Greece Joins Soviets in Urging Deep-Arms Cuts," New York Times, February 25, 1983.

11. Because of the difficulties of introducing the value added tax by the Greek authorities, a postponement of two years was permitted. "Anovoli tou Forou Prostitheme, nis Aksios Gia 2 Hronia" (Postponement of value added tax by two years), Oikonomikos Tahydromas, Athens, December 29, 1983, p. 19.

9

CONVERGENCE OF THE ECONOMIC SYSTEMS

Greece, with a basically market economy, and Yugoslavia, with a basically planned economy, have different economic systems. The economy of Greece is characterized primarily by private ownership of the means of production and a competitive market mechanism. Enterprises belong mainly to the private sector, and decisions are taken by individual entrepreneurs or boards of directors who are representatives of the stock owners. The Yugoslav economy, on the other hand, is based primarily on the planned economic system with a socialized or decentralized process of production and distribution. Enterprises are managed by the workers (self-managed enterprises). However, all the economic activities are coordinated by the overall national plan.

Both systems have learned from experience how to overcome some of their weaknesses and to adopt some of the advantages and benefits of the other system. Thus the Greek economy moves gradually away from extreme individualism toward more collectivism. The public sector, which includes central and local government and public enterprises, has already grown to almost half (48 percent) of the entire economy. On the other hand, the Yugoslav economy has gradually been moving away from strict state controls, especially after the reforms of 1965 and 1974, to a more competitive economy and the adoption of some of the techniques of the market mechanism for production and price determination via supply and demand. Through borrowing positive elements from capitalism and socialism, both countries have achieved a good degree of rapprochement between their economies.(1)

Both countries, and particularly Greece, have introduced measures to reduce inequalities in per capita incomes, especially between the urban centers and the poor provinces. Such measures mitigate also the sociopolitical superiority of the "haves" over the "have nots", which is a disadvantage of private capitalism. The use of fiscal and monetary policy and the manipulation of demand have contributed to continued progress in the market economy of Greece. Similarly, the use of planning in socialist Yugoslavia has made economic growth a permanent feature in the country. Investment and tax incentives, productivity guidelines, or price and wage controls to curb inflation, and various subsidies introduced in these two countries to achieve high economic growth and low unemployment rates, tend to bring their economic systems closer to each other.

The Yugoslav policymakers have realized that detailed economic planning and centralism are responsible for excessive bureaucracy, poor quality, and low efficiency. As the economy moves to higher stages of development, productive enterprises need more autonomy on such important matters as production, investment, financing, and sales promotion, which means more decentralization and movement toward a system of democratic socialism. Also Greek policy makers have realized that strict individualism is not conducive to modern methods of mass production and advanced technology. Emphasis on closer cooperation of small and middle-sized enterprises and even mergers toward larger and more efficient production units, as well as some form of collectivism in decision making, have been introduced so that the economy will be able to survive foreign competition. These concurrent trends and reforms seem to support some of the arguments of the convergence thesis, which states that gradually market and planned economies will adopt each others' advantages and move toward a middle-of-the-road economic system. In that type of social and economic system there would be less inequality and discrimination, more participation, less centralism, and more adherence to demo-cratic ideals.

RECENT TRENDS TOWARD CONVERGENCE

The growth of the industrial systems and giant corporations in both countries influences existing beliefs and ideologies. The growing number of large-sale enterprises and organi-zations in both countries require more autonomy from state controls and bureaucracy and more authority over the market mechanism. In cases in which a producer's sovereignty prevails, the state tends to become subservient to giant corporations, domestic or foreign, acting almost as a subor-dinate in providing training and education for the required manpower, stimulating demand for products through fiscal and monetary measures, and coordinating prices and wages to facilitate the productive operations of these corporations.

Material progress is gradually reducing the impact of ideological appeals upon the people, who are interested mostly in personal enjoyment and not so much in revo-lutionary changes and reforms. Technological development and educational advancement direct these two countries, as well as other Balkan countries, toward common goals and eventually to a new system that may incorporate the advan-tages of both capitalism and socialism and blend the ideal and the real.

Major changes have been made in the economy of Yugoslavia regarding structural organization and economic cooperation. Such changes include emphasis on managerial specialization with remuneration according to productivity, and stress of international trade instead of self-reliance. Likewise, important changes in Greece include the use of developmental, but not necessarily detailed, planning, the growth of public and semipublic enterprises, the strength-ening of producers' and consumers' cooperatives, and the socialization of decision making. The changes tend to create an economic system with common characteristics, that is, to speed up socioeconomic convergence between these two countries.

Trade cooperation and joint investment ventures be-tween Greece and Yugoslavia as well as among other neigh-boring Balkan countries liquidate lingering nationalism in the area and reduce regional conflicts, which have plagued these nations for decades.(2)   Convergence, then, may bring an economic and sociopolitical synthesis through peaceful co-operation and not through a conflict of opposites (thesis-antithesis, as Marx predicted).   A similar method of recon-ciling two different arguments into a new view that incor-porates elements of both was used by Plato in his Dialogues and was adopted by the Scholastics in ancient Greece.

The fact that machines, cybernetics, computers, and robots can substitute for muscular work, as well as for human brainpower, alludes to the vision of Aristotle, in the fourth century B.C., that:

> If every instrument could, on order received, or even intelligently anticipated work of its own accord, ... if shuttles could weave alone, if the plectrum itself could play the zither, then em-ployers would be able to do without workers.(3)

Furthermore, there are certain realities facing the world today which are expected to prevail over dogma, whether of the liberal or conservative variety. They include economic and political justice, respect for the environment, as well as concern for the world community in the present atomic age.(4)   All these elements point to the need for a socio-economic and even political convergence on a worldwide basis.

On the other hand, a middle way with respect to property acquisition, justified by the anxiety about livelihood was recommended by Aristotle.   The pursuit of wealth in excess of this limit was considered a corruption or an unnatural form of acquisition.(5)

A successful experience of economic convergence be-tween these two countries may be followed by other coun-tries with different economic systems or groups of countries such as the EEC and COMECON. Also, other developing and uncommitted nations that are anxious to avoid extreme capitalism or communism can search for such a converging system that combines the best elements of the two extremes. Although it is difficult to expect an optimum combination of the public and the private sectors in these countries in the near future, it is equally or even more difficult to accept what extreme apologists of either system suggest: that "convergence" is a camouflage for subversion.   However, there is always the possibility of serious setbacks of convergence by the short-run strategies and the long-run goals of the big powers, so influential in that region. As Victor Hugo said, though: Nothing is more powerful than an idea whose time has come.

Both countries are at roughly the same stage of development, somewhere between the self-sustained and the drive-to-maturity stages. Therefore, stronger economic ties between them are possible and desirable. To the degree permitted by the EEC, Greece can conclude separate agreements with Yugoslavia and leave the door open for other Balkan countries to join later. With cautious trial-and-error efforts, the two countries could prepare the ground for the creation of Balkan Economic Community (BEC) that would be a vital link between Europe and the Middle East. Furthermore, the dramatic increase in trade and investment among the Balkan and the Middle East countries during the last decade may eventually lead to the creation of a broader Eastern Mediterranean Economic Community (EMEC).(7) At present the formation of an expanded economic union among the countries of the region might be considered a utopian dream, but today's utopia may be tomorrow's reality.

NOTES

1. Comparisons of changes in capitalism and communism are in Jan Tibergen, "Do Communist and Free Economies Show a Convergence Pattern?" Soviet Studies 12 (April 1961), 333-41.

2. Serious efforts at closer cooperation and integration of the Balkan countries were made mainly by Rhigas Pheraios (Valestinlis), Alexander Ypsilanti, and the Pulios brothers (in Vienna) during the Ottoman occupation; Alexander Papanastassiou, Alex Milonas, and John Stephanopoulos (in Greece), Stefan Radish (in Croatia), Alexander Stambuliski (in Bulgaria), and Nicolai Titulescu (in Romania) in the 1920s; Stamatis Mercouris (in Greece) and Savas Gonofski (in Bulgaria) in the 1960s; and all the leaders of the Balkan countries, except perhaps Albania, in recent years.

3. Aristotle, Politika A^4 (1253^{b33}-1254^{a1}); and Angelos Angelopoulos, Global Plan for Employment: A New Marshall Plan (New York: Praeger, 1983), p. xviii.

4. For a valuable review of such socioeconomic and environmental trends, see Paul Tsongas, The Road from Here: Liberalism and Realities in the 1980s (New York: Alfred Knopf, 1981), chaps. 1-10. For the relationship of self-management and convergence see N. Gianaris, "Koinonikopoiesi: Tha Apodihti Apotelesmatikos Sygerasmos for Oikonomikon Systimecton?" (Socialization: Will Convergence of Economic Systems Prove to Be Effective?), Oikonomikos Tahydromas, Athens, November 17, 1983.

5. Earnest Barker, The Political Thought of Plato and Aristotle (New York: Dover, 1959), pp. 390-405; and T. Lewis, "Acquisition and Anxiety: Aristotle's Case Against the Market," Canadian Journal of Economics, February 1978, pp. 69-90.

6. For more doubts about economic integration and the possibility of negative convergence, see M. Mihojlov, Underground (New Rochelle, N.Y.: Caratjas Brothers, 1982), chap. 1. Also, Mike Pournarakis, "Development Integration in the Balkans," Balkan Studies 19 (1978): 285-312. For similar pessimistic views of John Galbraith and Arthur Schlesinger Jr., see N. Gianaris, The Economies of Balkan Countries: Albania, Bulgaria, Greece, Romania, Turkey, and Yugoslavia.

7. For a similar economic organization around the fifth century B.C.. see A. Zimmerman, The Greek Commonwealth (London: Oxford University Press, 1961). Further comments in N. Gianaris, "Prooptikes Oikonomikis Synergasias Sta Valkania" (Expectations of Economic Cooperation in Balkania), To Vima, Athens, July 9, 1982, p. 3.

APPENDIX A

STATISTICAL CORRELATIONS OF GROSS DOMESTIC PRODUCT WITH INVESTMENT AND EXPORTS

Table A.1. Simple and Multiple Correlations of Gross Domestic Product (GDP) on Investment (INV) and Exports (EXP) (1958-80): $GDP = a + b_1 INV + b_2 EXP$

	a	b_1	b_2	F	R^2
For Greece	68.9 (3.8)	3.6INV (20.1)		403	0.937
	100.2 13.4	1.7INV (9.6)	2.9EXP (12.0)	1,388	0.990
For Yugoslavia	22.6 (2.2)	2.9INV (32.6)		1,065	0.982
	69.7 (10.0)	1.9INV (15.6)	1.0EXP (8.8)	2,815	0.997

Note: Figures in parentheses are t-values.

As the above simple regressions indicate, a 1-unit change in investment is associated with a change in GDP of

245

3.6 units for Greece and 2.9 units for Yugoslavia. On the other hand, the multiple regressions show that for Greece exports are a better explanatory variable of changes in GDP than is investment, while for Yugoslavia investment is a better explanatory variable than are exports. It would seem, therefore, that postwar economic growth in Greece was based primarily on increases in exports, and not so much on capital formation, as was the case in Yugoslavia. In the simple regressions, the slope of change in output (ΔQ) over change in investment (ΔI), $\Delta Q/\Delta I$, does not show the productivity of investment, because other factors in addition to investment, primarily labor, contribute to the increment of product. Also, this slope $\Delta Q/\Delta I$ is not the inverse of the incremental capital output ratio (ICOR), $\Delta K/\Delta Q$, in which the numerator shows changes in total capital or cumulative investments. It simply shows the trend of changes in output over changes in investment over time. Moreover, changes in product or income over change in investment is a notion of the multiplier, but there is not a cause and effect relationship here as there is with the multiplier.

Another multiple regression of GDP on investment, exports, and population (POP) gave the following results for Greece (1960-80):

$$GDP= -1,022 + 1.65INV + 2.72EXP + 128.05POP \quad R^2=0.998$$
$$\quad\quad\quad (6.02) \quad\quad (9.63) \quad\quad (4.2) \quad\quad\quad F=3,777$$

Figures in parentheses are t-values.

Again, exports are a more important variable in explaining changes in GDP than is investment. The export regression coefficient is almost double that for investment. On the other hand, a percentage change in population is related to a 128.05 billion drachma change in GDP. Population growth during the period 1960-80 was small mainly because of extensive emigration, especially during the 1960s and early 1970s.

For all cases considered, the regression fit was very good. The coefficient of determination, R^2, was more than 0.930 for both countries. From that point of view, policymakers can use such reliable regressions for future economic projections.

APPENDIX B

STATISTICAL CORRELATIONS OF TAXATION WITH PRIVATE CONSUMPTION, IMPORTS, AND INFLATION

SIMPLE REGRESSIONS

In order to see whether private consumption, imports, and inflation affect tax revenue, I put their relationship to a statistical test. Simple and multiple correlations for the postwar years were used to determine the slopes of these variables and their reliability for the Greek and the Yugoslav economies.

As Table B.1 of the Appendix indicates, variations of local taxes with respect to the other three variables (private consumption, imports, and inflation) were small during the period 1950-80. The corrected coefficients of determination in all cases were high ($R^2 > .890$) indicating a good fit of the regression lines, for both Greece and Yugoslavia. However, the D-W statistic was lower than the critical value (at 5 percent level of significance) in both countries, particularly in Greece, indicating the existence of serial correlation. This means that tax policymakers in both countries can, with some degree of caution, extrapolate these trends into the future for projections.

The regression coefficient of total taxes on private consumption was higher in Greece (0.46) than in Yugoslavia

Table B.1. Simple and Multiple Regressions of Total Taxes on
Private Consumption, Imports and Inflation, 1950–80 (current prices)

	Constant	Regression coefficients			R^2	D-W
	a	b_1	b_2	b_3		
Greece	-14565.0	0.46 PRC (73.0)			0.995	0.623
	2881.2	1.15 IMP (42.7)			0.985	0.666
	-0.3	1.91 INF (15.3)			0.893	0.237
	-1.8	0.90 IMP (9.2)	0.59 INF (1.2)		0.984	0.518
	-4.7	2.04 PRC (8.6)	0.44 IMP (2.7)	0.80 INF (2.7)	0.996	0.400
Yugoslavia	1.9	0.38 PRC (73.0)			0.981	0.857
	5.4	0.76 IMP (20.3)			0.951	0.868
	-14.2	1.27 INF (35.2)			0.983	0.895
	0.2	0.56 IMP (2.7)	0.38 INF (1.0)		0.972	0.751
	0.1	0.46 PRC (0.8)	0.25 IMP (0.6)	0.19 INF (0.4)	0.971	0.671

Note: Figures in parentheses are t-values. For inflation, the ratio of current prices GDP over constant prices GDP was used. For Yugoslavia: 1953-80. Multiple regressions are in logarithmic form; that is: log TT=a + b_1 log PRC + b_2 log IMP + b_3 log INF; where a is constant and b_1, b_2, b_3 the regression coefficients.

Source: OECD, National Accounts, various issues; United Nations, Yearbook of National Accounts Statistics, various issues; N. Gianaris, "Indirect Taxes: A Comparative Study of Greece and the EEC, "European Economic Review 15 (1981): 111-7; IMF, International Financial Statistics, Yearbook, various issues.

(0.38). A 1-unit change in private consumption associated with a 0.46 change in total taxes in Greece and a 0.38 unit change in taxes in Yugoslavia.

On the other hand, the regression coefficients of total taxes on imports were higher than those of total taxes on private consumption for Yugoslavia and more so for Greece. This means that a unit change in imports is related to a 1.5 change in total taxes for Greece and a 0.76 change for Yugoslavia. In both countries, indirect taxes, which include customs duties on imports, are the largest part of total taxes, about 70 percent. Although imports are expected to continue to be high in the near future for both countries, the fact that Greece has become a member of the EEC means that tax revenue from customs duties will gradually be reduced. However, for Yugoslavia, tariffs will continue to play the same or a more important role in public finance in the foreseeable future.

In both countries the regression coefficient of total taxes on inflation was positive and higher than one. The regression results indicate that a 1 percent increase in inflation is associated with an almost 2(1.91) percent increase in total taxes in Greece and a 1.27 percent increase in Yugoslavia. As prices of commodities and services increase with inflation at each stage of production, ad valorem and other taxes increase at least proportionally to price increases.(1) Moreover, chronic inflation pushes taxpayers into higher income tax brackets where, under the progressive tax system, tax rates are higher, thereby transferring proportionally more and more income from the private to the public sector. Thus inflation--the vicious "hidden tax--helps the governments of these countries to increase revenue without introducing new tax legislation.

MULTIPLE REGRESSIONS

For a further review of the relationship between taxation and a few of the most important variables affecting it, multiple regression analyses of total tax revenue on imports and inflation, as well as total taxes on private consumption, imports, and inflation were used for Greece and Yugoslavia. Mutatis mutandis, identification of these relationships may be useful to other countries affected by similar problems. However, further research and more reliable data incorporating other variables affecting taxation are needed for

Table B.2. Simple and Multiple Regressions of Direct Taxes on Private Consumption, Imports, and Inflation, in Logarithms, 1950–80 (current prices)

	Constant	Regression coefficients			R^2	D-W
	a	b_1	b_2	b_3		
Greece	-5.53	1.21 PPC (46.83)			0.987	1.335
	-1.22	0.95 IMP (34.10)			0.976	1.242
	-14.99	4.47 INF (22.40)			0.947	0.322
	-5.20	0.70 IMP (6.90)	1.28 INF (2.59)		0.981	1.149
	-7.34	1.49 PRC (3.85)	0.28 IMP (1.05)	0.26 INF (0.55)	0.987	1.319
Yugoslavia	-0.44	0.48 PRC (9.72)			0.837	0.697
	0.16	0.43 IMP (9.22)			0.824	0.633
	-1.31	0.80 INF (9.54)			0.831	0.622
	-1.05	0.08 IMP (0.19)	0.66 INF (0.84)		0.821	0.620
	1.27	0.96 PRC (1.14)	0.51 IMP (0.77)	0.14 INF (0.16)	0.824	0.838

Note: Figures in parentheses are t-values. For inflation, the ratio of current prices GDP over constant prices GDP was used. For Yugoslavia 1953-80.

Source: OECD, National Accounts, various issues; United Nations, Yearbook of National Accounts Statistics, various issues; N. Gianaris, "Indirect Taxes: A Comparative Study of Greece and the EEC," European Economic Review 15 (1981): 111-17; IMF, International Financial Statistics, Yearbook, various issues; and United Nations, Statistical Yearbook, various issues.

Table B.3. Simple and Multiple Regressions of Indirect Taxes on Private Consumption, Imports, and Inflation, 1950-80 (current prices)

		Regression Coefficient			
	Constant	b_1	b_2	b_3	R^2
Greece	-0.58	0.23 PRC (62.73)			0.993
	0.29	0.57 IMP (37.03)			0.980
	-0.13	0.14 INF (0.33)			0.896
	-0.11	0.52 IMP (10.67)	0.93 INF (0.01)		0.981
	0.16	0.39 PRC (10.06)	0.32 IMP (3.58)	0.19 INF (0.004)	0.991
Yugoslavia	-0.10	0.21 PRC (29.78)			0.976
	0.35	0.42 IMP (31.50)			0.980
	-9.81	0.68 INF (21.72)			0.957
	-2.30	0.32 IMP (5.11)	0.16 INF (1.57)		0.982
	6.50	0.27 PRC (2.24)	0.19 IMP (2.27)	0.54 INF (1.64)	0.985

Note: Figures in parentheses are t-values. For inflation the ratio of current prices GDP over constant prices GDP was used. For Yugoslavia 1953-80. The regression equation used was: $INDT = a + b_1 \, PRC + b_2 \, IMP + b_3 \, INF$ where a is the constant and b_1, b_2, b_3 the regression coefficients.

Source: OECD, National Accounts, various issues; United Nations, Yearbook of National Accounts Statistics, various issues; N. Gianaris, "Indirect Taxes: A Comparative Study of Greece and the EEC," European Economic Review 15 (1981): 111-7; IMF, International Financial Statistics, Yearbook, various issues.

better projections and derivation of the related policy imple-
mentations.

For Greece, the multiple regression coefficients of
total taxes on imports and on inflation were 0.90 and 0.59
respectively, as Table B.1 of the Appendix shows. For
Yugoslavia, they were 0.56 and 0.38. respectively. This means
that for Greece, a unit change in imports was associated with
a change of 0.90 units in total taxes, while a unit change in
inflation was related to a change of 0.59 units in total tax
revenue. For Yugoslavia, the regression coefficients were
0.56 and 0.38 respectively. In both countries, throughout the
postwar period, the imports variable was more important
than the inflation variable in their relationship with total taxes.

The regression results indicate that for both Greece and
Yugoslavia the correlations of total taxes on imports and
inflation were high. The corrected coefficient of determination was close to one ($R^2 > 0.970$). However, the Durbin-
Watson statistic (D-W) at a 5 percent level of significance
was not high enough to signify the nonexistence of serial
correlation, and the results should be interpreted with caution.

In the multiple correlation with four variables, total
taxes were the dependent variable; private consumption,
imports, and inflation were the independent variables. Comparatively speaking, the regression coefficient of total taxes
on private consumption was higher than that on imports for
Greece and vice versa for Yugoslavia. Although the corrected coefficient of determination was high ($R^2 > 0.970$), the
D-W statistic was lower than the critical value (at a 5-
percent level of significance), indicating the existence of
serial correlation and making the results doubtful, especially
for Greece.

NOTE

1. Regressions based on cross-section data lent little
support to the argument that inflation is systematically
influenced by changes in the public sector or in the tax
burden. A. Peacock and M. Rickets, "The Growth of the
Public Sector and Inflation," in F. Hirsch and J. Goldthorpe,
eds., The Political Economy of Inflation (Cambridge, Mass.:
Harvard University Press, 1978).

INDEX

ABOUT THE AUTHOR

NICHOLAS V. GIANARIS earned his B.A. at the Graduate School of Economics and Business of Athens, his LL.B. at the University of Athens, and his M.A. and Ph.D. in economics at New York University. He has taught in the United States and abroad. At present he is professor of economics at Fordham University, Lincoln Center, New York.

Dr. Gianaris is a member of the American Economic Association, Royal Economic Society (U.K.), Economic History Association, and American Association of University Professors. Listed in American Men of Science and similar volumes, he has also received the N.Y.U. Founders Award for scholarly achievements.

He has contributed a number of articles to both American and international economics publications and has presented panel papers at symposia on southeastern Europe and other regions. Parts of his previous book, Economic Development: Thought and Problems (1978), were translated into French and Spanish by the International Monetary Fund for use in the IMF Institute's courses on financial analysis and policy.

His most recent book, The Economies of the Balkan Countries: Albania, Bulgaria, Greece, Romania, Turkey, Yugoslavia (1982), was also published by Praeger Publishers.